To John,

Thank you for

at my book signing

With Love

Helena

SILENT TERROR

Memoir

of

Helena Cowan

The two flags on the front cover show the official Hungarian flag in red, white and green, which was altered with the communist symbols during their regime. In the 1956 revolution, the devoted Freedom Fighters restored its original design.

www.trafford.com

North America & international
toll-free: 1 888 232 4444 (USA & Canada)
phone: 250 383 6864 ♦ fax: 250 383 6804
email: info@trafford.com

The United Kingdom & Europe
phone: +44 (0)1865 487 395 ♦ local rate: 0845 230 9601
facsimile: +44 (0)1865 481 507 ♦ email: info.uk@trafford.com

10 9 8 7 6 5 4 3

Dedication

Silent Terror is dedicated to the special people in my life: with unconditional love to my daughter, Beatrix Perry, who is part of this book; and to my editor, Heather Leask, who is an excellent teacher and the most considerate human being I have ever known. Thank you for making my dream come true.

Also thanks to my dear spiritual friends Priscilla Metcalf, Teresa Proudlove, and Brenda Prevost for their supporting love.

The book cover was designed by the author.

Table of Contents

Childhood and World War II

Teenage Years and Young Love

Engagement and Marriage

Pregnancy and Motherhood

Revolution and Escape

Canadian Life

* Some names have been changed to protect the innocent.

CHAPTER 1

I dashed into the steamy, hot kitchen with my two friends, Klari and Vali, tagging at my heels. *"Anyuka,"* I asked, "may we go to the meadow to play?"

Mother, bent over the washtub where she was rinsing the hand-embroidered tablecloth Grandmother Batta had given us, straightened up slowly. "Yes," she said wearily, "but take Julika with you. You'll have to look after her until I'm finished washing. You can play in the meadow, but don't go to the creek." The creek, which was about six feet wide and two feet deep, was our favorite place to play, but it was dangerous. This "mean creek's" rapid, strong current could sweep you off your feet and, to show her power, fling you to the big, gray rock anchored in the middle of her. We were not allowed to go there unless my older sister, Manci, was with us.

Carrying Julika, my year-old baby sister, we were soon in the lush, green meadow. She watched as Klari, Vali and I chased butterflies. Then we picked wild flowers, the pride of the countryside: white marguerites, red poppies with their grayish-green lobed leaves, and blue cupids. We braided them into wreaths, to circle around our heads like halos. Pretending that we were angels, we held hands, made a circle and danced happily bare-footed in the grass. Suddenly the warning siren went off. Allied fighter planes were approaching! We had no time to get back home. We panicked. Where could we hide?

Klari yelled, "The meadow is too open. They could shoot us!"

We had no choice but to run to the old log bridge that spanned the forbidden creek, knowing we would have some protection under it. Shaking with fear, I carried my little sister on my back. Several times I fell to my knees. Sensing my panic, she kept crying, *"Mama, Mama."* Finally, we reached the bridge and skidded underneath it on its loose dirt bank. After what seemed a long time, the siren stopped. Then the planes came, flying low with a horrifying, ear-piercing roar. We huddled together fearing to be killed. By this time Julika was screaming so loud we were terrified she would be heard.

In a panic to silence her cries, I fiercely rocked her and accidentally slipped into the creek. Instantly, she clutched to my neck so tightly that I was gasping for air. The swift-moving current quickly carried us down the river, as I desperately tried to stay at shore, so as not to be flung against the big, gray rock to unconsciousness. Water splashed into my mouth and eyes, momentarily blinding me. Somehow I managed to grab a willow branch, but fighting the forceful water I lost my footing and my sister was immersed in the water for a second. Fearing to lose her in my weakening left arm, while hanging on to the cracking branch with my right hand, I cried for help. Finally, my confused friends got a hold of my hand and miraculously pulled us out of the creek. My terrified, infant sister continued wailing; I didn't know what to do to quiet her. Mother was still nursing her, and that always made her stop crying. So, even though I was only eight years old, I had her suck on my nipples and she quieted down. Sitting there, drenched and cold, cradling Julika in my arms, remembering Grandmother's counsel – "When in a fearful situation, start praying and aid will come," the prayer of "Our Father" flew sincerely from my pleading heart. When my two friends joined me in prayer, I felt peace within, while staring into the savage water, which had almost taken our lives. We stayed under the bridge until the second siren went, indicating the raid was over. As we were crawling up the deep bank, our mothers ran to us. They were upset that we had gone to the creek. Mother was furious with me when she saw that my sister was wet and covered with mud. When we arrived home, I told Mother about breastfeeding Julika to quiet her. She looked at me questionably, "Ilona, who gave you that idea?"

"I don't know, *Anyuka*. It just came to me," I answered. She looked up, sighed and thanked God that Julika was safe. "How about my safety Mother?" I wondered. But that thought remained with my Savior.

My home country of Hungary, located in central Europe, was bounded on the north by Czechoslovakia, where I believe my ancestors originated. On the east was Russia (now the Ukraine), the eventual doorway through which Stalin's communism would enter Hungary. Austria and Yugoslavia bordered Hungary on the west and south respectively.

Hungary's 10.1 million people lived closely on only 93,030 km^2. Most of the population lived in large cities, such as Hungary's capital, Budapest, with a population of about 2 million. The majestic Danube River, connecting Buda and Pest, helped make this one of the most romantic cities in Europe. Virtually all Hungarians fluently spoke a single language - Hungarian (*Magyar*) - and the majority were Roman Catholics. Hungary's fertile plains, among the most productive agricultural areas in Europe, are broken up sparingly by low mountain ranges. The highest peak in Hungary is the Kekes summit (1,015 m) in the Matra range. Perched on the peak of the summit was the famous Kekes Hotel. On a clear day, from its tower you could use binoculars to see half of Hungary. The mountains' habitat included birch and oak trees, sprinkled with pine. There was an abundance of acacia and linden trees, where the cuckoo birds' calls could be heard. With their slender bodies, grayish-brown and white plumage, and pointed wings, they proudly displayed themselves among the lush, green branches. They were so unique: they laid their eggs in the nest of other birds, which then hatched and raised the baby cuckoos. When I return home to Hungary, I take a special trip to the woods to hear the cuckoo's two-note call that so closely resembles its name.

At the foot of the Matra Mountains is the city of Matraverebely-Kanyas. Nearby, in a quiet valley, sat the small village of Kanyas where I was born in 1934. My parents, grandparents, and the other fifteen families in our community farmed the fertile soil.

Mother, Mari, was tall and slim with dark hair, brown eyes and olive skin. She was a pretty woman with a very dictatorial personality. Father, Jozsef, was tall with blue eyes, fair skin, light wavy hair, and a neat little mustache above his neatly contoured lips. He was a loving, affectionate man. Sister, Maria, nicknamed Manci, was two years older than I. She took after Father with fair hair and blue eyes. Julika, who was seven years younger than I, inherited both of my parents' genes. Being the middle child, with dark skin, dark hair, and dark eyes, I was often called the black sheep of the family.

Our white, stuccoed, country house was divided into two large rooms, separated by a French door. Father and Mother slept in the kitchen part, with Julika next to them on a cot, folded in the daytime for extra space. The second room was a combination bedroom and living room. There were three beds, curtained off at night for privacy, and a fireplace embraced the corner. The oak dresser and two cabinets were against the opposite wall. The door beside the fireplace led into a 14'x15' storage room (*kamra*). Against the living room window, covered by Grandmother's white crochet curtain, sat a hand-carved oak bench. On its back panel, carved by Great-grandfather, was a grassy field with some shrubs in the background, as two rams butted heads. In front of it was a big table, with six high-back chairs. We only dined there when we had company. Other times we ate in the kitchen. We lived without the luxury of electricity. We had two petroleum lamps for light, which hung from the ceiling beam on a chain within easy reach to ignite and put out at night. A home-built brick stove in the kitchen was used for cooking and heat.

There were lots of chores to do on the farm. No one wanted to weed the garden, but feeding the animals was enjoyable. Well, except for Chestnut, whom I had to feed when Father was away. She was a beautiful horse with a shiny, reddish-brown coat, and blond mane and tail, but with a bad habit of biting everyone in range except Father. One day at feeding, to protect my face, I slowly approached her walking backwards, trying to calm her, and saying, "Nice horse, nice Chestnut." While easing closer, trying to toss the oats in her trough, she suddenly seized the clothing on my back with her teeth. With a quick lift, she shook me for a second and dropped me. While not hurt, I was furious. "One day I will outwit you!" I promised. Later on I built up courage and at feeding time I approached her confidently, with one hand pouring the oats in her trough, while in the other hand I held my pitchfork right in her face. Unable to terrify me, she furiously rolled her big, fiery eyes, stamped her right front foot, and snorted until I left her stall. It felt good as a young child to overcome my fear of the big, wicked horse.

Wood chopping was Father's task. Our task was to carry and stack the wood neatly in a pile. That is where that teasing, big, fat, brownish-green bullfrog, which I tried to catch for a while, lived. He would come out, sit on the lower board of the fence and just bellow. Regardless of how quietly I sneaked up on him, he would wait until he was just within my reach, then two or three hops and he was back under the old woodpile making funny noises. It was just like he was laughing at me. "But one day I'll catch you," I pledged. We also had to help Mother with meal preparation, as she was a seamstress. The nearest clothing store was seventy-five kilometers from Kanyas, so her services were much in demand.

I was greatly bound to my grandfather. Grandfather Batta was special; everyone agreed that he was a wise man. I spent much time with him; he had the patience to answer my endless questions. We had long walks around the fields checking if the grain was sprouting well. Later on he would tell me if we were going to have a good crop or not. And why. On our leisurely walks we saw mice, rabbits, and birds, and we would talk about them - especially about the cuckoo birds. Grandfather said because of their singing the cuckoo clock was invented. I was amazed when he told me how birds fly south thousands of miles, with only their God-given navigation instinct to guide them. On hot

4

summer days, resting, stretched out on the grass under the shady, old, oak tree, chewing on long stems of grass, looking up at the hazy, blue sky sprinkled with small fluffy clouds, resembling flocks of sheep, we discussed what was out there in the universe. And we talked about the Creator and His creations.

One day as we walked the three km to *Szentkut* Holy-well for healing water, Grandfather and I were reciting the famous Hungarian poet, Sandor Petofi's, patriotic poem: *Talpra Magyar hiv a haza!"* ("On your feet Hungarians, your country is calling!") Grandfather wanted to reinforce the patriotism in me, as a new generation for our beloved country. After quenching our thirst, with the clear, fresh water of *Szentkut's* well, we filled up our containers with holy water to take home to soothe Grandmother's ulcerated stomach. I asked, "Grandfather why we do call this a holy well?" While resting in the shade before our return, he revealed the story of the holy well of *Szentkut* and its "first miracle of healing."

A shepherd and his young son, who was dumb since birth, were tending to their grazing flock of sheep while advancing slowly through the valley. As the thirsty boy stayed behind to search for water, from the branches of the nearby oak tree, abruptly a beaming light blanketing the Holy Mari holding baby Jesus on her arm, appeared to him. She pointed to a crescent-shaped hole, where sparkling, clear water was arising. He quickly knelt down to satisfy his thirst, and then he called to his father. Startled to hear his son's voice for the first time, the skeptical father ran back, hesitantly asking, "What happened to you?" And the son recited the vision to his father fluently. The astounded, misty-eyed father hugged his son tightly, praised God for his miracle, fell to his knees, and gulped the cool, spring water.

"And my darling this is the first miracle and healing at *Szentkut's* Holy-well, which was documented as early as 1525," said Grandfather. (*Szentkut* still exists more than ever today, with thousands of pilgrims journeying to it on special occasions. The healing testimonials are endless as shown by the numerous grateful, burning candles and inscribed marble plaques left behind. This holy well remains in my heart to this day, even after 50 years in Canada. Upon returning to my home country for a visit, my first stop is at *Szentkut* to reflect on my early childhood with my beloved grandfather.) Before we proceeded home we ducked into the nearby 18th century, baroque-style church where I was baptized and named Ilona (Helena in English).

The church, nestled in a forested, partly landscaped, large valley, often echoed with the monks' harmonious Gregorian chanting. Regularly we made the hourly walk there to worship. The monks and nuns who cared for the church had land of their own to support them. The nuns traveled seven km from *Szentkut* to Matraverebely on bicycle to teach Catechism in our school, before the Communist takeover. Their robes and big white headpieces, resembling butterfly wings, fascinated me. I enjoyed being with them as we cleaned *Szentkut's* church. After dragging out the big carpets, and throwing them over a special rail, we beat the devil out of them with a wicker hand beater. "Beat the devil out of it." That was how the nuns phrased carpet cleaning to me. In the spring I visited the nuns and helped to plant the cement planters, mostly with red geraniums and white lobelias.

I had a special bond with Mother Rozalia, who cuddled and taught me while reading Bible stories. I would pretend that she was my mother and bury my face deep in her bosom, inhaling the sweet incense of her soft, black robe as she cuddled me. My dream was to become a nun, to be with her at all times. I was allowed to explore the church by myself: enjoying the pictures, statues, and the exquisitely detailed paintings of the Holy Mari, with the shepherd boy painted on the ceiling. It captivated me. I tried to copy this picture on a sheet of paper as Mother Rozalia had encouraged me to do. What frustrated me on Sundays was to sit quietly and pay attention to the Mass, part of which the priest conducted in Latin. I soon lost interest in the Latin words, but my *nagymama,* Grandmother Batta, next to me whispered, "You have to pay attention if you want to be a nun." But that was hard for my childish mind, since in my thoughts I was playing with the shepherd boy in the picture. The church was usually quiet on weekdays, but still people came endlessly to pray and drink the healing water, just as Grandfather and I did.

In 1941 I started school in the town of Matraverebely, walking the five km each way, every day except on severe winter days. Our schoolhouse was a red, brick building with white trimmed windows and boxes filled with crimson, trailing geraniums. These were the sun bathing pads for the ladybugs, and we were forbidden to pick them by our nature-loving principal. At the end of the wooden porch was our school bell, which we rang by pulling a string when needed. Our two outhouses were well camouflaged with tall, bright yellow sunflower plants, which we had to water daily. There were ten of us from our village in grades one through six, but we attended different classrooms. My sister, Manci, was two years ahead and she guided me through different events and team games.

One day at recess a boy pushed me off the swing and I landed on my face in the dirt. When I could see where the boy was, I grabbed him and slugged him a couple of times. That night at home my sister told Mother her version of the incident.

"Ilona was beating up a boy in school today!"

"That is not so! The boy pushed me off the swing, " I yelled.

"I didn't see that part," Manci answered.

What was worse was that Mother believed everything that Manci said. I was furious that she wouldn't listen to me. "Why don't you listen to my side of the story?" I cried.

"Shut up!" she said and turned away.

That night when she withheld my dessert of reconstituted fruit *compot* for punishment, I was still hungry and very angry. "It's not fair! It's not fair!" I shouted. She threw a cup of cold water in my face.

I ran out straight to the creek. Being very upset, I cursed both my mother and sister for not wanting to hear the truth of what really happened. Staying under the bridge until dusk, staring into the rapid, noisy water, I wondered where it would take me, if I floated downstream in the rushing current. Maybe it would take me to everlasting peace. It was dark and terrifying for me, as a young child trying hard to stabilize myself on a big rock near the river shore. Suddenly there was the sound of footsteps . . . I was startled . . . nearly slipping into the creek, thinking maybe the gypsies had found me, as their caravan was roaming the countryside, snatching everything in sight - even children. Then, more footsteps. I was shaking, fearfully holding my breath, *crunch-crunch*. By now the sound of footsteps was right above me on the bridge, and then silence.

A whispering voice called, "Ilona, Ilona, where are you? This is *Apuka* (Father). I came to take you home."

Ecstatic to hear Father's voice, I answered quickly. "Here I am, *Apuka*."

When he came down the bank of the river he hugged me tightly for a few moments and whispered, "Ilona, I love you dear. To be here in the dark alone is very dangerous; promise me you are never going to do this again." I promised and he held me in his arms for a little longer. And we strolled home together holding hands. As we walked in Mother gave me a harsh look. Father helped me to get in my pajamas, prayed with me, tucked the covers around me,

7

and kissed me goodnight. Shortly after, he returned with a small glass of milk and a piece of bread.

Later, I heard my parents arguing about me. Father said, "Mari how would it have been if Ilona had fallen into the creek, with no one to help her . . . and she had drowned?"

"Nobody sent her there," she replied casually.

"You have no compassion for her. Mari, you are creating a rebellious child!" Father exclaimed.

Mother's voice rose in anger, "Hush up! Just, hush up about her!"

"Mari you are so unfair to her. If anything had happened to her, I would never have forgiven you." Father seldom raised his voice and when he did it bothered me. I thought maybe it would be better if the gypsies would take me, and then there wouldn't be conflict between them.

Next morning I asked Mother if I could start walking to school by myself, just to the crossroad. She gave me permission. Even though we had mostly horse-drawn wagons, with only the odd car, I still had to wait for the other children and my sister before going on to the main road. I was happy to go earlier by myself, because at the crossroad was a small hill. On top of the hill was a weathered cross, on which I saw an imaginary Jesus looking down at me every time we walked by. I wanted to go up and see it for myself. I was fascinated during my first exploration: the black, rugged cross anchored in the hill was real, as my imaginary white Jesus figure beamed down at me, capturing my six-year-old heart. Sitting on the grass in front of the cross, I shared my heartache over missing my mother's love and understanding with my secret Friend. I felt secure and safe there, in a world of my own. Later I found a small hole at the foot of the cross where I met my other new friend: a cricket I named Maestro. Holding him in my open palm, I admired his motionless, shiny, black body, but was really fascinated by the rapid, searching movement of his wiry, black antennae. When I cried out in frustration and loneliness, he came out of his hole and played his best for me.

After several visits to the cross, Mother asked me, "Ilona, why do you always want to walk alone just to the crossroad?"

"I just want to be alone," I replied, not wanting to share my secret with anyone who wouldn't understand. Having never told Mother about my crossroad talks, I was surprised that she agreed whenever I asked to go there. Usually, she wouldn't let me go anywhere without my older sister. I didn't like being with her. She always bossed me around; at times she was worse than Mother at handing out orders. So I became a loner and spent much precious time at the crossroad: braiding wild-flower wreaths and hanging them on the cross, as my friend Jesus smiled down at me.

CHAPTER 2

Hungry at all times, I was forever plotting ways to get more food. Just before the war reached Hungary, Mother collected the limited amount of sugar we got on stamp rations. The sugar was kept in a locked chest in the living room. Only Mother had the key to the chest, since our money was also kept there. She had the key tied to her apron string. Whenever Mother was close I looked intently at the chest key, until I had its shape engraved in my mind. In the tool shed I got a piece of hard wire and formed a key from my mental image. I hardly could wait to be home alone. Finally I was. I rushed into the living room and tried my wire key in the lock; to my amazement it opened on the first try. Before I got control of myself, I had eaten most of the sugar cubes. By the time I could stop myself, I had nearly emptied the whole container. Approximately two weeks later, with Easter approaching, Mother decided to do her baking. To her shock, there was hardly any sugar left in the container. Rage reflected from her sparkling eyes and red face, as she asked my sister and me which one of us had taken the sugar. She knew it wasn't Manci, as she was always around her. Having admitted taking the sugar cubes because I was hungry, I was startled when Mother grabbed the stick that she always kept near at hand.

"You have to be punished for stealing," she yelled. Ignoring my cry, she whipped me furiously. "You have stolen from the whole family, not just from me," she screamed. "You'd better go to the crossroad." Which I did, sobbing all the way. I had to tell my Friend on the cross the pain I felt and admit that it was wrong to steal the sugar. Sitting was too painful so I just lay on the ground sobbing. Maestro came out of his hole and played for me, rubbing his feet against his wings. He fascinated me and helped me to momentarily forget my troubles. Listening to him, my heartache slowly eased, allowing other thoughts to fill my mind. Suddenly I realized my mother must know about my crossroad talks; that's why she sent me there. When I arrived home I asked her about it.

"Yes," she said, "I know what you do when you're there." She told me that one day she followed me to the crossroad and hid behind the bushes and listened to my heart-felt pleadings. "I'm happy about your conversations with Jesus," she said. That made me feel even worse for stealing and deceiving Mother.

When my father heard about my deed, he took a different tact. Curious about how a young child could make such a key, he said, "Ilona come to the tool shed with me, and show me how you made the chest key."

"Okay Father. I can make it; come and see." He watched me closely. When I finished, he took the key and put it in his pocket saying, "I will try it tonight." Later, he found out the key worked.

Father was always quiet, gentle, fair, and loving, so different from Mother. When school got out, Mother often sent me to Grandmother's for the summer, but not Manci. That puzzled me. Why? Maybe because I wasn't the boy that she hoped for. While feeling rejected by Mother, I was delighted to visit Grandmother Usak in Budapest.

Her name was Rozi, and we loved each other deeply. She looked after a disabled lady, since Grandfather Usak had passed away long ago. She was my mother's mother, but they did not get along.

Before I left to Budapest I asked Father to look after Maestro for me. He was in a jar in the shed. "Yes dear, I will take care of Maestro for you," Father promised.

I was fascinated by the train ride; I gazed out the window enjoying the villages, towns and countrysides as the train zipped by. I was amazed at how different everything was compared to our small village.

Arriving in Budapest, for the first time on my own, I felt so grown up. Grandmother waited for me at the station and we rode the streetcar on Rakoci Street to Grandmother's apartment. The multitude jumped on and off the streetcar as they commuted across the city, without saying anything to each other. The overhead, electrical wires, powering the streetcar as they crackled and sparkled, fascinated me. I felt like I was in a totally different world, far away from Kanyas.

After supper, while Grandmother washed the dishes, I bathed using Grandmother's fragrant soaps and shampoo in the huge bathtub, which had shiny, chrome taps. I dreamt of how nice this would be at home, instead of our washbasin, which was in constant use between the five of us.

The first time I went for a walk with Grandmother around Budapest, she explained how Budapest is really two cities - Buda and Pest - divided by the majestic Danube River, the same river that was the inspiration for Johann Strauss' famous *Blue Danube Waltz*. The cities were unified in 1873. We explored Buda's terraced plateau, which still contained relics of the former

11

Turkish occupation. As a child, the structure of the thick walls, towers, and drawbridges of the old castles intrigued me.

After lunch we crossed the Danube using the Chain Bridge, one of the many bridges connecting Buda and Pest. The House of Parliament, built on a plain, overlay four acres in front of us. Grandmother explained there were many institutions inside this magnificent structure: the Academy of Sciences, the Museum of Fine Art, the Palace of Justice, the University of Budapest, the Custom House, and the National Museum. We would spend many days discovering the treasures hidden within this building. At night, the glistening lights of the Parliament building created a captivating reflection on the shimmering Danube.

Budapest's tree-bordered boulevards and inventive, landscaped, wide squares, edged by old and new buildings, gave Budapest the reputation of being one of the most beautiful cities in Europe. One of our favorite places for picnics was Margit Island, a public park in the middle of the Danube River. I can still taste Grandmother's egg salad sandwiches with her tangy, home-made spread, her mildly flavored coffee cake, *kuglof,* and the sweet taste of her home-made raspberry drink, *malnaszurp.* While resting in the shade of an acacia tree on hot summer afternoons, Grandmother educated me with stories about old churches, castles, and the museum of Buda.

Throughout my visit we had many interesting adventures. I particularly enjoyed teasing the crafty monkeys in the zoo at the park. People would cover rocks with candy wrappers and toss them to the monkeys, who would quickly open the packages and throw the rocks right back at their tormentors. They amused the public. When we went to the circus, I especially enjoyed when the young children performed. I wished I could do that. The amusement park was where my pleasure and fear laid: thrilled by the small rides, but petrified by the big roller coaster. I loved being with Grandmother; she satisfied my curiosity about many interesting things and events. We enjoyed each other's company, going to the market, on picnics, and to church.

I especially treasure the memory of going to church one Sunday in my favorite outfit: a white dress with little red daisy prints; a white ribbon in my dark hair, which Grandmother had French braided; and white shoes, which Grandmother's friend had given me. All dressed up, going to church, I felt like a princess, and I walked like one, as Grandmother taught me. When I was in church, I prayed to God mostly for two things: first, for my mother's love and second, for Grandmother to come and live with us. I also wished for the boy, sitting in front of me with his grandmother, to turn around and smile at me, which he did occasionally. On our way home we always stopped by the corner bistro to have espresso for Grandmother and a *malnaszurp* for me.

I learned with Grandmother how to get around in our neighborhood. Later I was able to go to the market by myself on the streetcar, feeling very independent.

My precious visit ended and I was very sad to leave Grandmother. At the station she gave me a hug and kiss, and whispered, "Don't cry dear. I will come and live with you some day." Even with her promise, I had to catch some of the rolling, salty tears with my tongue since I had no wipes. When I boarded the train, I sat by the window staring out into the emptiness, saddened deeply to leave my peaceful, loving grandmother to face my unloving, domineering mother. With the queasy feeling in my heart, aching for my dear *nagymama,* I reached Nagybatony station, where Father waited for me. With a big tender hug he said, "I missed you Ilona."

So few words, but they were enough to soften my aching heart. I smiled at him. He reminded me so much of Grandfather Batta. Surely the love in my heart shone in my eyes, but too shy to tell him how much I loved him, I asked instead, "*Apuka* how is Maestro doing?"

He shook his head. "Sorry, but Maestro got away, as I accidentally left the jar open." Knowing he didn't like to see anything captured, I didn't protest my loss. Thinking instead of finding another pet: perhaps I'll be lucky and catch that big, teasing, yappy bullfrog hiding under the woodpile.

When we arrived home, Mother pointed at me and remarked, "Trouble is home!" Nothing had changed. It tormented me. Why didn't she love me, like she loved my sisters? As a child, and even later, that was beyond my comprehension; only Mother knew.

Five months passed and W.W. II reached Hungary in 1944, and with it my dream came true: Grandmother Usak came from Budapest to live with us. But she wasn't as excited as I was, so I asked her why not? Hesitantly she said, "Time will tell with your mother." Knowing how difficult Mother could be, I felt sorry for Grandmother. Nevertheless, I loved her more for that very reason. To my delight she allowed me to sleep with her. In bed we discussed Bible stories, and reminisced about our favorite places in Budapest. Later she tried to explain the dangers of the war we were facing and that she had felt a

13

strong urge to be with me at wartime. While all that was really beyond my comprehension, just having my *nagymama* so near was enough to make me feel secure and content.

One night after supper, my sisters and I were sent to bed in a hurry. Always curious, I snuck out of bed and with ears glued to the door I heard my father and our neighbors planning to build a shelter in which to hide, when the battle reached our valley. I was excited to hear we would be sharing the place with many people, especially with my friends. But I had no idea what the war was all about.

The next day, on our way to school, some of the older children said German and Russian soldiers were coming with guns and tanks and would be fighting for territory. They were old enough to understand that we would be trapped between the two armies. The way they described what would happen sounded scary, but for me, in my innocence, I thought it would be a great adventure.

It wasn't long before the war reached our valley. We had to run and take cover, carrying food and blankets with us. My best friend, Terri, and I were the only ones who seemed happy to be there. Now, with no school, we could play all day we thought. But our happiness was short-lived.

Two days after we escaped into the bunker, we heard pounding on the door and yelling in a foreign language. In his frightened state, my father had a hard time opening the door. Another intense bang from the outside forced the door open. Two German soldiers barged in with a Hungarian interpreter. They looked frightening. Their piercing eyes scowled at us. Through the interpreter, we found out that they were looking for Jewish people. Later I heard of Hitler's attempt to eliminate the Jewish nation. This saddened me deeply, but we weren't allowed to talk about that. Grandmother said the only thing we could do was to pray for them.

We stayed hiding for three more days and nights, existing on the food we had carried, while the Germans and Russians battled around us. The whistle of bullets and large artillery scared me. Not knowing where they would land, we realized we could all be killed at any time. All we could do was whisper prayers.

The morning of the fourth day, everything was dangerously quiet. We waited anxiously, not knowing what had happened outside. Suddenly, German soldiers wearing swastika armbands burst into the bunker again and forced us out. Having been in the dark so long, the soldiers' shiny silver rings attracted me: the crown of the ring was formed by a skull and crossbones - the symbol of Hitler's security police, the feared SS troops. They searched every inch of the bunker, walking on our straw-stuffed mattresses, while poking their long knives into them to make sure no one was hiding inside. After the search we were forced back into the bunker. Two soldiers stayed outside, guarding the door. We were not allowed to go out - not even to relieve ourselves. We had to use buckets hidden away in one corner. The putrefied, foul odor from the buckets saturated not only the air, but also our bodies. We all gagged frequently. That was the only time I didn't feel hunger.

Late in the afternoon the battle started again. This time, the shells landed very close to where we were hiding. Two soldiers came in and killed the petroleum lamp, our only source of light, and left us in the darkness. Suddenly, dead silence. Abruptly, the deafening whistling of a shell caused us to cower together on the tattered mattresses. A violent explosion ripped through the air and shook the whole place. Grandmother held me in her arms and covered me with a blanket. I couldn't breathe. I was so terror stricken, I wet the mattress where we were crouching. Feeling the warm liquid, Grandmother whispered, "Hush, darling, hush," as she pulled me closer to her. Knowing and feeling the power of her faith, I knew we would survive.

The following day the German army was forced out by the Russian Cossack soldiers. One of the men bravely opened the door and looked outside to see what was happening. After a few minutes he slammed the door shut and reported what he had seen, his voice shrill with terror.

"The Russians are coming down the hill like ants. They are being slaughtered, but they just keep coming."

Later that day the fighting ceased. The Cossacks had taken over our village. They were much different than the Germans, who had neat uniforms, high boots, carried only hand and machine guns, and traveled with tanks and motorcycles. The Cossacks, on the other hand, were the front line for the Russian Red Army. Wearing baggy pants, short boots, round furry hats and carrying their short rifles in a sling on their backs, they also carried short swords in cases, which were attached to their belts. Instead of having a mechanized army, the Cossacks rode bareback on medium-sized horses.

Once our fathers were satisfied that the firing had stopped, we crept out of the bunker. Stupefied from the fresh air and bright sun, we saw the destruction of the village. Relieved to see that our house was still standing, we rushed to it.

15

But to our shock, it had been looted. Our down duvets, the good dishes stored in the cabinet, and the linens were stolen. Mother was furious when she discovered that her sewing machine was also missing. Grandmother calmed us, telling us to be thankful that we were alive. Unfortunately, most of our neighbors suffered alike. Later we discovered that the thieves were civilians from other villages nearby. After some detective work Mother found her sewing machine.

The Cossacks were apprehensive and thoroughly combed the village barns and lofts for hidden Germans. They scanned our house, with eyes like searchlights, while two of them held us in the kitchen. My terrified ten-year-old eyes were focused on the soldier's trigger finger as he held the barrel of his machine gun about 15 cm from my face. He was growling at Father in Russian. To hold back his anger, Father squeezed my shoulders, as I stood between the two of them, utterly terrified. When they were satisfied with their search, they left. Days went by and more soldiers passed through our village.

One afternoon, we heard a disturbance outside. Mother fearfully peeked through the window and said, "Three Cossacks are getting off their horses. They are staggering toward the house, drinking from bottles. They are drunk." The sound of their guttural Russian and coarse laughter frightened us even more. Mother ordered my older sister to stay quiet and pushed her back to the wall on the bed we were sitting on, and she quickly covered her with blankets. She told her not too move, peek or utter a sound. I didn't know why she wanted her to stay hidden, but I dared not ask any questions. While sitting on the bed together, Mother seized Julika in her arms, and Father sat me on his knees and held me tight. It wasn't until I felt his body shaking against mine that I realized we were in great danger. The five of us huddled on the bed, with my twelve-year-old, restless sister, suffocating under the blankets. I didn't know what was going on.

Within minutes the intoxicated, grinning, red-eyed soldiers were in the house looking in every room for something or someone, while talking loudly in Russian. Scanning us with their wicked eyes, one of them pointed at Mother. Instantly, Father took one of his arms from me and pulled Mother securely to us. We were terrified. Nevertheless they laughed, staggered around, and mumbled in Russian for a while before they left.

Shortly after they left the yard, our neighbor Mrs. Szabo stormed through the door. She was speechless, gasping for air, with her torn blouse and loose hair flying. Mother quickly led her into the other room and closed the door. I wanted to follow them, but Mother pushed me out and sent me outside for firewood. I realized something terrible happened, but Mother kept denying it. After a few days of hush-hush, I heard from the other neighbors that Mrs. Szabo and her thirteen-year-old daughter were raped: by those drunken soldiers. Shortly after, her young daughter died, because of that horrible ordeal. Then, I realized why my sister had been hidden and why Father had held me so tight.

Grandmother realized my perplexity, and with rosary in hand she led us in prayer, but I could not concentrate: the rape, death and funeral left an indelible mark on my soul. It left me with a very deep hatred for war and the gruesome word *rape.*

About two weeks later, the Cossacks moved out and the Russian Red Army took over our village. It was difficult to communicate with them, so we learned to use gestures and facial expressions until we gradually learned to communicate. With the invasion of the German and Russian armies we were very short of food. One day, my parents told me to play outside and let them know if anyone came into our yard. When I saw them going into the tool shed, securely closing the door behind them, my childish curiosity arose and led me to tip toe to the shed and peep through the door crack to see what was going on behind that closed door. Shocked at the sight, I just oozed to the ground. Creeping up and looking into the gloom of the shed again, I could see a deep hole, lined with a wooden box containing food: beans, corn, potatoes, a smoked ham, and dried fruit. "Food! Food!" I screamed. Mother ran out and clasped her hands around my mouth. "Hush! People can hear you miles away." But luckily no one did, and she made me promise not to tell anyone about the hidden food.

It became a normal routine for one member of the family to watch out the window for unwanted visitors, while the rest of the family ate secretly and quickly. The soldiers were constantly searching for food. The soldiers had even carted away the dead horses that our fathers had wanted to butcher. Being hungry most of the time, my thoughts centered mostly on food. Every little bit we ate made us greedy for more. "We don't know how long the war will last. We have to ration," Mother warned us. Later we discovered that our neighbors had also hidden food and eaten secretly.

One night we each had a small piece of ham for supper from the hidden treasure box. My tiny ration just disappeared in my mouth, leaving me with an even deeper hunger. Granted, it was the best tasting ham I had ever eaten, but it just wasn't enough. As a growing ten-year-old, I was still extremely hungry, craving for more. Lying in bed that night, I started plotting ways to steal a big piece of that ham.

The next day, with Father's jack knife in my pocket and no one in sight, I ran into the tool shed, my mouth watering, already tasting the sweet, salty, flavor of the smoked ham. To my surprise there was straw and a big boulder sitting on top of the box to camouflage it. The hunger flashed; that boulder wasn't going to stop me. I tried to move the boulder, but it didn't budge. Powered by hunger, pushing, pulling, I finally managed to move the boulder halfway off the box. Suddenly, I heard Mother.

"Ilona, are you in the shed?'

I forgot to lock the door!

Mother called, "I'm bringing the key right now."

My fear of Mother's anger if she caught me stealing again was greater than my hunger. With strength I didn't know I possessed, I managed to get the boulder back in place just as she came through the door.

"Ilona, what are you doing in the shed?"

"Just playing," I answered, bent over pretending to tie my shoelace to hide my flushed face, and deceit.

"From now on I forbid you to play in the tool shed. Come into the house right now."

"Yes Mother!" Exhausted, and furious that she had disrupted my ham feast, I followed her, but I didn't give up about the ham.

CHAPTER 3

The Russian soldiers had been occupying our valley for several months. By then we were used to having them amongst us. One miserable, rainy, Sunday afternoon two young soldiers barged into our house and gave Mother a live goose to cook. They tried to explain to her in Russian that they would be back for supper. Behind the tool shed, Father was reluctant to kill the goose, which I recognized as our neighbor's mother goose. She had been sitting on four eggs, which were hidden under a big willow basket locked up in the chicken coop. Father said we couldn't save the goose; the hungry Russian soldiers wouldn't understand or permit it. Hesitating for a second, Father used his axe to quickly silence the mother goose, before all the neighbors would hear her cry. Soon after, the goose was plucked; Father quickly buried the feathers and said, "Listen dear, not a word to anyone about the goose not even to our family."

"Yes Father."

Soon the goose was roasting in the oven. The lingering, savory aroma was enough to drive us insane. We were all so hungry. But there was no thought of stealing it - we knew only too well what would happen if we crossed our unwelcome guests with their loaded machine guns. I fantasized how heavenly it would be to have that goose all to myself. My dream didn't last long.

A few hours later, five soldiers came back bringing bottles of wine, drinking straight from the bottles. I ignored them, trying to figure out how could I steal a piece of the goose. Drooling wild-eyed at the big, golden, brown drumstick Mother was basting, I closed my eyes and fantasized about sucking the bone and chewing the gristles. Shortly, the two young soldiers returned and joined the other five in our living room. They brought some bread and two bottles of *palinka*, Hungarian whisky. Now I was really worried. How could there be anything left for me after seven soldiers finished eating one goose?

At last the goose was done and Mother carried it into the living room and set it on the table. She asked me to get plates and cutlery, which I did gladly. I brought the plates and utensils in and positioned myself between two soldiers, with my elbows and hands on the table ready to eat. Mother called me several times to come back to the kitchen, but I pretended not to hear her. I had no other thought but to stay close to the savory goose, with the crispy drumstick. My father came to take me out, but I refused to go. I clung to the older soldier with the mustache and he held my hand, indicating that I could stay. My father had to leave me there, but I could see my parents were keeping an eye on me from the kitchen. Once Father had left, the mustached soldier lifted me up on his knee. Somehow he was different from the others, with his warmer smile, and cleaner nails and boots. He started to feed me and gave me a hug. The word "rape" flashed through my mind; with deep fright I pushed him away. I wanted to run out, but my overpowering hunger kept me back. I was eating the morsels they gave me so quickly that I choked. I couldn't believe how quickly the goose was disappearing as the seven hungry soldiers tore at it.

"Bring some for us," Mother whispered as she was staring at me. But how? The soldiers were giving me just one piece at a time. Sometimes it was goose meat and other times I would be fed bite-size pieces of bread dipped in the gravy. I had an idea. I took every other piece in my hand and pretended that I had accidentally dropped it under the table. Then I casually got down from the soldier's knee to find the meat and put it in my apron pocket, before I straightened up. The soldiers continued to eat and drink, and then they began to sing. The harmony of their voices, especially one of the younger ones called Sasha, filled the house as they sang one Russian song after another about the Ural Mountains and the Volga River. They kept feeding me, but I was getting nervous that they would notice that I was ducking under the table too often. There were still some scraps in the pan, and I needed more for my family. The only way to have more was to stuff some in my cheeks.

When my cheeks and pocket were full, I slowly got off the soldier's knee and walked back into the kitchen. I gave a hug to Mother while I spit the goose meat into her hand. She started to feed Julika, who was waiting with an open mouth like a little bird. All this time the soldiers paid no attention to us. Father said in a low voice, "We are proud of you for getting some food for us."

By now the soldiers were highly intoxicated. They stopped singing and sounded like they were arguing. Their voices were loud and harsh. We were in danger. I saw my father's face tense, as one of the younger soldiers came to us and grabbed Mother by the arm, trying to pull her into the bedroom. Father jumped up and tried to wrestle her away from the soldier, but the other younger soldier put his rifle against Father's chest, pushed him roughly to sit down and held his gun on Father.

At this moment, Mother panicked. She quickly seized me and clutched me in her arms.

"Hang on to me!" she screamed. "Don't let go of me." Tears streamed down her face and I felt the wild beating of her heart, as she held me tightly. We were both petrified with terror. The soldier grabbed me roughly and tried to rip me out of my mother's arms. Barely able to move because of Mother's desperate embrace, I yelled at him.

"You savage beast. Let my mother go!"

The gruesome word of *rape* flashed in my mind. I was screaming and hitting the soldier with my two small fists while crushed between him and my mother's arms. As the soldier dragged us towards the bed in the other room, the mustached soldier yelled. It became louder and louder as Mother and I were forced closer and closer to the bed. I was still crying and screaming. Then, the mustached soldier jumped up, grabbed his rifle, and fired a shot into the ceiling. Instantly Father ran into the room. The young soldier, who had attacked Mother, furiously turned on him, throwing him to the floor. The mustached soldier cocked his rifle again, holding it on the two young soldiers and forced them out of the house.

Grandmother seized me in her arms. Father cradled Mother in his. The five soldiers who remained lowered their voices, talking among themselves. Still distraught, Mother slumped onto the bed and covered her face with her hands, as she rocked back and forth.

"Thank God we are safe. Thank God, thank God," Mother mumbled to herself.

After this rape attempt, the tension in the room was unbearable. Sulfur fumes from the discharged rifle mingled with the smell of liquor and the gray haze of the cigarette smoke of seven soldiers permeated the whole house. Mother was unable to control herself; she rushed to the washbasin and vomited violently. Watching her, a pool of acid rose in my throat, and I had to share the basin with her. In the other room, the remaining soldiers quieted down and whispered among themselves. The mustached one came into the kitchen. He approached Mother as she leaned over the basin and gently stroked her shoulder, saying something in Russian, which we couldn't understand. Then he took a photograph out of his wallet and showed it to Mother. It was a picture of a lady holding a young girl about my age. When the picture was passed to Father, he looked deeply into the Russian's eyes, silently thanking him: one father to another.

21

Eventually the soldiers dozed off, some sleeping on our beds in their clothes and boots while the others dozed on the chairs. In the kitchen, Mother pushed me into the corner of the bed with Julika. Mother, Father and Grandmother, were sitting on the outside edge. Then Mother said to us, "We have to be silent about this episode, not a word to anyone, not even Manci," who was hiding in our neighbor's attic with her friend. Still frightened, the five of us huddling on one bed waited for the terrifying night to end.

Still fearful, awoken by loud voices, I thought the horror of the previous night was about to continue. I quickly ducked under the bed. Just then one of our neighbors burst into the house with the news we had been waiting for: "The war is over! The war is over!" We hugged, cried, and sang the Hungarian Anthem.

CHAPTER 4

Now, for Hungary, a new era was about to begin. The Red Army took over and brought with them their notion of freedom. The post-war cooperation between Russia and the West collapsed, and the cold war began. With Soviet support, Hungarian Matyas Rakosi, who had been trained in Moscow, began to establish a communist dictatorship. And the communist terror in Hungary was enforced.

Under Communism, we were not allowed to listen to foreign radio stations, especially "Radio Free Europe." Anyone caught listening to that particular station was subject to severe punishment. Our fathers met secretly, crouching over a radio in the darkened room, trying to get news of the political situation in Hungary. Outside, late at night one of the fathers patrolled to alert the others if anyone approached the house. We were all terrified of the Hungarian undercover communists. We were prisoners, not only in our country, but also in our homes.

Those known to the Party leaders as faithful communists were paid to report on anyone they suspected of engaging in any activities against the state. Whomever they reported simply disappeared. Within a short time, the government instituted a radical land reform program. Gradually, the mines, electric plants, heavy industries, and some banks were nationalized. Freedom of the press was strictly curtailed. We were forbidden to be in groups, either in our homes or on the streets, that reached beyond the immediate family.

Our precious church in *Szentkut* was looted. Some of the nuns were raped, the monks tortured or brutally abused and humiliated; later they just vanished. After this terrible crime we went to church seeking solace, but it wasn't the same. My mind could not concentrate on praying, when all I could think about was what had happened to the nuns, especially to Mother Rozalia whom I loved so dearly. What humiliation for any human being to endure, let alone these godly people, whom we had known and respected. Now that they were gone, without the spiritual presence they had radiated, going to church wasn't the same. I couldn't understand why this desecration had to happen, but as a young child it was deeply ingrained in my heart. What I needed more than anything else was for my God to help me to regain my faith; I yearned passionately to recapture the spiritual joy I had always felt in our precious church in *Szentkut.* Even though there was no priest to say Mass, we went to church regardless, praying and singing hymns with tear-flooded eyes and much sobbing. The tragic events suffered by the congregation during the war and under the tyrannical Communist rule, bound us together as if we were one family, striving to maintain our faith.

Before long, the government opened a coalmine in our village. People who worked in the mine were promoted or demoted according to how fast they adopted the Communist system. Some adjusted very quickly, not because they believed in the system, but as a means of survival. Father got a job at the mine, but his wages were very low since he wasn't in favor of the Communist system. There was no livestock, or seeds to plant; everything had been consumed by the German and Russian armies.

In the spring, people came to the village trading potatoes, sunflower seeds, corn, and wheat. These products were available only on the black market. Desperate for seeds, Father had no choice but to give them whatever they demanded for their products. Reluctantly, he was forced to give up some of his tools and some of our household goods. They even took my precious winter coat! I thought my heart would break when I saw Father finally hand it over to them.

In spring, we had to cultivate the land by hand. This took days, since the Communist regime had confiscated all the harnessing animals and machinery. This left very little time for us to play after school. We had to rush to finish our homework and then go out to the field. It had been decided that since Manci had more homework, she could stay longer at home to finish her schoolwork.

One day Mother sent me home for drinking water. As I approached the house, the smell of Grandmother's potato *paprikas* made my mouth water. She knew I was always hungry, and with her usual warm smile she gave me a small *paprikas* to taste.

"My poor, hungry darling," she said, watching me gulp down the delicious, stove-hot morsel. Eating hoggishly I asked, "Where is Manci?"

"She is in the other room studying," Grandmother replied.

I went to see, and she was in bed sound asleep. I was furious. It was a very hot afternoon.

When I gave Mother the water I burst out, "Manci is sleeping at home and I have to work in this heat. She's two years older than I am. Why isn't she working here with us?"

24

Mother didn't seem to be concerned. "Maybe she's tired," she stated as she turned to walk away from me.

"It's not fair! It's not fair!" I yelled at her through my tears. "You always favor her over me!" But she kept on walking away. I was angry with her and went to hoe at the other end of the field, about three-quarters of a kilometer from her. I was hungry, tired, and my back ached. I couldn't stop crying. I wished horrible things for my mother and sister. My only solace was thinking of the crossroad where I always found peace.

At suppertime I brought the subject up again, but there was nothing to discuss as far as Mother was concerned. The next Saturday Manci worked in the field with us. Later, Mother sent her for drinking water - a fifteen-minute walk away. It took her almost an hour to come back. When I complained to Mother about it, she continued hoeing as if I wasn't there. When I kept staring at her, she finally stopped, looked crossly at me and said, "She's slower than you are. So what?" She always made excuses for her.

I felt like running away. I had a bitter fight with Mother and finally she sent me home. On my way home from the field, I made a detour to the crossroad. Sitting in front of the rugged cross I prayed for Mother's love, hugs, and understanding. After doing everything I could to protect her from the soldiers, I couldn't understand what more I needed to do to win her love. Her constant unfairness proved to me that I was an unwanted child. I beseeched the Lord to guide me in my thoughts, so as not to wish evil things upon my mother and sister.

CHAPTER 5

I attended high school in Kisterenye, a larger town than Matraverebely, where I had finished elementary school. The town of Kisterenye circled around a low mountain on which the town's majestic church was perched. The church could be reached by climbing 124 brick steps, lined with acacia trees. Their fragrance permeated the whole town.

Dr. Nadasdi, the old-fashioned, friendly doctor, still made house calls as he looked after the townspeople. With population growth the small theater badly needed expansion. The town hall, located in the middle of Kisterenye, was where the people very carefully tried to sort out their different views on communism. The one corner and one general store were sufficient, because under the Communist system food was scarce and there was no competition: one pound of coffee or one pound of margarine was the same price all over the country. Our transportation was by foot or train. Since it was seven km from Kanyas, it was arranged that I would live with my godparents and Aunt Anna (*Panni Mama*). I went home to Kanyas only on weekends.

My godmother was my mother's cousin. She had no children of her own, so she was happy to play the mother role for me. Godmother Julia was a kind, heavy-set, red-haired lady. Godfather Istvan, also called Pista, was a tall, thin, haughty person. He was an excellent miner at the Kisterenye coalmine. Aunt Anna, Godmother's mother was like a mother hen who folded everyone under her wings. She was a lovely, soft-spoken, good-hearted lady in her eighties. Godfather, who was very difficult to live with, didn't pick on her, because she was hard of hearing and most of the time she just ignored him.

I was glad to get away from my mother, but sad to be apart from Father and Grandmother Usak. Arriving in Kisterenye, I was curious about my temporary new home and hoped my life at Godmother's would be easier. That hope vanished the first evening. Sitting at the supper table, Godfather announced, "Ilona, since your parents are not paying for your room and board, you have to work for it."

"Room-and-board?" I thought. "We are related!" After all, they often stayed at our house and I had to give up my bed for them and sleep on the floor.

Godfather continued, "You have to do your own laundry and help with the household chores. And I expect you to get water before and after school," he finished with a wicked smirk. Since they had no well of their own, water had to be carried from a community well half a kilometer down the road. Having delivered his demands, he went back to eating, trying to avoid my angry, piercing eyes. Sensing his hostility, I was frightened and confused. But after remembering Grandmother's advice, I decided I would do what ever it took to get my education.

The next morning was registration at the school. Large pictures of Communist leaders, including our Moscow trained leader, Matyas Rakosi, as well as Stalin and Lenin, looked down on us from one wall of each classroom. A very large map of Russia dominated the opposite wall. From the first day it was made clear to us that we were to learn how to become faithful Communists. We were taught about the "Glorious Bolshevik Revolution" and the "Great Soviet Army." Our patriotic red, white, and green striped flag was altered to bear the symbol of Russia - a hammer and sickle on a red star - in the middle of it. Our new comrade principal gave us a lecture on how lucky we were to live in a free country under the "Glorious Communist Regime." He declared, "There is zero tolerance in my school for disobedience." Then he announced that the student youth group, *Disz*, would be organized and he ordered everyone to participate. With this new system we found ourselves living in a different country, or more like a different world.

When I came home from school, Godmother asked me how I had managed. I told her what we did and how nervous I was not knowing anyone. While we prepared supper, she tried to assure me that everything would work out just fine.

At the table, Godfather dished out the food for each of us. I wanted more; I was still hungry. But, I wouldn't dare to ask him for more. As he rose from the table, he looked sternly at me and ordered, "Ilona, you have to clear the table and do the dishes. Don't forget, you have to work for your room and board." The words "room and board" got to me again, but remembering I was there to get my education, I swallowed the words I wanted to say.

By the time I finished the dishes, my only desire was to go to bed, but there were only two rooms in the house: the kitchen and the bedroom. Since I slept with Godmother in the kitchen, I could hardly wait until Auntie and Godfather went to bed in the other room. Their beds were curtained off for privacy. Godmother did not sleep with Godfather because the room wasn't heated and he kept the windows open summer and winter, regardless of how cold it was.

The next day on my way to school I heard two men talking about our deteriorating political situation.

"It is getting worse day by day. The Hungarian Communist Party is gaining more and more authority over the country and the people," said the bearded man.

"That damn party dominates us whether we like it or not. I despise them, but we have to be silent if we want to keep our job and our lives," the other man complained.

"Even our own countrymen betray us. We could just simply disappear like so many have already," the bearded man replied.

I kept quiet as I followed them closely.

In school we had to be on guard about what we said. We didn't know which students were Communist and which were not. Some were informers. They knew how to be friendly and talk nicely to get your opinion on communism, only later to betray you. If you voiced your beliefs freely, such as I like democracy or I hate communism, you could be reported and pay a very high price for it - your life. Even the walls had ears. We learned to be voiceless, especially in school.

One day, Mrs. Bognar, our next-door neighbor, came over to ask Godmother if I could babysit her two-year-old son, Gyurika. She got an evening job at the railway ticket office, and her husband didn't get home until seven p.m. I would have to go to her house right after school, and she would give me supper and pay me by the hour. I was delighted that Godmother agreed. I was awake most of that night counting all the money I would earn.

The next day I approached Godmother, "The youth group is going to have ballroom dance classes on Saturday nights. If I save my babysitting money, can we go to Salgotarjan and buy me a new dress for the opening night?" I held my breath, while waiting for her answer.

"Of course, darling, and I will help you out if you don't have enough money." With a fearful look she added, "But not a word of this to anybody. If your godfather found out we would be in trouble." Even she feared Godfather.

"My lips are sealed," I whispered. Astounded by Godmother's generosity, I gave her a tight hug for which she cried, "Ouch!" Knowing how unpleasant Godfather could be, it was hard to believe she would take such a risk for me. It was beyond my wildest dreams that I would be able to pick out my own style and color of dress, and pay for it with my own money.

The following afternoon I went to Mrs. Bognar's house. Eating our supper of bean soup and cabbage noodles, I couldn't help but notice Gyurika looked so cute with most of his supper on his face. We laughed and played little games together as I fed him. He was such a delight. After putting him to bed I washed the dishes and did my homework. Being trusted to be responsible for such a young child filled me with pride. I lay down on the chesterfield and closed my eyes. Quickly I was in dreamland: the land of Cinderella, dancing in my new turquoise-blue dress at the opening night of the dance class. The sound of the door opening put my dream on hold. Mr. Bognar had just come home. We said goodnight and I went back to Godmother's. Walking into the house my eyes widened and my throat tightened as I saw the pile of dirty dishes in the washbasin. Godfather looked at me with a sly grin.

"Yes, they are waiting for you," he said coldly. I gave him an evil look, but I had no choice. Washing the dishes, scraping the dried-on grease scum, my eyes misted, wishing evil things would happen to Godfather.

Later in bed Godmother said, "I wanted to do the dishes, but Pista wouldn't let me." I was too upset to answer. "I have to obey him, Ilona, otherwise he will send you home. I'm happy that you are here with me. This way, I can mother you, for which I have a great desire, since I have no child of my own." Feeling her tensed body as I lay beside her, I realized even she was threatened by Godfather.

The following morning before school, I had to make three trips to fill the water barrel, as it was washday. The problem was I was short and the buckets touched the ground when I straightened my arms, causing some of the water to splash out with each step. I was angry, but the thought of my new dress helped to ease my anger.

The next weekend I went home, but I didn't tell anyone, not even Grandmother, about my new dress. I wanted it to be a surprise. Or was I afraid my mother would kill my dream? In the afternoon, Father and I went for a long walk. He must have missed me. Now a teenager, almost as tall as he was, he still held my hand as we walked to our destination: an owl's nest with three little, fuzzy chicks in it. Excited, I reached into the nest, but Father held me back. "No, Ilona. Their parents would miss them, just like I miss you." Again, I could only smile at him, still too self-conscious to tell him how much I loved him. We left the nest untouched.

That night, lying in bed beside Grandmother, I couldn't keep my secret any longer. I told her about my dream dress, which I would buy with my babysitting money. It would be a turquoise taffeta to compliment my olive skin. The sweetheart neckline, and sleeveless bodice would add elegance, while the gathered waistline would ensure the skirt flared about me as I danced. She was delighted for me and amazed by my imagination.

After the weekend, I went back to Kisterenye. The week passed, and early Saturday morning I went to Mrs. Bognar's to get my money. She said that she couldn't pay me for another two weeks. I was very disappointed, but there was nothing I could do about it. Calming myself with the thought that two weeks would go quickly, I realized that I would have even more money then.

Monday we registered for dancing school. The next weekend I delayed going home to Kanyas. I had to do my laundry and get ready for the Saturday night dance. Hanging my clothes on the line, I called over to Mrs. Bognar who was hanging her laundry as well.

"Mrs. Bognar, I'm going to a dance tonight." She stopped and asked what I would be wearing to the dance. I showed her my wet, white blouse and navy skirt. I told her about my dream turquoise dress that I would have bought for the opening dance, if she had paid me. Hearing what I said, a troubled look came over her face; she hesitated for a moment, then she ran into her house. I stood there stunned, wondering about her actions, but I was too busy to think about it any further. I still had to wash my hair and iron my clothes to get ready for the dance.

My chaperone, Godmother, was just as excited as I was about our night out. She French braided my hair, then stood back to look at me and said, "You look pretty, Ilona." Then she went in the bedroom to dress.

Godfather came into the kitchen where I was admiring my hair in the mirror, hanging on the back of the kitchen door. He came up behind me and grabbed my hair, pulling it so roughly that my head flew back. "You look ugly," he muttered in my ear.

Angry and humiliated, I spun around facing him and yelled, "Get away from me, you wicked man." His face contorted in fury. His hand shot out and I felt his nails dig in, as he twisted the soft flesh in my upper arm. I screamed with pain.

Godmother ran out of the bedroom, asking me, "Ilona, what are you yelling about?" Godfather put his finger to his lips, indicating to keep quiet. I didn't

30

want an argument. Afraid that he would keep us home from the dance, I snatched my jacket and ran outside, waiting for Godmother to come out.

Even with the burning pain in my arm, I was excited when we walked into the ballroom. I had never danced with a boy before, but I wasn't alone. Many of the girls in the group were in the same situation. The dance instructor, Zoli, fascinated us by showing the different dance movements, while flexing his thigh muscles in his tight, black pants. Later he paired us girls with boys. The music started and we began to move: one, two, three, one, two, three. I was thrilled with my partner, Barni. He was older than I was and seemed very self-assured. We moved awkwardly at first, but we caught on fast. I glanced over at Godmother and she returned my smile, enjoying playing the mother role as she visited with the other mothers.

Sunday morning I got up early and rushed home to Kanyas for the day. I could hardly wait to tell my friend, Ilcsa, about dancing school. At her house, we went out into the garden where no one could hear us. I told her about Barni - how tall and handsome he was - and how tense I became as he held me close. I tried to explain my feelings to Ilcsa when I looked into his big, blue eyes: my heart raced, the palm of my hands got damp with perspiration, and I stumbled over my own feet. But it was so magical! We giggled and talked about boys and the feeling we got when they touched us. I had never experienced this feeling before, but Ilcsa said she had. All too soon I had to rush home.

Mother and Manci didn't ask me any questions about school or about living with my godparents. Julika, however, now a seven-year-old, was so happy to see me she wanted to know when I was coming home for good. Father was away, but Grandmother let me know with her warm hugs that she was pleased to see me. I wanted to talk to her privately, but someone was always around. I started back to Kisterenye in the early afternoon and asked Grandmother to walk with me to the main road. Away from the house, I told her what Godfather had done to me. She couldn't believe that he would do such a thing, until I showed her the black and blue mark on my arm. She was shocked and told me to keep away from him and that I should not be alone with him in the house at any time. She promised to pray for my safety and try to think of some way to solve the problem. At the main road she held me close to her and assured me that she would talk to my parents about the situation.

Walking on the main road I caught up to two ladies who had made a pilgrimage to the shrine of *Szentkut's* church. They had gone there to pray for the younger lady's six-year-old daughter, Marika, who was in the sanatorium with tuberculosis. They were going to Kisterenye to take a train to their town, Novak.

The older lady, Marika's grandmother, asked me, "Would you please help me to carry one of my bags?"

"Certainly," I replied, taking the bag from her hand. She asked my name and I told her.

"Do you believe in God Ilona?" she asked as we continued down the road.

"Yes," I answered with conviction.

"Then we can pray together for Marika's recovery." As we walked we recited the rosary. In her free hand she held the beads with the cross in the middle. When we reached my godparents' house, they sat down beside the road to rest and asked if I would bring them a drink of water. I ran into the house and told Godmother about my traveling companions sitting outside, and asked if I could take some water out to them. She put a pitcher of water and glasses on a tray with two freshly baked buns, and she handed the tray to me.

The ladies were so grateful for the refreshments. When they had finished, they departed and the older lady put her arms around me saying, "God bless you, Ilona." I felt her put something in my pocket. As they carried on down the road I felt a bond between us, a spiritual bond. Maybe it was because of our collective praying on the road. When I took the tray back into the house, I felt inside my pocket and was amazed to find a ten-forint bill: hmmm, a down payment for my dream dress…yes!

"You did a good deed, Ilona," Godmother said as I was showing the money to her. "It's a lot of money, but you deserve it for carrying her bag."

At that moment Godfather walked by me and snatched the money out of my hand.

"This is mine for the buns and water!" His face showed more evil than ever before.

"Give me back my money, you monster!" I cried out, but he just laughed and put the money in his pocket.

Godmother pleaded with him. "Pista, give the money back. Ilona earned it. The lady gave it to her." She tried to convince him in a quiet voice, but to no avail.

"I'll give it back tomorrow," he said with a tone that meant no one should talk to him any more.

I ran to the garden where I asked God to change Godfather and take away his ruthless spirit. He was terrorizing me. I didn't know how to take his irrational behavior. After crying in the garden for a while, I was still too angry to go in. Finally, Aunt Anna came out and pleaded with me to come inside before I caught cold, by lying on the ground. In bed I told Godmother I wouldn't talk to Godfather until he gave back my money. She warned me that wouldn't be a good idea, but I had no intention of speaking to him until he returned it.

For the next few days I kept my distance from him, answering only "yes" or "no" and only when I absolutely had to. One morning we were in the kitchen alone, and he said that he would give me back my money if I would be nice to him. I looked straight into his eyes and blurted out, "I would rather die!" After that episode I just ignored him.

My one source of happiness was to look after Gyurika. He was so adorable and good-natured, my frustration eased when I cared for him and we played baby games. When Mr. Bognar came home, I dreaded having to go back to the house where I knew Godfather and a pile of dirty dishes would be waiting for me. But one night to my surprise the dishes were done. When we were in bed I asked Godmother who had done the dishes. She answered, "Aunt Anna did." I said my prayer, and thanked God for helping me to cope with my anger.

In order to stay away from Godfather as much as possible, I joined the girls' soccer team and the church choir. The beautiful hymns we sang helped me to recapture some of the deep feelings I had experienced in our church in *Szentkut*.

The Saturday night dances were always exciting. During the first half of the night, Zoli, our instructor, chose partners for the girls. The boys had their choice of partners for the second half. Most of the time Barni chose me. Being just fourteen years old, it pleased me very much to have an eighteen-year-old partner. One Saturday night he asked Godmother if he could walk home with us. Godmother gave her permission, and on the way home they had most of the conversation. At the gate, she left us alone. I was nervous and speechless, not knowing how to act with a boy. However, Barni had a way of making me feel not quite so shy. He told me that he watched me play soccer and he thought that I was a good goalie. He offered to give me some tips on soccer, and he moved closer and embraced me. I thanked him for his offer, quickly said goodnight, and rushed into the house. I felt uneasy being alone and that close to him.

The next day Godmother told me that they were going out of town to a wedding. This left Aunt Anna and I home alone. We had long talks together and enjoyed each other's company. On our last free evening Aunty was unusually quiet for a long time, as if she had something on her mind. At last, with a deep sigh, she turned to me.

"Ilona, I have to tell you about the mysterious episode in your life when you were a baby."

"What about my life Aunty? What about my life?"

"You were born on October 11, as a healthy baby, but in December you developed a fever and a bad cough. Your mother thought it was just a chest cold. Since the nearest doctor was five kilometers away, she didn't take you to see him. Later, as your health got worse, your mother brought you to us. You didn't eat and had severe diarrhea that must have caused you a lot of pain, because you cried constantly. Godmother and I took you to the doctor, and he said you had a gastrointestinal problem that was causing the vomiting and diarrhea. And it could be fatal in such a young infant. He gave us a prescription, but it didn't help. You still couldn't keep any food down and you were losing weight rapidly. You were in our arms constantly. The only thing we could do was to pray and ask the good Lord to save you. A few days later we took you back to the doctor again. He examined you and said you were just skin and bones. You were suffering severe malnutrition and dehydration."

"He gave us a special formula to feed you and a new prescription. As we were leaving his office he told us if that didn't help you, there was nothing more that he could do. We brought you home and tried to force feed you, but you couldn't swallow the formula. It just drooled out of your tiny mouth. You were so exhausted, you couldn't even cry any more. Your little face was like wax, with deep dark circles under your closed eyes, and you were cold to our touch. We put you in your wicker basket and covered your face."

Hearing all this I just sat there motionless and breathless. Gathering my thoughts I interrupted to ask questions.

"Hush, hush," Aunty said. "Wait until I'm finished," and she continued. "It was around 10 p.m. as we prayed the rosary for you. We decided that in the morning we would take you home to your mother (as your godfather constantly demanded), and we would stay for your funeral. We left you in the cold

34

bedroom and kept praying all night. Around 4 a.m. we heard a frail cry. I went to your basket, uncovered your face and nearly fainted. To my amazement, your eyes were wide open and you moved your bony little hands. Your eyes showed such tranquillity that we were astounded. Instantly, we praised God and thanked him for this miracle we were witnessing. Your godmother picked you up and started to feed you with the formula the doctor had given us. To our amazement you kept it down. We continued to pray and thank God for his divine act. It was just before Christmas and we felt we were witnessing another miracle, like the birth at Christmas so long ago. We kept you for another week and you progressed day by day. Later, we took you back to your mother. That broke your godmother's heart, she wanted to keep you for good, but your godfather was dead set against it. We had planned your funeral, but God overruled.

When my godparents came home, I could hardly wait to be alone with Godmother Julia to question her about my illness.

"Where did you hear that?" she asked in a surprised voice.

"Aunt Anna told me the whole story."

"You should ask your mother about it," and she quickly walked away from me.

This story shocked me. How was it that I'd never heard it before? I knew the next time I went home I would have lot of questions for my mother. Why hadn't she looked after me? Why had she given me to Godmother? Even Grandmother Usak didn't know about what had happened to me, because she had lived in Budapest at that time. When I asked Mother about my illness, she told me nothing. She absolutely refused to discuss what had happened. She was angry with Aunt Anna and said, "She shouldn't have told you." No one wanted to talk to me about my illness, so finally I let it go, thanking God that He had given me a second chance to live. Later, I heard vaguely that Mother and Godmother had even discussed my adoption.

Finally, the time came to collect my babysitting money from Mrs. Bognar. Godmother had said we would take the 9:15 a.m. train to Salgotarjan to buy my dress. Early in the morning I was watching through our window, waiting for the Bognars to wake up. When I saw their light on, I ran over and knocked on their door. Mr. Bognar answered, and I said, "I've come for my money so I can buy my new dress." He said he would wake up his wife. When he returned he told me that Mrs. Bognar had given the money to my godfather, as he demanded two weeks ago. He said the money was his for my room and board. Perhaps that was why Mrs. Bognar acted so nervous and ran into her house when we were hanging our laundry.

I walked home with evil thoughts churning in my head. While I was telling Godmother what had happened to my money, Godfather walked in and admitted that he had it. He had no intention of giving it to me. That was all there was to it. When I saw the smirk on his face, I wished him in hell.

Outraged, I shouted at him. "You are a malicious, evil person, and you are definitely insane." He lunged forward to slap me, but I was too fast for him. I stormed outside and stumbled down the five steps to the ground. I hurt my leg so badly that I couldn't get up. Mr. Bognar, driving by on his motorcycle, saw me fall down the steps. He stopped and took me to the doctor as I requested. The doctor examined my foot and said that I had sprained a ligament. He bandaged it and handed me a pair of crutches, telling me to stay off it until it healed. As we were leaving the doctor's office, I begged Mr. Bognar to take me home to Kanyas. We went back to Godmother's, and I asked her to pack my clothes and books. I was going home. She was very upset, but we didn't say anything because Mr. Bognar was present. She knew it wasn't safe for me to stay there right then. I had to leave before something even more drastic would happen.

On the way home, with my leg hanging down on the motorcycle, the pulsing pain was so unbearable we had to stop. Resting at the roadside, I elevated my foot on a large rock. As we were resting, Mr. Bognar informed me about our progressively worsening political situation. The bitter fight between the Catholic Church and the state had reached a dangerous point. The head of the Catholic Church in Hungary, Cardinal Jozsef Mindszenty, had been arrested and sentenced to life imprisonment. Since most of the Hungarians were Catholic and highly honored Cardinal Mindszenty, there was great conflict between the Catholics and the Communists. However, afraid we would suffer Mindszenty's fate, we were silenced. In addition to persecuting the Catholics, the government also exterminated all army officers and any other people who were suspected of disloyalty to the Communist regime.

This terror continued throughout Hungary, as it did in my own life.

CHAPTER 6

I hopped into our house on crutches, while Grandmother ran to help me. She cried out, "What happened to you?" Not wishing to tell the true story in the presence of Mr. Bognar, I merely said, "I tripped on the steps and sprained a ligament in my leg."

When Mr. Bognar left, Grandmother instantly blurted out her withheld curiosity. "Ilona, now the truth. What really happened to you?" With the family together, I told them about my traumatic episode with Godfather. Hearing the story Grandmother got furious, "How could he do such a thing? Taking her money away?"

Glancing at Father she said, "Jozsi, you have to talk to Pista about this unfair situation. She could have broken her neck."

"First thing in the morning I will go and confront him about it," Father replied. Hearing this, Mother yelled, "Oh no, you won't! I will go and find out the truth."

As usual, Father was helpless against Mother's strong will. The morning before Mother left to Kisterenye, I asked her to go see my teacher and get some homework for me. All day I anxiously waited for Mother's return. Late in the evening she finally arrived. I asked if she brought me any homework. Her brief, harsh, "No," infuriated me.

Father immediately questioned her, "What did Pista have to say?"

Mother shrugged and looked at me accusingly, answering, "He said it was just a little misunderstanding on Ilona's part. He was just teasing her."

"What about her injured leg? And where is Ilona's money?" Father questioned.

Mother stared at me as if daring me to challenge her. "I got it," she said, turning away from us.

Father asked, "Mari, had you made an agreement with Pista to take Ilona's babysitting money and give it to you?" Mother ignored that question.

Father was quiet for a moment, and with a strong conviction he stated, "Ilona is not going back to Pista's, and that is final!" I had never heard him speak so harshly. For once Mother was silent, and for the rest of the evening they didn't speak to each other. I felt bad to see my peaceful father so infuriated, but he had shown his unconditional love for me. I felt content.

The next morning, I found a big envelope on the kitchen table. There was a letter and school material from my teacher. I realized Mother had kept it from me all evening, just to torment me. But my teacher's kind words inspired me. She wished me a speedy recovery and good luck with my home studies.

Later, I asked Mother for my babysitting money. Her stinging reply was, "Forget it. I'm keeping it." I gave her an evil look through my teary eyes. My dream - my passionate dream - of buying my turquoise dress was my mother's pleasure to destroy.

When Grandmother heard Mother's refusal to return my money, she was furious and approached her. "Mari, we need that money for transportation. Ilona has to finish the last semester of the school year."

"She will go back to Pista's to finish school," Mother insisted.

"Not if I can help it!" Grandmother raged. "Even if you won't give us the money she worked for, I will find a way for her to finish school from home!"

Wondering how Grandmother, at her age, could find a way to make any money, I asked her what she would do. She replied, "We have to make good use of the time while your leg is healing. I will teach you to embroider." Her eyes shone with excitement.

I agreed to learn, knowing that embroidering and studying would help me to cope with my painful leg. Grandmother herself had an ulcerated sore on her right ankle and had to stay off her feet as much as possible. Unable to move comfortably, she kept herself busy doing the most beautiful crocheting and embroidery. With her guidance I learned quickly, enjoying working with the bright-colored threads to make different designs and stitches.

Despite the pain in my leg, I treasured this time with Grandmother. It also provided another blessing. Since I was somewhat helpless, it brought Julika and I closer, as she eagerly did whatever she could to help me.

One day Grandmother insisted on walking to Matraverebely, about an hour walk away, to mail a letter to her friend in Budapest.

Mother looked suspiciously at her. "You can't walk all that way with your sore leg. I will do it for you." She put her hand out to take the letter from Grandmother, but Grandmother inscrutably put the letter into her pocket, and out the door she went.

A few days later there was a knock on the door. When Mother opened it, a lady carrying a suitcase stood outside. She asked for Mrs. Usak. "What do you want with Mrs. Usak?" Mother asked. Hearing their voices, Grandmother shuffled to the door.

"I'm Mrs. Usak. Come right in," Grandmother said, pushing Mother aside. She led the woman to the kitchen table and invited her to sit down.

The woman laid the suitcase on the table and said, "Mrs. Usak, I saw your ad on the post-office bulletin board that you embroider monograms. Would you do some for me?"

"Of course. I'd be happy to do that for you," Grandmother answered with a smile.

The lady opened her suitcase and brought out two snow-white linen tablecloths with twenty-four matching napkins. She asked Grandmother to embroider her daughter's monogram on them with gold thread. Grandmother told her boldly how much she charged, and a price was agreed upon.

When the lady left, Mother erupted in anger. "Mother, how could you do this behind my back?"

Grandmother folded her arms and looked at her placidly. "Mari, I did it right in front of you, and you can't do anything about it! Ilona and I will do the embroidering, and with the money we earn we will buy a bicycle so she can go to school." Ignoring Mother's raving, she carefully put the linens back in the suitcase and carried it into the bedroom. From then on we spent many weeks embroidering and singing our favorite hymns together.

Before we were done, another lady, who also saw Grandmother's ad, came to the door and hired Grandmother to embroider some towels, face cloths, and pillowcases. This time, when Grandmother was negotiating the price, Mother remained strangely quiet in the background. When the lady left, Mother tried to convince Grandmother that she should give her some of the money we earned by revealing her own dream: to save enough money to buy a lot and build a house at the peaceful shrine of *Szentkut*. But Grandmother firmly stood her ground, "Mari, Ilona's schooling comes first. You don't get any money from me until we buy a bicycle for her to finish school."

By this time, Barni had heard in school about my accident and came to visit me. He had talked to my teacher and she sent some more homework for me. He offered to tutor me every Saturday, which I gladly accepted since he was four years ahead of me in school. With my inability to get around, the only thing I could do was study, embroider, and patiently wait for Saturdays.

My family was fond of Barni because he wasn't a Communist. He enjoyed teaching me, especially when we were alone. Often he distracted me, when he insisted on putting his arm around my shoulder. I was only fourteen; I didn't understand why he wanted to sit so close to me. Manci often irritated me when she hung around us, chatting with Barni like I didn't exist. I guess she understood him more, since she was sixteen and Barni was eighteen.

Finally, the day came to see the doctor again. He was very pleased to see how well my leg had healed. He gave me instructions for exercises to strengthen my leg muscles. Later on, Barni helped us to pick out a bicycle, since he had one of his own. On the way home, I got my first lesson on how to ride a bike. Barni was patient and while he was holding the bicycle, as I was trying to pedal, he asked me if we could be friends. I didn't know what he meant so I said, "We are friends already." He just smiled and moved a little closer to me. That night before I went to bed I polished my bicycle, not because it needed it, but because I was overjoyed. After a thankful prayer, a blissful feeling came over me. I realized that I was no longer angry about not getting my turquoise dress. I did what Grandmother had been asking me to do: I forgave my mother for keeping my babysitting money. She also wanted to accomplish her dream, a house in *Szentkut*. I commuted to school on bicycle until I finished.

As soon as I finished school, Mother urged me to find a job. In our small community that wasn't easy, especially since it was known that our family did not favor communism. I applied at our newly opened grocery store, but no luck. Finally, I got a job at the mine, re-charging batteries in the miners' lamps for the approximately one hundred miners, who were bussed in from neighboring villages. Three of us worked with the lamps on each shift.

The job wasn't easy: we handled fifty to sixty lamps on one shift, each of which weighed five kg. We had to clean the lamps of mud and sand, especially the connecting points so the batteries could be charged with electricity. We had to wear rubber gloves and boots to keep from being electrocuted. I got zapped hard several times. I despised my job, especially the afternoon shift from four until midnight.

Our Communist supervisor regularly made a point of checking up on us. There was no doubt in our minds that he was spying on us. He grilled us constantly about reforming our attitudes towards communism. One day he announced, "There will be a two-week political lecture in Budapest. All free!"

40

Hearing the word "free," sarcastic grins appeared on our faces. When he looked up, we quickly masked our expressions, as we wouldn't dare let him see our disbelief. The Communists removed the *free* from *freedom:* the condition of not being under another's control. While lecturing us on how wonderful it was to live under the freedom of Communism, while we were terrorized, they enforced curfews and eliminated all political opposition. Amazingly, they believed that their total control of the social and cultural life of the people was *freedom.* Sadly, they brutally tried to convince the Hungarian nation of that absolute truth.

It was clear to us that if we went to the seminar it meant a raise in pay; if we didn't, we would lose our jobs. And if, at the seminar, we adopted the Communist system, there was nothing to stop us from having a better job and life. For us it meant simply selling our souls and betraying our country and peers.

The seminar caused a real problem with my parents. They were afraid if they let me go I might be brainwashed to be a Communist and turn against them. This had happened in many families. Children reported relatives to the authorities, who then sentenced the family members to a Siberian labor camp - for life. There was chaos, not only in the country, but in families as well.

I pleaded with my parents to let me go and tried to assure them that they had nothing to worry about. I believed in God and in my crossroad Friend. Regardless of what I said, Mother was skeptical as our eyes met. I continued pleading, telling them I could not be persuaded, because I didn't believe in the kind of system that denied God. Father had faith and trusted me to go, but Mother did not. She continued to argue that it wasn't safe to allow me to go. I thought for a second, "Maybe Mother realizes that I could get even with her for all her unfairness towards me." Finally, Father and Grandmother convinced her that it was safe to let me go, and that they trusted me and that I could get a better job. I was relieved and delighted to be getting away from Mother for two whole weeks.

Before we left Grandmother asked Iren, a friend from work I traveled with, to look after me, since I was sixteen and she was twenty-two. During our long wait at the station I was anxious to get on the train. When the train finally arrived, I was pleased we had a compartment to ourselves. Quickly opening my suitcase I started shortening my pink-flowered dress to about 15 cm above my knees.

Iren, stunned, with her eyes wide, yelled, "Ilona, hold it! Hold it! Your mother will kill both of us, if you cut it off."

"Relax Iren, I'm just turning it up to be in style."

"I hope that your mother doesn't find out."

"She won't, if you don't tell her about it." She kept glaring at me silently, offended, while I quickly shortened my clothes. I had to explain, "Iren, don't worry. On our way home I will let them down."

In Hatvan we had a half-hour wait for connecting trains. In the washroom I changed into my white and pink floral skirt, that I had just shortened, put on soft, green eyeshadow and pale satin, pink lipstick. I pulled back my childish, naturally curly hair and tied it with a pink ribbon, and applied soft, pearl nail polish. Meanwhile, the people were bustling in and out of the washroom, paying no attention to me. With a final glance in the mirror I admitted to myself, "Ilona, you look like a city girl. So glad you left the country one behind for two weeks."

I walked up the train to face my judgmental, old-fashioned friend, Iren. For a second she didn't recognize me. As I was sitting down, she said, "This seat is taken." When she took a second look at me she gasped, "Ilona, what have you done to yourself?"

With a snicker I said, "Just updated myself to Budapest standards." She eyeballed me from head to toe, and startled further when she noticed my pink toenails peeking from my sandals. From the expression on her face, I thought she would pass out. Silently staring at me for a long time she finally spoke.

"Ilona, I have to admit you look good. I wish I would have the courage to do it."

"Iren, this is not courage. I learned about fashion when I was in Budapest with Grandmother Usak." I felt elegant and content.

When we arrived at our location in Budapest, we met so many others who came from different parts of the country for the seminar. Greeted by a devout young Communist, we were left without a doubt that he was in command. We were shown to a dormitory: ten girls assigned to a single room with only one bathroom, which was endlessly occupied. Four comrades, who lectured us on how well the Communist system worked and all the benefits it offered, conducted our daily seminars. We learned about Russia and the Bolsheviks, and about famous people in Russian history, who had been involved in the revolution. We had lectures on Nikolai Lenin, a Russian Marxist, who created the Bolshevik Party, and later on Joseph Stalin, whom we had to glorify - or face the consequences. We also had to listen to a lecture on our despised, Moscow-trained, Hungarian, Communist leader, Matyas Rakosi. Fortunately, after a day of lecture, we were allowed to go out with an 11 p.m. curfew.

Just as I remembered, Budapest was absolutely breathtaking in the reflection of the glittering night-lights, as lovers strolled the Danube River shore in the fragrant jasmine summer breeze. The evening view of Pest from Buda hill was magical, as the carpet of light covered the city as far as the eye could see. The quiet amusement park came alive in the evening with the blare of music, shrieks from the Ferris wheel, and screams from the steep-inclined roller coaster. I, like the rest of my group, especially Iren, was mesmerized by it all. By the time the seminar was ended most of us had fallen in love with Budapest. However, after the intense two weeks of Communist lectures we were anxious to go home. We said our goodbyes and boarded the train to Nagybatony.

Iren and I were afraid to discuss our true feelings about the seminar. The train was packed with people and we knew only too well that informers were everywhere. Instead, we talked about the ancient, architectural castles in Buda, and the many bridges over the Danube River. I found it interesting that these were the largest suspension bridges in Europe.

Upon my arrival home, my parents instantly questioned me about the seminar. A long conversation ensued before I could convince my family that I had not been brainwashed, and I assured them that I still loved them.

Mother looked uneasy and asked, "Ilona, would you like a piece of your favorite cheese cake?" I was shocked by her offer, which she had never done before to my recollection. I was frustrated with her unfairness towards me, but I always forgave her in my heart.

When I went back to work, I was called in to our Communist leader's office for questioning, about my liking of the seminar.

My answers, about the seminar were well liked and I got my raise in pay. This made Mother happy as it meant more money for her. It is custom in Hungary to have a dowry at marriage. Therefore I had to give my earnings to Mother, so she could start collecting one for when I got married.

Two days later, an announcement on the loudspeaker said, "An important lecture will be held after work." It was mandatory for everyone to attend. We were all curious what new piece of propaganda they would try to brainwash us with this time. Of course, there was no choice but to listen to what they had to say.   While waiting for the speaker, the workers began griping amongst themselves, becoming increasingly agitated. At last, our speaker approached the lectern and he was introduced, "And here is your Communist leader."

His voice was loud and his eyes darted around the gathered workers, as he spoke about the advantages of living under Communism: the soon to be worldwide system, that would wipe out capitalism. Most of us didn't believe this rubbish, but we had to listen. The topic of his lecture suddenly changed to "atheism," which he, knowing the religious convictions of Hungarians, seemed nervous in presenting.   His hands shook, as he rifled through his notes, occasionally pushing his straight, brown hair out of his fiery, red eyes as he delivered his speech. Everyone listened in silence until he made a fatal mistake. Raising his voice, harsh with conviction, he told us that our belief in God was a myth; there was no God. Within seconds, profanity filled the air and a fistfight broke out. Many of us quickly left the room, not wanting to be involved.

After this incident some workers were fired, and others were suspended. Later, posters appeared announcing that in the future everyone had to be absolutely silent at all lectures. We read these notices and murmured, "That's what they call living in a *free* country," but no one dared express the longing, we all had, to live again in the Hungary we had once known.

CHAPTER 7

To cope with the drastic political changes we had undergone, we turned to soccer games for entertainment. There we could yell and scream to release our hate and anger. Nagybatony vs. Kisterenye, to the people of these two towns, these games were important; the local boys trained intensely to qualify and to win. Sunday afternoon our group of friends decided to go and cheer our team to victory in Nagybatony. After the game, we all went to a bistro for ice cream. While we were visiting I was introduced to a young cadet named Janos. This young man in uniform made an instant impression on my teenage heart. I was immediately attracted to him, not only because he was in uniform, but also because he was very handsome, with dark curly hair, which coiled up on the edges of his military hat. When I secretly glanced at him, his sparkling, hazel eyes seemed to be focused on me, making me uncomfortable, but curiously excited.

When it was time to leave, he and his friend walked with us almost to home. We didn't want them to walk any further, because we knew our parents would not approve of us being accompanied by boys they did not know. Just before they said goodbye Janos stared at me and asked, "Ilona, are you coming to next week's game? I would like to see you again." He totally took me by surprise. I was hesitant in the presence of my friends, but thrilled. I blurted out, "Yes! Yes! I will be there."

He pleasantly smiled at me and said, "Good. I'll be looking for you."

At home I told my parents about him and his nice uniform. Mother immediately asked me to describe his uniform, which I did. Mother with her wide-open eyes, and her face two inches from mine said, "I forbid you to see him!"

"But why, *Anyuka?*" I wailed.

"Because he is a cadet in training to be a Communist officer!"

"That isn't fair. You don't even know him," I said, trying to keep the anger out of my voice.

"Whether I know him or not, for me he is a 'Communist Cadet' and I forbid you to see him again. I would not allow a Communist in my family, regardless of what you say or feel."

When she spoke like that, I knew it was useless to argue with her. I ran into the other room to hide my anger and tears. That night in bed, Grandmother was sympathetic, but I was inconsolable.

"Forget about him," she said gently. "Your parents will never agree to your friendship with a Communist Cadet."

"Grandmother, when you fall in love with someone you can't just blink your eyes and forget about him. Have the years made you forget about when you were my age and the feeling called *love*? *Nagymama*, he captivated my heart."

"Yes dear, I didn't forget, I believe in *love at first sight* darling, but sorry dear, I can't help you. With this situation you need a miracle."

Regardless of what they said I was determined to see him again, and with that thought I fell asleep.

Monday it was back to work with those dreadful lamps. I despised my job and had to force myself to go to work. During my lunch break, I read an advertisement in the newspaper. It read, *Privately teaching shorthand and typing in my home. Please contact Mrs. M. Biro at the address below.* At home I excitedly read the ad to Mother. Of course, her reply was, "No, you cannot go. If it is private, it will be too expensive for us. The answer is no! Period." I tried to plead with her but she would not listen.

She had never supported me, nor recognized that I was ambitious and wanted a better job. Why did she always have to kill my dreams? I wondered endlessly about that. Being upset, I went into the flower garden and found *Nagymama* reading her Bible. I told her about the newspaper ad and Mother's response. She was silent for a long time. . . Finally I asked, "*Nagymama*, don't you have anything to say?"

She pulled me closer to her. "Yes, I do darling. You just sit here beside me and listen." Then, opening the Bible to Romans 12:12, she read, "*Rejoicing in hope, persevering in tribulation, devoted to prayer.*" After our prayer she said, "Now, let's go inside and I will write a letter to Mrs. Biro." Shortly afterwards, she called to me and handed me a sealed envelope, saying, "Ilona, get on your bike and take this envelope to Mrs. Biro, and wait for her answer."

Arriving at the location, I rang the doorbell; Mrs. Biro appeared with a baby in her arms. I handed her the letter. She explained that she was on maternity leave from her job at the school board. She handed me the baby while she read the letter. When finished, she sat down and wrote one back to Grandmother. She handed me the sealed envelope, addressed to Grandmother, and took the baby from my arms. I rushed home, praying all the way that my problem had been solved. When I gave Grandmother the letter she opened it and exclaimed, "Thank God! She accepted my offer."

"What did you offer, *Nagymama*?" I asked, picking up on her excitement.

"I offered to crotchet her a regular size tablecloth and six twenty-five cm round doilies with white cotton thread in exchange for your lessons (under Communism bartering was a way of survival). Now, come with me, and we will go and break the news peacefully to your mother."

In the house, Mother was cleaning vegetables for supper. When Grandmother handed her the letter, her eyes blinked rapidly and her mouth turned down in a way that signalled she was extremely angry.

Grandmother motioned to me, "Ilona, go and do some weeding in the garden. Your mother and I have something we need to discuss." Mother's loud, harsh voice echoed from inside. I was worried. At last Grandmother, seemingly unperturbed by the confrontation, came out to the garden and said quietly, "It's all settled, Ilona, you can take your typing lessons." I had been so distraught at the sounds that had echoed from the house, I could only hug my dear grandmother and whisper my gratitude.

The next day at work, I told everyone that I was going to take a typing course, and when I finished I would apply for an office job at the mine. Some seemed happy for me, but a few of the others tried to discourage me. I thought they were jealous, but it didn't matter. I didn't let that burst my enthusiasm for pursuing my dream.

On the following Wednesday, I went to Nagybatony for my first typing lesson. It was not at all what I expected. Mrs. Biro covered the keyboard with a special cover, leaving just enough room for my hands to go under it. She told me this was her way of teaching speed typing. I didn't learn very quickly, but she encouraged me to carry on. By the end of the lesson, I had gained enough confidence to believe that perhaps, one day, I really would be able to master the keyboard.

I left Mrs. Biro's house going home as quickly as possible, as I still had to work the afternoon shift. At the stop sign I heard someone call to me, "Hi Ilona," and I turned around. To my surprise it was my cadet!

"So nice to see you. What are you doing in Nagybatony?" As he moved closer I blushed, while he gently laid his hand on mine as I clasped the handlebar of my bike. "Are you still coming to the soccer game?" My mind indicated that I should move my hand, but my teenage heart overruled. We intently gazed into each other's eyes, enjoying our magical bliss. It took me a few moments to collect my thoughts. Bashfully I answered, "Yes I will be there," and quickly rushed away. On my way home, my mind was so consumed by the magical nearness of him that I nearly ran over my little sister as she was playing in the yard. She jumped out of my way yelling, "What's with you Ilona? Are you out of your mind?"

I ran into the house, snatched my lunch bag from my waiting grandmother's hand, and ran to work. I felt so blissful, even the dreaded lamps didn't seem so heavy. But I couldn't tell anyone about my secret rendezvous.

On Saturday, Barni came for his regular visit. He enjoyed talking to Father, and he knew my parents liked him. For me, he was just a friend who had helped me with my homework. When I told him about my course, he encouraged me so I could get a better job. As usual, Mother invited him to stay for dinner, which he was more than pleased to do. But my mind was on the uniformed young man, thinking "How can I see him without Mother finding out?"

With five females in the house, Father enjoyed having Barni, another man, to talk to. They often discussed our fearful political situation, and both foresaw the approaching revolution. After exhausting the possibilities for change in the Communist system, we played *zsiros,* a Hungarian card game, which originated with the ancient Turks. But I could not keep my mind on the game. Preoccupied with my rendezvous, I finally asked Mother to play my hand for me. Mother, Father, Manci, and Barni sat at the table playing and chatting together, while I tried to read Julika her bedtime story. She brought me back to reality saying, "Ilona you read the story wrong. It doesn't end with kissing." Then, I realized that my mind was really wandering away to romanceland with my cadet.

Two days later I asked Mother if I could go to the soccer game with my friends.

"I know what you are up to, you want to see that Communist cadet again. I forbade you to see him, but it looks like you refuse to listen. Therefore, you are not allowed to go anywhere without your sister, except to work."

"But *Anyuka,* I love him, " I cried.

"You don't know what love is. You're too young," she huffed.

"Maybe I am young, but I feel love in my heart for him." But she just ignored me, rose from the chair and walked out of the room. How I wanted to

48

tell her that I too have feelings and confront her. Why doesn't she love me and try to understand me? But she gave me no chance to say anything. And that always infuriated me, and for me that was a mystery. With a broken heart, I went to find Grandmother, as usual in the garden. I sat on the grass at her feet with my head in her lap. She stroked my hair as I poured out the story of my broken heart. With a deep sigh, she said, "Obey your mother, *darling*. This time I can't do anything for you, and neither can your father. Have faith, and know that the good Lord will give you strength." Comforted by her words, as much as by her touch, I asked myself, "*Why has this fear of Mother cast such a dark shadow on my life?*"

CHAPTER 8

Two weeks before I finished my course, I heard that there were eight applications at the mine for two jobs: one for typing, and the other for receptionist. Since the comrades at the mine knew my family's feelings about communism, I thought my chance of being hired was very slim. Regardless, I applied and prayed to get one of them.

Each time I finished typing class Mother was waiting for me. She pretended that she was doing some shopping, but she didn't fool me, she was spying on me. On our way home we had a fight and I said nasty words to Mother. Later I sought refuge with my spiritual Friend at the crossroad.

I thought how unfair Mother was, not even trying to understand my heartache, but knowing how intractable she was, I also knew I had to resign myself to it. Then it became clear: she preferred Barni. That is why he came to the house more frequently by Mother's invitation.

Barni ignored my wishes that I had no feelings for him and I wished that he would stay away from me; but he kept coming by Mother's encouragement. One night he suggested a card game again, but this time for money, which I didn't care to play, but Father and Manci agreed. As the game progressed, I lost my patience with Barni. We were a team and he secretly instructed me what card to play, and when we lost he blamed me. Playing this way made me upset, as I knew he couldn't stand to lose. Finally, we reached the point where he was playing my cards. At that point, I gave up and Mother took over for me.

I went into the other room, and I got out my sketchpad and started drawing. Grandmother came in, sat down at the table across from me, and we discussed my typing exam scheduled for the following Monday. Shortly afterwards, Barni joined us and proceeded to tell me that if I had played the cards the way he wanted me to, we would have won. I was angry and told him that I didn't like card games, especially when he played my cards. His smile mocked me, as if I was childish. When he left, Grandmother said, "Ilona, it looks like you don't care for Barni very much, do you?"

"Just because he helped me with my studies, it doesn't mean he can boss me around. I wish he would stop coming here."

On Saturday nights our young group of eight gathered for dancing, while our neighbor, Mr. Sandor, played the accordion. I was the only one who had taken dancing lessons, so I taught the others to waltz and tango. One night at the dance, Barni told me excitedly that there would be a harvest ball, *Szureti tanc,* in Kisterenye on October 11th. He wanted all of us to go as it was going to be a big event. We had never been to a harvest ball before, and Mother allowed Manci and I to go. She asked Barni to stop at Godmother's on his way home and ask her if she would chaperone us.

The following Monday I got time off work to take my typing test. Four of us waited nervously for Mrs. Biro to hand out the results. I passed the test with the highest percent; my family was very happy, even Mother, who gave me a hug.

I took a second test in the mine office for speed and accuracy and got the best mark - but not the job! This upset me so much and I blamed my parents for their Communist resentments. I was angry and went to see our Communist leader, as he had urged me to attend the seminar, in order to get a better job. I told him that it was unfair that someone else was hired, when I had the best mark. He explained that the matter was out of his hands. Since our family did not favor the Communist system, the vote had gone against me. Resentfully I asked, "How about the political seminar in Budapest? None of those girls were there. This is about me, not my family, and it looks like the Communist system failed me."

He paused for a minute, and then said, "I will look into it, Ilona."

For the next few days I avoided him completely. After a few days, he appeared at my work place and asked, "Ilona, why are you avoiding me?"

I shrugged. "I have nothing to say, except that I'm still disappointed that you convinced me to go to the seminar, so I could get a better job, but then I didn't get the job." To my surprise he gave me a big smile. "You don't need to be disappointed any longer. You start the receptionist job tomorrow. I told you I would look into it."

Hearing this, I was so flabbergasted that I dropped a five kg lamp on my foot. With a handshake I said, "Thank you Comrade for the opportunity." Then he added, "You will have some typing to do between phone calls and you will also get a raise in pay."

When I broke the news to my family, everyone was delighted. Mother made an announcement, "Since you have a new job with a raise in pay, Manci and you can get new dresses for the harvest ball." I couldn't believe Mother had had such a change of heart.

That night I couldn't sleep for the throbbing pain in my foot, the same foot that was damaged by Godfather's wickedness. Grandmother got up and wrapped a towel soaked in cold water and apple cider vinegar around my foot. My pain gradually eased and I drifted off to sleep.

In the morning, awakened by a quiet noise in the kitchen, I glanced through the partly opened French door to see Grandmother ironing my blouse. With great excitement I realized this was the first day on my new job. Quickly I ran into the kitchen, and Grandmother said, "Darling, from now on you will have to dress neatly for your new job. I will crochet a few different colored tops for you to wear with your skirts."

I leaped to her and gave her a big hug and a kiss. "Thank you, thank you, *Nagymama*. You're the one who made it possible for my dream to come true."

A gentle smile crossed her face as the iron moved up and down on the white cotton blouse. With Grandmother's help I was soon ready to go to work. When I arrived at the office, I realized there was a lot to learn. Looking at the switchboard, with so many cords, made me very nervous and afraid I would make a terrible mistake. But I had a good teacher, Sari, who had handled switchboards for many years. With her patient coaching, I felt more confident, and I knew I was going to love my job.

Now Barni came to our house more often, even on weekday evenings. The big topic of conversation was the harvest ball. He had previously attended other harvest balls and was enthusiastic about the Gypsy band that had been hired to play. He told us there would be wine for adults and fresh grape juice for minors.

When I got my first pay in cash, (to my recollection under Communism there were no cheques issued to anyone at the mine) Mother and I went by train to the city of Salgotarjan to buy our new dresses. Manci couldn't get away from her nanny job, but told Mother the kind of dress she would like to have. Going from store to store fascinated me, as it was the first time I had gone shopping for myself. It didn't take long for Mother to find a nice raspberry-colored dress for Manci. Since I was rather well developed on top for my age, it was difficult to find a dress that fit me. I was trying on dresses when Mother said, "Ilona, I'm tired from all this shopping. You'll just have to wear one of your old dresses."

"No!" I said loudly. "I'm going to have a new dress too!"

"I have an unopened box of dresses in the stock room. Just wait a minute and I'll go get it," said the clerk.

When she returned, she handed me a dress. "My dream dress!" I exclaimed cheerfully, as I was holding a gorgeous turquoise dress with a large scalloped collar. I could hardly believe it. Here was the turquoise dress I had dreamed of for so long. To my disappointment, it was too big in the shoulders and needed to be altered. Mother looked at the price tag and said, "With the cost of the alteration, your dress would cost more than Manci's, so you'll have to forget it."

She picked up her packages and started to walk out of the store. I looked at the clerk helplessly, while the tears were rolling down my face. Before Mother had reached the door, the clerk called after her, "Lady, if you buy the two dresses we will do the alteration free of charge." Mother paused for a moment, then came back and gave her assent. The clerk looked at me with a small, conspiratorial smile. Mother paid for the dresses and the clerk assured her she would send mine by mail in a few days.

On our way home on the train, I looked out the window at the blue sky, sprinkled with huge, white, fluffy clouds. While admiring the heavenly creation, I thanked God for my turquoise dress, which I had dreamed about for so long.

At home Grandmother was delighted and reminded me, "Ilona, don't forget to thank God that your dream has come true."

"I already have, *Nagymama*."

Just before the harvest ball, Barni arrived with the dreadful news that he would be drafted into the military soon. There was no escaping the draft. It was mandatory for all twenty-year-old males to serve in the military. He was upset. "I despise the military. I will get out of it somehow," he vowed.

"That is impossible, Barni," Father said. "You are tall and physically fit. I can't see how the military would let you off. You must be insane to think that you can deceive them." We all knew that the Communist military training was strict and ruthless, especially if they found out that you did not favor communism. "Don't be foolish, Barni," Father continued, "you could be jailed for the rest of your life, or sent to Siberia."

"At least I'll be at the harvest ball on Saturday," he said as he left to catch the train back to Kisterenye.

The day of the ball arrived and we began to get ready early in the afternoon. Julika was just as excited about the dance as we were. She held a towel for me as I washed my hair. She was fascinated watching us get ready. I wanted to put on some makeup and blush, but Grandmother told me not to, because with makeup my dark skin wouldn't look natural. When we were ready, Grandmother helped us into our dresses. Manci looked beautiful in her pink dress, which matched her lipstick. It made her look more like an adult. After Grandmother had zipped up my dress, I twirled around and the skirt opened up like an umbrella. It felt like I could fly away.

Father regarded us as we were leaving. "You girls look beautiful. I can't believe my little girls are young ladies already." He gave each of us a hug. "Have fun."

"Don't forget to pick up Godmother on your way," Mother added.

Walking like ladies, but acting silly, like young people laughing and giggling, we found Godmother waiting for us when we arrived at her house.

"My, oh my," she exclaimed. "I hardly recognized you girls, all dressed up; especially you Ilona, since you're such a tomboy."

At the dance hall, Barni looked handsome in a navy blue suit and light blue shirt that matched his eyes. He was waiting for us and showed us all to the place he had saved. Godmother walked across the hall to join a group of chaperones sitting together. When everyone was seated, Barni called me aside. I was wondering what he wanted, so it was a surprise when he said, "You look ravishing tonight, Ilona. I'm glad you are mine."

I frowned at him to let him know that I didn't care for him to talk to me like that. The dance began with the *Blue Danube Waltz,* which was most people's favorite. Barni asked me for the first dance and for a few minutes I forgot his remark. He was a wonderful dancer and as we moved so effortlessly together, I abandoned myself to the rhythm of the music.

At intermission, he led me over to his mother and introduced us. His mother was an attractive woman, obviously the motherly type. As soon as she had said she was pleased to meet me, she reached over and began to straighten the belt on my dress. The music started again and we joined in a *Csardas,* a popular Hungarian dance. I was happy to meet so many of my school friends again. And, seeing Godmother sitting with the chaperones, it was as if I was back in Kisterenye at the dance classes.

During the second intermission I went to the ladies' room. I was in one of the cubicles when I heard some girls come into the room. One of them asked, "Who is that girl with Barni?" I listened, holding my breath as another girl replied, "Her name is Ilona. She's just a country bumpkin." The other girl thought her friend's remark was very funny, as they giggled together. They talked about their makeup and which couples were dancing together. I stayed quiet until they left, feeling humiliated and degraded.

While washing my hands, I looked in the mirror. What I saw discouraged me. Maybe I should have worn some makeup after all, just like the city girls. But quickly I changed my mind. No! I did not want to look like them. Some of the girls had so much makeup on they looked like painted clowns. I stared into the mirror, asking myself, "Do I look like a country bumpkin?" Suddenly Grandmother's advice came to me. "If someone is degrading you, just remember you're as good as anyone else. So, straighten up and walk like a princess."

With my head held high I walked past the painted girls, noting with satisfaction their envious looks when Barni took my hand and led me to the dance floor. At the end of the affair no one wanted to go home, even though it was after midnight. The ball had been a great success, beyond anything I had imagined.

Barni walked back to Kanyas with us, even though it was an hour-and-a-half walk. Mother invited him in and served refreshments. When Barni was ready to leave I walked outside with him where he hugged and kissed me goodnight. I stayed outside for a moment to think about the difference between him and my cadet. When I was near Barni I was frustrated, but with Janos I felt a magical bliss I call love. I knew Barni and I would never be anything more than friends.

The next evening Barni came to the house, and to our dismay he was intoxicated. Father asked him why he had been drinking and he said that he had received his final notice; he had to be at the military base in Debrecen in two days. The draftees had gotten together for a party, but he had left because he wanted to come to say goodbye to me. He sat down in a chair close to me, but the smell of liquor and cigarette smoke made me move away. At that he got up and went outside. When he didn't return, Mother looked at me. "Ilona, go and see if Barni is all right."

I went outside and called to him, but he didn't answer. Finally, I found him lying spread out on the damp grass to cool off from the liquor. It was a cold October evening and I was worried that he would catch a cold without a jacket. When I spoke to him he said, "Come and sit beside me." I tried to persuade him to come back into the house with me, but he grabbed my hand and pulled me down beside him. He put his arms around me and began to kiss me. The more I struggled to get away from him, the more his arms tightened around me. Gasping, my mind churning with the thoughts of the Russian soldiers' rape attempt of my mother, I yelled at him, "Barni if you don't let me go I will scream." His grip only tightened more.

Suddenly Grandmother's voice broke the tension. "Ilona, Barni, coffee is ready. We're waiting for you."

I tore free from him and ran straight into my bedroom. Father went out to bring him into the house. Mother sat him down and put a piece of cheesecake, *turoslepeny,* and a cup of black coffee in front of him. Grandmother came into the bedroom and shut the door behind her. I sat on the bed, still shaking; she took me protectively in her arms.

"I heard everything through the window. That is why I called you." I clung to her until my heart slowed down and I was able to breathe normally.

"My dear *nagymama,* you never fail me. You're always there when I need help," I whispered.

As Barni was leaving, I shook his hand and wished him good luck.

Later, as I snuggled close to Grandmother in bed, she said, "I heard everything and I don't like Barni's aggressiveness. Definitely I will talk to your parents about Barni's behavior." I shuddered in her arms. "Life is not very kind to you, darling." Pulling me closer to her she whispered, "Hush, now, and go to sleep. I will pray for you."

CHAPTER 9

Two days after the incident in the garden with Barni, he left for the military. I was still perplexed and angry at his behavior. My one consolation was that Grandmother would talk to my parents about him. Since she had heard me struggle with him, she knew exactly what had happened. And I hoped she could convince Mother that Barni was the wrong choice for me. It seemed as if most of my life I had relied on my *nagymama* for protection and comfort.

That same day she gave me a lacy, pink crocheted top to go with my pink skirt. I was so delighted I kissed her hands to thank her for working so hard to make me happy. The top looked perfect, but my skirt was too long, ten cm below my knees. The new fashion was ten cm above the knees, but Mother wouldn't allow me to shorten it, regardless of how much I pleaded with her. "If she would let me dress properly," I thought resentfully, "maybe the girls at the harvest ball wouldn't have called me a country bumpkin." It upset me that my mother would never allow me to dress like the girls in Budapest. "Because I'm a country girl," she said. At work I got complimented on my pink top, but criticized on my skirt.

The topic of conversation at work was the political situation. All resistance parties had been forced to integrate with the Hungarian Communist Party to form the Hungarian Worker's Republic. We followed the Soviet constitution, and created the Hungarian People's Party. The economy was rearranged to adapt to the Soviet model. All the changes forced upon us led to serious economic problems. We followed all these changes in the only newspaper available to us, the *Szabad Nep* (Free People). Political lectures became mandatory at work places. At our lectures, one of the Comrades said we had to get our young generation ready for the new and better system. He further declared, "Whether people like it or not, *Communism is here to stay.*"

At home, Mother questioned me periodically about communism at work, and I let her know what I heard: Communism is here to stay whether we like it or not. And I told her I had to agree with the Comrade, because we were powerless to do anything about it. With that, Mother became angry with me. "Ilona, you're becoming much like a Communist yourself."

A *knock-knock* on the door hushed our conversation. "Letter for Ilona!" said the mailman. As he walked through the door, Mother snatched the envelope out of his hand and turned it over to see who had sent it. "Well, at least it's not from that Communist Cadet," she said rudely. I gave her one of my mean looks, for being so rude to the mailman and me.

I went into the bedroom to read the letter in privacy. It was from Barni. First he apologized for his behavior in the garden, and then he wrote that he was coming home for Christmas. When I told the family the news, Mother was so pleased that it made me curious what she was thinking. Obviously Grandmother hadn't talked to my parents about Barni's behavior in the garden, or she wouldn't have been so excited about the news. "Never mind," I said to myself, "Christmas is a long way off."

Later an unmarried couple moved into our neighborhood. Jutka was a chubby forty-year-old woman with a charming personality. She wanted very much to marry her younger, handsome boyfriend, Andras, who had an attractive dimple on his chin, so she would have a father for her two young girls. Piroska, age six, was a very pretty little girl, with a velvety complexion. Her sister, Magdus, was eight, with two buckteeth and a freckled face.

Andras worked at the mine as a special mechanic, operating and repairing the mine's cargo elevator. The mine was about three hundred fifty meters deep and the elevators went up every fifteen minutes. One box container was loaded with coal at the bottom, while the other was being unloaded up in the yard.

One day Jutka asked Mother if I could babysit for her children on weekends. They discussed my wages, which Jutka agreed to pay directly to Mother. I didn't know how much I was to make, but I didn't mind as Mother was collecting items for my dowry. Also, since Mother didn't allow me to go dancing after Barni left for the military, it helped me to pass the time on weekends.

The first Saturday I went to Jutka's, the girls were thrilled to see me. Andras introduced himself with a strong handshake and a cheerful smile. When Jutka came into the room, I could see the frustration on her face as she handed me her curling iron. "Ilona would you please curl my hair at the back?" I did as she asked and did some quick adjustments on the top. When she looked in the mirror she was very pleased. "Ilona, if you do my hair when you come to babysit, I will pay you without your mother knowing. I can see how domineering she is about your money." I readily agreed.

Finally, they left for the dance. I enjoyed staying with the girls, curling their hair and teaching them to draw. Since they had electricity we were able to play records, so I also taught them dancing. Magdus did all right, but six-year-old

Piroska was a born dancer. Exhausted after the dancing, I put the girls to bed. I dimmed the lights in the living room for a romantic atmosphere and put on my favorite record, the *Blue Danube Waltz*. I visualized my cadet and I dancing closely. Mesmerized by his hazel eyes, and the soft pine fragrance of his shaving lotion, I felt the rhythm of my heartbeat rising as Strauss took me away…

The sound of the key turning in the lock ended my fantasy. Jutka and Andras were home. Andras walked me home as my parents had insisted. At home Grandmother was still up reading, waiting for me as she always did. To show her my appreciation for all her support, I gave her the money that Jutka had given me for doing her hair. It was a small token for the wonderful love I got from my *nagymama*, as she tried to replace the lack of love I received from my mother.

Back at work I glanced out the window and saw a new poster on the bulletin board. It read, "Influential comrades coming from Budapest to lecture, Saturday from 10 a.m. to 4 p.m. in the Nagybatony School auditorium. Attendance is compulsory for anyone not working on that day." Not wanting to jeopardize our jobs, Iren and I decided to attend the lecture. We were wondering if the speakers would be the same as we had heard in Budapest.

When we got there, we had to wait in line to register. As we got closer, I realized cadets were handling the registration. To my heartfelt happiness, I saw Janos among them. I wanted to run to him and give him a hug and a kiss, but with Iren with me it was impossible. I was afraid she would tell Mother.

As usual, the lecture began by mocking democracy, followed by a speech about the positive benefits of communism. The speaker spoke loudly to intimidate the crowd, telling us that it was our duty as young people to build a new nation. Behind us someone murmured, "To build a new nation, while our grains and coal are shipped to Russia as *surplus*, while we have to ration and stand in line for food. It is an outrageous takeover and we are too terrorized to do anything about it." Another voice whispered, "You had better shut up before you end up in Russia unloading those shipments." The first man replied," I don't care!"

The speaker warned us with conviction, "Stop that undertone muttering or I will eliminate the instigator permanently." His eyes scanned us for a long time, searching the rows, which had become deadly silent. We were terrified even to breathe. Finally, he called for an intermission. That is what I was waiting for, so I could go by the cadets. I wanted to go to the washroom alone but Iren said, "I insist on going with you."

"Why?" I asked.

"Because your mother asked me to." I was furious at Mother for going that far, to ask my friend to spy on me.

Hardly waiting to reach home, I confronted Mother. She admitted her action. I was hurt, and fighting and raging with Mother, when Grandmother walked in. "What has happened? Why is Ilona so upset?"

I left the house before Mother could answer and walked to the crossroad to see my spiritual Friend; it was the only place where I could find tranquility. Sitting on the grass, resting my throbbing head on my knees, through my tears I asked God to help me.

The family was eating supper when I returned home. Mother glanced at me. "Come and have supper," she said, as she dished out my potato soup. I glared at her.

"I'm not hungry," I stated and went straight into the bedroom and crawled into bed with my street clothes on. When Grandmother came in she brought me a slice of bread smeared with some honey.

I was so unhappy at home; I spent most of my free time visiting with Jutka, even though she didn't need me for babysitting. We played records and she taught me how to do French manicures and pedicures, and how to pluck my eyebrows. She had lived in the city and was a hairdresser and manicurist before she moved here. When I came home wearing nail polish, Mother had a fit and we had a bitter argument. In her eyes, wearing nail polish at my age was a cardinal sin, and I had to go back to Jutka's to take off the polish with her remover, since we didn't have any.

Jutka and I talked a lot and she told me that women have to look after themselves to be attractive to men. After the children were in bed she told me about her love life, the kind I had never heard before. She explained menstruation to me, which I had yet to experience. She wanted to give me a book on sex and pregnancy, but I didn't dare take it for fear Mother would find it and stop me from going to her house again. I wanted to learn more and told her that I would read the book when I came to babysit.

One day when I was there she cut her daughters' hair. After she was finished she motioned for me to come and sit down. Jutka looked at me critically. "It's time you had a new hair style." I readily agreed. She cut my shoulder length hair to a very short pixie cut. When I looked in the mirror, I thought that this time I would surely perish when Mother saw me. My hair was just a little longer than Father's.

Looking at me Jutka said, "Ilona, the short hair suits you. It makes you look like a sophisticated city girl. Come and I will polish your nails again."

"Not on your life you don't! It will be hard enough to face Mother with my new haircut." On my way home, scared of Mother's reaction about my hair, I knew I had to talk to Grandmother before I went into the house. Gently I tiptoed up the steps, peeked through the window, and saw Grandmother crocheting in her favorite chair, close to the fireplace. Father was reading the newspaper and Mother was writing at the kitchen table. It was such a peaceful scene, but sooner or later I had to face the inevitable.

"Oh Lord," I prayed, "I need your help." Just saying the words gave me enough courage to walk into the house, and say a quiet hello . . . Grandmother looked at me without saying anything. Father looked and wrinkled his eyebrows as if he didn't recognize me. Mother stared at me with her infuriated look.

"I didn't give you permission to cut your hair like that." I knew she would be upset. I responded firmly.

"Mother, I am sixteen and not a child any more. I have the right to choose my own hairstyle. You can't control everything in my life."

Her eyes narrowed. "We will talk about this tomorrow," she asserted. She picked up the pen to continue writing, as if there was nothing more to say.

Thinking quickly that this was my chance to talk while I wasn't alone with her, I blurted out, "Mother, if you think tomorrow you will punish me, I will run away!"

Father quickly cut in, "Ilona your mother will not punish you for a silly hair cut. Would you Mari?" Mother ignored Father's question. "As a matter of fact I like your haircut. It looks nice on you." This time he turned to Grandmother, "Don't you think so, *Mama*?"

Grandmother smiled at me and said, "It looks very nice, Ilona. You look more grown up with this style." At this, Mother, having lost the battle, walked out to get some firewood.

The next day when Manci saw me, she exclaimed, "Ilona, you look like a boy." Julika laughed at that, and gave me a hug saying, "Now I have a brother as well." But Mother was still furious with me. "I am going to Jutka tomorrow and give her a piece of my mind. She had no right to cut your hair without my permission."

To take the blame from Jutka, I told Mother that I had asked her to cut my hair. "And another thing, Mother," I added, "you can't dominate everybody."

Mother was quiet, but speared me with her raging eyes.

The following day, Mother, Father, Grandmother, and I sat at the kitchen table to discuss the incident with Barni. Grandmother told them what had happened in the garden and because of that event I feared Barni. At first it seemed Father wasn't going to take any action. Finally, he spoke up. "Ilona, you know how we feel about the Communist system. Please, dear, you have to understand that to bring a Communist Cadet into our house would cause a major conflict. And for now, forget about Barni. He will be in the military for a long while and many things can happen in that time." I sat with my head bowed, relieved that he had spoken up, but not convinced that Barni was out of my life. Father went on, "I assure you that when Barni does come home I will definitely confront him about the way he frightened you in the garden. Drinking or not, how dare he force himself on you like that! I will not tolerate that kind of behavior, and if he continues, he had better stay away from you." I was delighted to hear the "stay away from you" part of the sentence.

I was surprised that Mother didn't respond to his outburst. I waited for her to say something, but she just smiled - a smile that aroused my suspicions.

CHAPTER 10

The weather was very cold by the end of November. To get fuel for our heater at home we had to go to the mine yard to pick coal, from the mud and dirt that the dockworkers had dumped as waste. Even those of us who worked at the mine couldn't afford to buy our winter supply of coal, which was extremely expensive. It really aggravated us that our country was forced to ship coal to Russia as surplus, while we had to pay a high price or search through mud in freezing temperatures for pieces the size of walnuts. People even came from the city and picked with us through the icy mire all day long. We kept an on-going open fire nearby to warm up our frozen bodies. With Christmas in mind, some of us even sold the coal for extra money.

In the cities not only heating fuel, but also food was very expensive, especially meat. We were fortunate to live in the country; at least we could raise some of our own meat, such as chicken and rabbit. Also we grew produce: mostly potatoes, turnips, and sugar beets for the winter. This made life a little easier for us country folks. Periodically I went to Budapest and took some food to Grandmother's friend, Mrs. Nemet, who was having a hard time supporting herself in the big city.

After Mass on Sunday afternoon, in preparation for the holiday season, we made *szaloncukor* - hard candies wrapped in white-fringed tissue paper lengthwise and red foil across the middle. Hung on the green tree with white thread, they were showy. We baked cookies shaped like bells, angels, and stars, and we also made ornaments using pinecones, small apples, and walnuts wrapped in colored foil. In previous years, we could have purchased these things, but under Communism they were not available in our store. So, we made our own. At work, however, there were no Christmas decorations or celebrations.

By this time we had mastered the art of being two-faced, showing acceptance of the Communist system on the outside, while hiding our hate for everything it stood for on the inside. Some of the brave Hungarians, who dared to reveal their true feelings, paid with their precious lives. Knowing the consequences of dissent, some workers who had faithfully celebrated Christmas before the Communist takeover, now publicly stated that they no longer believed in Christianity.

During all this uncertain time, I wanted desperately to see my cadet. Schemes came and went in my mind, as I tried to figure out how I could find an excuse to go to Nagybatony. Desperate to go, I asked Mother if she needed anything from the bigger store. She shook her head. "I know what you're scheming about! Barni will be home and you can go with him anywhere."

"I don't care about Barni," I declared with anger.

She looked at me coldly. "You'd better! You have no choice."

I was furious, but too afraid of her to carry the conversation any further. Walking to work, I realized that as I grew older the conflict with my mother became more and more serious. I had to do something. I was sixteen and it wasn't right that she treated me so unfairly. My only hope seemed to be to run away from her. But run away where? At sixteen, I was still under age; I could be forced to come back. And if that happened, I was afraid to think of what Mother would do to me. Maybe the only solution was to make the sacrifice and marry Barni. He would be home shortly. I wasn't looking forward to seeing him, but perhaps, with God's help, I could reconcile myself to the thought of spending the rest of my life with him, just to get free from Mother's domination.

The next day Grandfather Batta asked me to go with him to cut our Christmas tree, as was our tradition. I was happy that he still thought it was important that we carry out our usual custom of the two of us bringing home the tree. As we trekked through the deep snow, big fluffy snowflakes fell around us. It was exhilarating to be out in the woods with Grandfather; I felt like a small child again.

"Grandfather! It looks like the angels are having a pillow fight again and the fluffy down from the broken pillows is falling on us. That's why it's snowing. Isn't it Grandfather?" I asked him cheerfully.

He nodded. "Ilona, you still remember the angel story I told you so long ago. You were a small child and now you are all grown up."

"Yes, I know, *Nagyapa*," I replied. "I will never forget our times together."

As the snow fell softly on us he gave me a warm hug. He cuddled me for a moment, and turned his face away, but not before I saw his misty eyes.

We scouted silently for a while, and then suddenly we spotted our perfect tree. While Grandfather was cutting it down I pondered about the short life of this tree. Our glorified evergreen, which we adore at Christmas, is the baby Jesus' birthday bouquet, according to my grandmother's teaching during my early years. On January 6, we would take down all the decorations and divide the edible ones amongst the children. And there would be no further use of this precious tree that we had glorified for only a short time. After Christmas some people just threw it into the garbage dump, but not my grandfather. He burned it. When we burn the tree the sweet scent of the pine smoke ascends to the Creator, according to Grandfather's teachings.

Awaking me from my reminiscing, he called, "Ilona, I need your help." We lay the tree on the sleigh and we headed home, knowing we were bringing with us one of the symbols of our delightful ancient tradition.

Shortly, we put the tree up in the living room, which also served as a bedroom. The wonderful smells from Grandmother's baking mingled with the fresh scent of the evergreen, filling the house with the undeniable aroma of Christmas.

In the afternoon, we children decorated the tree with the *szaloncukor* ornaments and Grandmother's freshly baked cookies. As we trimmed the tree, when we thought no one was looking, we purposely broke some of the dainty cookies. Since they were no longer suitable for the tree we would be allowed to eat them. Pinches of white cotton, resembling snowflakes, put the finishing touch on the tree. Father put candles on the branches, which he would guard while they were lit for a short while on Christmas Eve. With the tree decorated, I took Julika for a sleigh ride so she wouldn't see who put the presents under the tree. With child-like innocence, she truly believed in the magic of Christmas. As adults, we were captivated by its spiritual message.

It was a tradition not to eat meat on Christmas Eve, so we sat down to a dinner of home-made mushroom soup and Grandmother's especially fine-cut, home-made noodles mixed with ground poppy seed and dusted with icing sugar. For dessert, walnut and poppy seed rolls were the traditional pastry, which was always carefully portioned out by Mother.

After dinner, we stayed in the kitchen and waited for Baby Jesus to come. Father went into the living room and lit the candles and a sparkler that he placed under the white angel that crowned the tree. When he rang the secret little bell we walked into the room singing *Csendes Ej,* (Silent Night). The moment was truly magical, with the candles and the sparkler lighting up the tree. We wished each other Merry Christmas with a hug and a kiss, and Grandmother led us in a special prayer. Julika mumbled the last words in a hurry, holding her present ready to open.

For her gift she received a toque, scarf, and mittens. She also received a book, *Csipke rozsika*, a story similar to Sleeping Beauty. Grandmother's present was a book, *Valamit Visz a Viz* (*Something is Floating on the River*). Mother tried on her new blouse, and Father was more than pleased with his new tools. Manci's gift of a hand-knit blue and white striped pullover looked very nice on her, as it matched her blue eyes. My gift was a dark green and white knitted pullover. I tried it on, and it fit me perfectly. When Julika was absent Grandmother confessed she had knit them secretly while we weren't home.

Midnight Mass had been abolished since the Communist takeover, so we stayed home, playing games for walnuts and singing Christmas carols.

On Christmas day Barni arrived before noon. As he walked in my back was turned to him. After he finished greeting the family he came over to me and gave me a hug. Then, he noticed my haircut and he looked pleased.

"I love your haircut Ilona. It looks very stylish. In Debrecen most of the girls wear their hair short." And he ran his fingers playfully through my hair.

After the greetings, Father called to him, "Barni, come with me; I want to hear all about the military." They went into the other room and Father closed the door. I assumed that there was another reason why Father wished to speak to Barni alone. I hoped he would question him about his behavior in the garden and realize that, in spite of what Mother thought, he would not be a suitable husband for me. When they came back into the kitchen, Father came over to me and whispered, "Barni apologized for his actions, and promised it won't happen again."

Barni could not accompany us to church on Christmas day, because of military restrictions. So he stayed home with Mother, as she had to cook our dinner. In church I enjoyed singing Christmas carols, and thinking about the possibility of loving Barni as I love my cadet. My mixed feelings puzzled me. Barni looked so handsome in uniform. I don't know why, but the uniform did something for me. (Still does.)

After church, as we approached our house, we could smell the aroma of the roast goose with Grandmother's savory stuffing. In the kitchen, we girls had to help Mother with dinner since Barni had to go home early, because he had to go back to his military base the next day. After dinner, he asked me to go for a walk with him, as he wanted to talk to me desperately. We left the house and walked along the road to the meadows. We had gone only a short distance when he stopped and handed me a gift wrapped in red paper, tied with a white bow. He wished me Merry Christmas, held me close, and gently kissed me. I briefly returned his embrace and then opened the box. Inside was a bottle of lilac cologne, my favorite fragrance. He looked pleased when I opened the bottle and put some on my wrists.

"I love it," he said, and he held me closer. "From now on this will be our fragrance." I gave him a quick hug and thanked him. And he kissed me again.

"Dear Ilona, I love you so much. I will be home soon and I will be with you all the time."

I was startled. "What are you talking about, all the time?"

He took my hand and I saw a light in his eyes that I had never seen before. "We will get engaged as soon as I am dismissed from the military."

"Engaged . . . and dismissed? Barni what are you talking about?" I was becoming increasingly nervous at this turn of events. "Barni, I'm not ready to get engaged and you have to serve a year and a half yet. Why would you be dismissed?"

His body stiffened and a dark look crossed his face. "I can't stand the military, especially the drilling," he said harshly. "I will be out shortly. You'll see."

"But how?"

"I disobey all the rules. At roll call everyone has to be in the line-up, fully dressed and ready for inspection. But I shuffled in late with my shoes untied and my shirttail hanging out, with no belt or hat. The whole unit burst out laughing and the commanding officer had a hard time controlling the brigade." He smiled briefly at the thought, and then he continued, "Two officers came and took me away, beat me, and . . . put me in jail. The day I was released, we had target practice; everyone was given a rifle and a round of shells. When I got my rifle loaded with all the shells in the magazine, I cocked the rifle and fired all the bullets in the air without stopping . . . rat-a-ta-ta." He made the sound like a machine gun. "Everyone was terrified. But for me, I thought it was so hilarious I just had to laugh."

I could hardly believe what he was telling me. "They must have thought that you were crazy. Then what happened?"

"They took me away again and put me in jail. I was ordered to have daily sessions with the military psychiatrist. However, he was upset with me too."

"Why was he upset," I asked, almost fearful of his answer.

"Because I never showed up on time. And with the things I had done, he came to the conclusion that I'm mentally disturbed. But I don't care."

I was totally flabbergasted. Words failed me. I couldn't tell him how I felt. I just stood staring at him, rigid as a statue. Finally, we returned home. Then he grabbed my shoulders and shook me. "Ilona, I want you to swear not to tell this to anyone." Now there was a pleading in his voice. "They would exterminate me if they knew I was faking the insanity to get out of the military." I was wondering if he really was faking it.

When we reached the house, the coffee was brewed and Mother put a slice of poppy seed roll on my plate, but gave two to Barni. I was hungry, and that upset me beyond humanity. I could not eat, or even utter a word, stunned that she had given him two slices. As Mother was eying me, I slowly pushed my plate away; instantly she picked up my roll and put it on Barni's plate, and they exchanged a snickering smile.

I was hurt, deeply hurt, at Mother's action. Grandmother silently witnessing Mother's behavior slowly rose from her chair, went to Mother's side, took the knife out of her hand, went to the counter, cut off a big chunk from the one last roll, and went into the bedroom and closed the door. By her crimson face I thought Mother was going to die. Instead she poured another cup of coffee for Barni, who was chatting with Father, as if everything were perfectly normal. Mother and Manci made a fuss over Barni, but I was too distraught to say anything.

Before Barni left, Father shook his hand and warned him, "Barni, don't do anything stupid at the military base." Then Barni came over to where I was standing by the open door. Outside he kissed me goodbye. I quickly turned away from him, thinking, "You really are insane."

"I'll be home soon. You'll see," he whispered in my ear. I shivered, not only from the cold outside, but also at the thought of what the future might hold for him in the military.

When I came in Mother exclaimed, "Isn't Barni a wonderful, handsome man?" Father's brow creased into a small frown. His eyes were thoughtful, as if he had been confronted with a problem he didn't quite know how to handle.

"I don't know what it is, but there's something wrong with Barni's thinking about the military. He doesn't seem mentally stable to me."

Mother glared at him. "Nonsense. Barni is a very fine, young man."

Still shocked about Barni's actions, quietly I said goodnight and went into the bedroom, where Grandmother handed me the chunk of poppy seed roll. "Eat this since your Mother wanted to cut you short of it. And now, I demand you tell me what happened with Barni, while you two were walking. When the two of you came back, you looked like you just saw a ghost. Tell me what happened?"

"Nothing, nothing Grandmother," and I stuffed my mouth with the roll so I could not talk. I couldn't discuss Barni's secret with anyone. I vowed to keep his secret. If he were killed or disappeared because of me, I would never forgive myself. I feared for his life, plotting against the brutal Communist military.

CHAPTER 11

Barni's abnormal behavior at the military base was very serious, and I was greatly troubled by it. I promised to keep his secret, but for how long? I had to consider all the implications of revealing his scheme. Trying to outwit the Communist military could have very serious consequences. What could he be thinking of? I began to think that perhaps he truly was mentally disturbed. As the days passed, it became more and more urgent that I talk to Mother, to beg her not to force me to marry such an unstable man.

Depressed, but determined to tell Mother everything, I thought about how to plead my case. I sat at the kitchen table peeling potatoes rehearsing in my mind, as I had many times, how to begin the conversation. No matter how anxious I was about the outcome, I had to talk to Mother, and this was the right time.

"*Anyuka* I have to discuss a very urgent problem with you."

Before she could respond, Julika called, "Ilona, please come and help me with my Russian language studies." Looking at Mother's unconcerned face, I hesitated for a second. "I'm coming," I called rising from my chair. The moment had passed and the opportunity was lost - an opportunity that could have changed the course of my life, if Mother would have realized Barni's true mental state.

Julika was waiting for me with her textbook open. Learning Russian was now mandatory in school. Before the Communist establishment the students had a choice of foreign languages. I had learned German, but now in our "free" country, only Russian was taught in our schools. I enjoyed teaching her, because she had a great desire to learn and her childish Russian pronunciation was amusing.

Grandmother returned home from our next-door neighbor's, Mrs. Dobos, who owned a weaving loom. She and Grandmother were weaving yards of linen for tablecloths, tea towels, and sheets, as well as for clothing. I had to talk to Grandmother about Barni's scheme, because it was killing me. Just then Manci raced in looking for Mother, who had just walked in.

"*Anyuka*, I just heard there's going to be a dance in Matraverebely, and our group is planning to attend. Can I go with them?"

Without hesitation, Mother answered, "Of course, dear."

"Please, *Anyuka*, can I go too?" I begged her.

She looked at me sternly, "You are Barni's girlfriend and he wouldn't like it."

Instantly angered, I nearly blurted out his secret. Instead I said, "*Anyuka*, your notion about Barni is all wrong."

"Regardless, you are not going." She paid no attention to me while she finished cooking supper. I tried to withhold my anger, but allowed my evil thoughts to take over about Mother. I stared out the window with misty eyes. I felt Father's hand on my shoulder. He patted me gently, "Ilona, after supper I would like to talk to you privately."

"What about?" Mother asked with great curiosity.

"You will find out later," Father answered.

I thought, "Now I will have a chance to discuss Barni's situation with him." I had to tell someone before it drove me insane. I rushed through supper and followed Father into the other room. He closed the door and sat beside me at the table.

"Ilona, this has to stay in the family. If our neighbors were to find out that I'm interested in the Russian language, they would assume that I'm secretly a Communist." His serious expression aroused my curiosity. He continued, "I would like to learn the Russian language and I want you to teach me." Only then did I notice that Julika's Russian textbook was on the table.

I was so astounded I jumped up and gave him a hug and a kiss.

"Dear *Apuka*, I will gladly teach you what I know. I'm very proud that you want to learn." With a bright smile I added, "I love you." I had finally expressed my true feelings and shown my deep love for him. This small incident was the beginning of our deeper relationship. I felt honored to teach him, and I treasured the times we spent together. I was ready to tell him about Barni, but he was so immersed in his study that I had no intention of stopping his progress. So, I waited.

Since we had no telephone, Jutka's private messenger, her daughter Piroska, delivered a note for me asking if I could babysit for her on Saturday night. I thought since Mother would not allow me to go dancing, at least I would have an opportunity at Jutka's to listen to records. But I tried once more to get Mother's permission for the dance, but she said, "I know the Communist Cadet will be there; that is why you want to go so badly, but it is not going to happen, because you are not going."

With anger I yelled at her, "You are evil; you are an evil Mother."

I left the house muttering to myself, "It's not fair! It's not fair!" Arriving at Jutka's, she gave me a lecture about being late. Little Piroska listened for a few minutes, then said, "Mother, leave Ilona alone. She just had a fight with her mother. I could hear them outside."

At that, Jutka looked at me more closely, "I'm sorry, Ilona. I should have seen that you were upset." She called to Andras, "Would you make some tea for us?"

When he handed me my tea, he asked, "Why aren't you going to the dance? All the gang will be there."

"Mother won't allow me to go," I said curtly. His face softened, and he nodded understandingly. He left, leaving me to do Jutka's hair and nails.

After they left, Magdus started the record player. She put on a rumba and the three of us danced until we were exhausted. We ate some compote, and afterwards huddled together on the sofa as I read the girls a story.

Later, I put them to bed as Piroska was already dozing. I returned to the living room, dimmed the lights, and stretched out on the sofa. Instantly I began thinking about Barni's dreadful situation, which haunted me. Gradually, my turmoil eased as I turned my thoughts to the crossroad cross and beseeched my Lord and Friend to guide me in my turbulent life. I napped until a gentle touch awakened me.

"Ilona, we are home," Andras said, smiling down at me. "Come, I will walk you home." He paid me for babysitting, and I put on my coat and followed him outside.

On the way home I asked him if he had a good time at the dance.

"No," he said, "It was a disaster."

Curious, I asked, "What happened?"

"Jutka was angry with me, because I danced with several other girls."

"But, Andras," I protested, "that's not fair. I would be upset too."

He stopped and turned to face me while gently caressing my arm and said, "If you would have been my date, I wouldn't have danced with anyone else." Totally taken by surprise, I had no idea how to respond. And I didn't. But I was puzzled by his touch.

When I walked into the house, I was surprised to see a young man talking to my parents. Manci introduced us, "Ilona, meet Josef."

I acknowledged the introduction, poured myself a cup of tea, and hastily said goodnight. In the bedroom I shared my tea with Grandmother, who spoke soothingly to calm me down. I handed her the extra money Jutka had given me for doing her hair and nails. Desperate to tell Grandmother Barni's secret, I asked Grandmother to come to the early Mass with me the next morning. We were almost asleep when Manci came to bed. She wanted to tell me all about the dance, but I pretended that I was sleeping. The dance was the last thing I wanted to hear about.

Walking to church the next morning, we were joined by our neighbor, Mrs. Orvari, which prevented me from discussing my problem with Grandmother. As we sat in church, I made a silent plea with God: asking for help to sort out my life and for forgiveness for my evil wishes for Mother. With prayer, a sense of tranquility permeated my being, banishing my resentment and frustration, as if my soul had been cleansed. In my heart I knew this was the sign of the Lord that I had been forgiven for my evil thoughts. More importantly, I knew I was not alone with my problems.

After church, Grandmother and I waited until everyone had left, so we could walk home alone on our quiet country road and talk privately. We had not gone far when two young men riding bicycles caught up to us. When they continued to stay close behind, we turned around to see who they were. We didn't know them and they didn't introduce themselves. One was tall with dark hair, searching blue eyes, and a large Roman nose. The other was shorter, with red hair and a kinder face. The tall man ordered Grandmother, "Old woman you walk ahead with Frank! I want to talk to Ilona privately."

Grandmother stood her ground. "Who are you? And why do you want to talk to Ilona? I've never seen you around here before."

"We are from the military," he said, "and I want to talk to Ilona about Barni, alone."

Grandmother frowned at him. "What about Barni?" she asked.

The man's Roman nose seemed to twitch as he growled, "Old woman, do as I tell you before I lose my temper." At that, Frank grabbed Grandmother by the arm and forced her to walk ahead with him. I saw the fear in her eyes that reflected my own panic, when I realized that these men were the ruthless AVO, the security police in civilian clothes. They had unlimited authority; these men interrogated anyone they suspected of defying the Communist system. I was well aware that if I confessed what Barni had told me, he would be killed.

The man turned to me. He asked so many questions about people and my friends that I became confused. I tried to stay calm and answer without giving anything away that might incriminate anyone. But it was obvious; it was Barni that he was interested in - particularly what his intention was in the military. They were obviously afraid of an uprising. As his questioning continued, I grew more fearful.

"Why are you so nervous, Ilona," he asked sharply, as his eyes stared into mine. "What are you hiding?"

"I'm not hiding anything. I don't know anything. Barni didn't say anything about the military to me," I replied. When he continued to stare at me, I added, "I'm nervous because I'm not interrogated by the secret police very often."

He shouted at me, "We are not interrogating! We just want information. I want you to engrave that in your mind, so you will never forget it." And he pushed me so hard that I lost my balance. Grandmother saw me tumbling, quickly ran back, and held me protectively.

With fury she voiced her opinion. "Since Ilona is a minor, I insist on being here if you are going to question her any more."

My interrogator went over to her. With his face only inches from Grandmother's, he ground his teeth, twitched his jaw muscles, and growled at her, "Even if you are a grandmother, you don't insist on anything with me," and he gave her a push. She pushed him right back.

By this time I was ready to attack him, to protect my grandmother, but the carrot head seized me. Grandmother calmly said, "We haven't done anything illegal, so you can't talk to me like that and push me around!" She clasped my hand tightly. "Come, Ilona, let's go home."

"Yes *Nagymama*." I clutched her hand and we walked away, scared to death, but brave in our flight.

He shouted after us, "I'm warning you, old woman. Don't cross my path again or I guarantee you will never see your home again." Shortly afterwards they jumped on their bikes and rode off.

We were in the countryside in the open air, but we were suffocating, overcome with fear. We clung to each other as we made our way to the side of the road, where we sat down, terrified and exhausted. When we had collected our thoughts I told Grandmother about Barni's outrageous behavior in the military: how he had ignored all the rules and had violently discharged his firearm at target practice. She listened in silence, with disgust on her face and with a deep sigh she whispered, "No wonder the AVO is so furious. They are afraid of a revolution and that Barni could be an instigator. He must be insane to behave like that," she said, agreeing with me about his mental condition.

Leaning against her comforting body, I asked, "*Nagymama,* what are we going to do?"

She patted my shoulder reassuringly. "Nothing, right now, dear. Barni will be in the military for a while. Right now we have to be silent. We won't say anything about the AVO interrogating you."

"But how did they know we would be going to the eight o'clock Mass instead of the usual eleven?"

Grandmother sighed again, "Informers, dear, informers." She said it sadly. "It could have been one of our neighbors. We have to be discreet about it. This could be a disaster for you." I shuddered, remembering the furious wicked eyes of my interrogator.

"I know," I agreed. "And because they are in civilian clothes, they are undetectable. They could follow me anywhere. *Nagymama*, I am terrified. How can I escape this fearful situation?"

"Dear child," she said gently, "only with devout prayer to God, only with devout prayer." I nodded, huddling closer to her. And we prayed earnestly for my safety.

CHAPTER 12

With the interrogation by the Communist secret police still shadowing our minds, my dear *nagymama* and I walked home from *Szentkut* arm in arm. Deep in my heart, I believed the purpose of her life was to protect me, as a divine guardian. When I tried to express my gratitude to her she responded, "I will always be there for you, dear, but right now we have to decide what we are going to do about this fearful situation." The shock was too great for me to offer any suggestions.

Just before we came to our yard, she cautioned me, "Don't say a word to anyone about this. I will investigate on my own and find out who is our betrayer. It has to be someone who lives close to us and watches where we go."

As we walked into the house, I was glad to see that Manci's boyfriend had come for a visit. While Manci and Mother entertained him in the kitchen, Grandmother and I had a peaceful rest, which we desperately needed.

Back at work we were informed that we had to split up our two-week holidays - one week in the spring and one week later - to avoid a summer staff shortage. I decided to take a week at Easter and go to Budapest to see Grandmother's friend, Mrs. Nemet. I desperately needed time to get away from my mother and the interrogation episode. Mrs. Nemet was the perfect answer to my prayer. She was alone and she loved to have company. She especially enjoyed the food parcels I brought her on my visits.

I asked Grandmother, "Do you think Mother will let me go to Budapest and stay with Mrs. Nemet for a week?"

Without hesitation, she answered, "Yes." When I asked her how she could be so sure, she replied with a smile, "Because we are not going to tell her that you are going for a week. It would be good for you to get away, especially after our ordeal with the secret police." She walked over to the chest where she kept her personal belongings and pulled out a small purse. "Here is some of the money you gave me. I saved it for you, so you would have spending money when you needed it." I was grateful and gave her a thankful hug.

Glancing out the window, I saw Mother chatting with Mrs. Orvari. I called to Grandmother, and when she saw them she shook her head and frowned. "That old buzzard. If she's the one who betrayed us, she will not live to regret it. What she put us through with those AVO men is unforgivable."

I agreed. "Maybe she is the one. By squealing on people she could easily make good money."

"That is a disgrace," Grandmother said indignantly. "What kind of a person would sell out her own people?"

Just then we heard Mother say, "Come on in, Mrs. Orvari, and I will put the kettle on."

When they came into the house, we strolled into the kitchen.

"I will join you," Grandmother said. Mrs. Orvari's face remained placid as she said, "I like to visit with the neighbors and discuss our frightful political situation." At that, Grandmother and I exchanged glances.

"Ilona," Grandmother said, "you asked me to remind you to spend more time on your drawing."

I got the message. "Yes, I'm going right now," I replied. I went into the other room, leaving the door open a crack, so I could hear what Mrs. Orvari was saying. I sat down at my easel and continued working on the drawing of *Szentkut's* glorious eighteenth century church. In the meantime I listened to Grandmother's questioning of Mrs. Orvari.

The next day at work, I was luckily informed that I had to take my holiday at Easter. That meant that I had to leave for Budapest in three days. When I told Grandmother the news she rushed to get some baking done, and Mother gathered some preserves, honey, dried fruit, and eggs. The day before my departure, Mother butchered and dressed a chicken for Mrs. Nemet. This was a very generous gesture on her part, as we had only a few chickens left for us until next summer. While Mother and Grandmother were busy preparing the food parcel, I secretly packed extra clothes so that Mother wouldn't get suspicious that I would be gone for more than two days. I was brimming with excitement, not only to see my beloved Budapest, but also to get away from my dire situation.

As I came home from my last day at work, happy at the prospect of being free for a week, Mrs. Orvari called to me from her open window. "Ilona, what train are you taking to Budapest tomorrow?"

I came to an instant stop. "Who told you I'm going to Budapest?"

"Your mother," she answered.

Thinking of the possibility that she might have been the one who had squealed on us to the AVO, I quickly said, "I changed my mind. I'm going to leave on Sunday instead of tomorrow."

Outraged at Mother for telling Mrs. Orvari my plans, I let her know my rage when I arrived home. It was only when she said that she didn't think it was a crime to tell people where I was going, that I remembered Mother didn't know anything about the encounter with the AVO. I instantly apologized to her for my outburst. Grandmother, obviously sensing that a rescue was necessary, called from the bedroom, "Ilona come here and show me which suitcase you want to take," despite already knowing I was taking the burgundy case, which I had packed the night before.

The next morning we finished packing the food hamper. All that was left to do was to take a bath and wash my hair. In the meantime Grandmother advised, "Don't worry about anything dear, just think about Budapest and the good times we had there together."

On the way to the station, I thought I was leaving all my troubles behind. While waiting for the train, I bought a teen magazine and a puzzle book. When the train arrived, everyone hurried to get on. Luckily, I found a seat by the window and tried to immerse myself in my magazine, but I couldn't concentrate. All of the distressing events that had recently happened in my life, continued to torment me. I tried to shut out those turbulent thoughts by reminding myself of my good fortune: having one whole week in Budapest, away from Mother and all my troubles. My greatest desire was to live a happy life with my cadet, free from anxieties.

In Hatvan, there was a half-hour delay, waiting for a connecting train. I left the magazine and book on my seat to reserve it, and got off to stretch my legs. After boarding the train again, I was surprised to find a well-dressed, dark-haired, young man wearing sunglasses and a black leather jacket had taken my seat. His smile looked cold and sly. In my mind I named him "Slicker." When I approached, he slid away from the window seat, just far enough that he would be sitting next to me. He handed me my books and said, "My name is Arpad. And yours is…?"

"Ilona," I answered briefly, opening my magazine and beginning to read. I didn't want to talk to him. He gave me this dreadful feeling, but he kept asking more questions.

"What is your destination, Ilona?"

"Budapest," I replied.

"Where are you staying in Budapest?" I tried to ignore him, but he continued his questioning. "Where are you from?"

78

"Matraverebely," I answered impatiently. Remembering the interrogation with the secret police, I thought, "If he is one of them, he can't do anything to me while we were on a train filled with people." This gave me enough courage to look straight into his eyes and say, "What is this questioning all about? I would like to be left alone, if you don't mind."

By now I was sure he was with the AVO. Even though my heart was beating rapidly, I tried to appear calm to show him that I was not afraid of him. I turned away from him and looked out the window. After a long silence, he touched my arm to get my attention and offered me a candy, which I refused.

When the train reached the last stop before Budapest, Slicker got off the train. I felt free. Gazing at the people outside, as they were rushing to their destinations, my attention was drawn to the baskets hanging from ornamental lampposts. They were filled with red geraniums with vivid green leaves and trailing white lobelia. The colors reminded me of our patriotic red, white, and green Hungarian flag, before the Communists restyled it with their large red star, and a hammer and a sickle in the middle. Then, I noticed Slicker, half hidden by the lamppost, talking intently to an older man. I watched him anxiously until the train started to move. Quickly he leaped back on the train, before it gathered speed.

When he returned to the compartment, I closed my eyes, leaned my head towards the window, and pretended to sleep. I buried my thoughts in the pulsing motion and sound of the clickedy-clack, clickedy-clack of the wheels. But, not for long. Even turned away from him, I could feel him staring at me. Resigned and resentful, I turned to face him.

"I was waiting for you to wake up, Ilona," and he offered me another candy. I took it and put it in my purse, saying, "I will eat it later." Could I trust him to give me a candy without a narcotic in it?

When we arrived in Budapest he offered to share a taxi with me. Terrified, and sure he was an AVO man, I refused. I chose another taxi, and while the driver loaded my luggage, Slicker continued to insist that I go with him. I got into my own taxi and tried to close the door, but he blocked it with his foot. His eyes were now cold and threatening, and his face was centimeters from mine. He said harshly, "You'd better stay in Budapest. If I find you in Debrecen visiting Barni, unpleasant things might happen to you." With that, he slammed the door shut and the taxi driver hastily pulled away from the curb.

As I gave the driver Mrs. Nemet's address, he glanced in his rearview mirror. "That man is desperate. His cab is following us."

I shuddered at the thought of how easily the secret police had found me. These people would do whatever it took to keep political control. Now, due to Barni's bizarre behavior in Debrecen at the military, I was a target for their terror. If I told them that I had nothing to do with his actions, would they believe me? I doubted it. I feared them because they had their own cruel methods of interrogation, including having people confess to crimes they did not commit. Being completely distraught, I didn't notice that my cab driver had taken a different route to Mrs. Nemet's to lose our following cab.

When we arrived at the apartment, still upset I asked the driver to help carry my suitcase and hamper up to the second floor. Seeing how frightened I was, he readily agreed. As I paid him, he warned me not to go out alone at night.

Mrs. Nemet greeted me warmly. Unpacking the food hamper, she was ecstatic with the contents. When I put some of the food into her little icebox, I realized why she was so happy. It was almost empty. Not wanting to spoil the joy of the moment, I decided not to tell her about my experience with the AVO man on the train.

I watched her as we drank tea and nibbled on Grandmother's linzer cookies, which she calculated, at one a day, would last her about a month. As she rolled the cookie in her mouth, savoring its last crumb, she remarked, "This is definitely Rozi's baking. I can tell by its special flavor." Her eyes misted. "I love your grandmother, Ilona. She's the best friend I've ever had. I miss her so much."

I solemnly nodded, knowing how lonely she must be since Grandmother left Budapest. "She is my best friend, too, Mrs. Nemet. I couldn't live without my dear *nagymama*."

"Yes, I know how it is," she replied. Then brightening, she added, "You've had a long journey. Go and have a hot bath while I start supper." She rose and went into her little kitchen and held up the fresh chicken I had brought. "We are going to have chicken paprikas for supper," she exclaimed, "which I haven't had in a long, long time."

I could hardly wait to get into the bathtub. The warm water felt superb. The lingering fragrance of the apple blossom bath salts, which Mrs. Nemet had given me, filled the air. She had also thoughtfully lit a candle for me to enjoy.

Its warm glow cast soft shadows around me, while the soothing of the warm water eased the tension from my body. Mesmerized by the candle's flickering light, I was torn with emotions. Uppermost in my mind was how happily I could live with my Communist cadet, instead of with the non-Communist Barni who secretly terrorized my life. Why can't my mother see that? Why did life always have to be so tormenting? What was I going to do about Slicker during my stay in Budapest? There was no way I could report him to the authorities, because he was obviously one of them. There was nothing I could do, but keep silent. Maybe, I rationalized, it would be best if I went home after the weekend so Mrs. Nemet would not get caught up in the AVO net. She was too old and fragile to have to deal with such a heavy problem.

After supper she asked, "Ilona, would you like to go to church with me tomorrow morning?" I paused. The Communists despised church and religion. If I went, that would be a strike against me. But I had to turn to God. He was the only one who could truly help me.

"I'd love to go to church with you, Mrs. Nemet," I replied. "It will bring back the wonderful childhood memories of being here with my dear grandmother." Later in bed, we prayed together, not only for strength to cope with our daily lives, but also for our troubled country as well.

Next morning in church, it seemed as if I had never left. The strong faith of my childhood remained. Envisioning myself in church wearing my white dress with the red flowers, red ankle socks, white patent leather shoes, and a white ribbon in my hair, with Grandmother by my side, I remembered how it felt to be a little girl, with no fears and worries. But today was different. I was grown up and full of fears.

For the hour we were in the cathedral, I became thoroughly captivated by the magnificent interior and uplifted by the harmony of the music. As I participated in the rituals that were so much a part of my being, I forgot my problems, content to revel in the tranquility that seemed to radiate from the very walls of the ancient building.

Some of my Budapest girlfriends attended Mass that day as well. It was so delightful to see them again. After the Mass, they joined Mrs. Nemet and me when we went to our favorite bistro for *malnaszurp*. We spent the next hour catching up on what had happened since we had last been together. The girls invited me to go to a movie with them, but due to my encounter with Slicker, I had to decline, saying I was returning home early the next day.

81

When Mrs. Nemet heard that, she looked shocked and disappointed. "But Ilona, your grandmother said in her letter that you would be here for a week."

I hated to disappoint her, but my encounter with Slicker had left me feeling too vulnerable to stay in Budapest. Regretfully, I apologized, "Sorry, but I've decided to go home tomorrow." Even though she didn't understand why I had changed my mind, she didn't argue with me.

In the morning, before I left, she handed me an envelope addressed to Grandmother and gave me some pocket money. As she kissed me goodbye, she said gravely, as if she had noticed the strain I was under, "God be with you, Ilona. I will pray for you."

"Thank you, Mrs. Nemet," I replied as I threw her a kiss.

Since I didn't have the food hamper, I took a streetcar on Rakoczi Street to the train station. Along the way, childhood memories resurfaced, as I stared out the window at the bakery and the butcher shop, where the owners used to give me carob pods (*szent janos kenyer*). But sadly since the Communist takeover, the shops were owned by the state and they were almost empty due to the shortage of food.

Boarding the train, I hoped I had left the secret police behind and chose a compartment already occupied by a young mother with two children. She told me her name was Anna. Her children were Erzsike, a girl of about eight, and Misike, a little boy of about four, who was crying softly, cradled in his mother's arms.

Hatvan was a connecting station where we always had to wait. I went to the station cafeteria to buy a fresh croissant (*kifli*). It smelled so delicious I ordered two, along with an apple and a bottle of *malnaszurp*. Anticipating the pleasure of eating the croissants, I hurried back to my compartment. When I opened the bag, the children stared at it so intently that I realized that they were hungry. Unable to bear the pleading in their eyes, I handed them the bag. The way they tore it open and devoured its contents, confirmed my suspicion that they were indeed very hungry.

Later, Anna told them to lie down on the opposite bench, and she gently covered them with her well-used coat. She looked so sad. To start a conversation, I asked where she was going. She said she was going to Paszto to see her mother and to leave the children with her.

"Now, I am a single mother. Without my husband, on my wages I can't support my children."

I felt her pain as if it were my own. "Where is your husband?" I asked.

Afraid of being overheard, she whispered in my ear. "He just disappeared. He went to work and he never came home." I didn't dare ask any more questions, but Anna volunteered, "He didn't hide his feelings about our traitors and our dishonest politicians."

Sick at heart at what I had heard, I said, "I understand, Anna. I truly do."

We sat in silence for a long time, infuriated by the Russian marching music that blared over the train's loudspeaker. Eventually, she dozed off and her head fell lifeless on my shoulder. Careful not to wake her, I looked at her beautiful children sleeping so peacefully, unaware that soon they would be without their mother. I could only imagine how devastating it would be for Anna to leave her children behind. Weeping, I prayed to God to help them.

With Anna's head resting on my shoulder, my arm soon became numb, but I tolerated the discomfort to allow her to sleep. As we approached Paszto, I had to wake her. She quickly roused the children, who were unhappy at being wakened from their deep sleep. Before she left, she gave me a goodbye hug and I handed her the money Mrs. Nemet had given me. She didn't want to take it, but I put it in her coat pocket so she couldn't refuse. They stood on the platform and waved to me as the train pulled out. I waved back until they were lost to my view.

I sat down and closed my eyes, my mind in turmoil, trying to understand the meaning of my meeting with Anna. It came to me that I had been led to be in the same compartment with her, to feed the children, and to help them with the money that Mrs. Nemet had given me. Certainly they needed it more than I did. Having heard often from Grandmother, "God works in mysterious ways," I now understood what she meant.

As I got off the train at Nagybatony, all my fears and troubles still with me more than ever, I also had to bear losing what should have been a treasured week in Budapest to the stalking of the Communist secret police.

CHAPTER 13

Finally, I arrived back home where I felt safe. Jutka saw me walking home and shortly caught up to me. She looked so agitated; my immediate thought was maybe Andras had left her. However, when she reached me she told me she had to go to Paszto to see her mother, who was very ill, and she asked if I would look after the children for three days. I was willing to help her since I had come home early from Budapest. I loved to be with the children and this was my chance to stay away from my domineering mother.

"I'll come to your house as soon as I can," I assured her.

Walking into the quiet house, I was shocked to find Mother and Andras having coffee alone. For a minute we all looked at each other, not knowing what to say. They both looked so nervous at my unexpected arrival. I didn't know what to think. Before I could say anything, Andras jumped up and said he had to go. Mother grabbed her sweater and said she had to go to the store. I was stunned. Hoping they weren't having a love affair, I tried to think of another reason why they would have acted so nervously. But I couldn't.

To ease my whirling mind I slumped into a kitchen chair. A little while later, Father came home. Now was my chance to tell him about the AVO agent. After he had greeted me, he poured a cup of coffee and sat down beside me.

"Now, dear, tell me about your trip."

"Father, you wouldn't believe what happened to me in Hatvan. A well-dressed young man got on and sat next to me, asking all kinds of questions."

Just then, Mother came home with her friend. I had to change the subject so they wouldn't know what I was talking about. I continued, "He was a very nice old man, and he kept me company all the way to Budapest."

"Who kept you company, Ilona?" Mother asked curiously.

"An old gentleman," I answered quickly, and signaled Father with a wink that I was changing the subject. Although I was desperate to tell Father the rest of the story, I had to wait. While having tea with them, Grandmother came home and eyed me like I was a stranger. Then she questioned, "Ilona, are you sick? Why are you home?"

I couldn't tell her the real reason for my early return, so I said with a smile, "Grandmother, have you forgotten? I live here."

The cover-up worked and everyone laughed at my remark. She gave me a kiss and felt my forehead to satisfy herself that I wasn't sick. To stop her from asking any more questions, I handed her Mrs. Nemet's letter.

"Oh, it is from my dear friend. I have to read this in private," she said as she limped into the other room. It broke my heart to see her dragging her painful leg.

Within seconds of closing the door, she called for me. As soon as I walked into the bedroom she closed the door behind me. Without hesitation, she asked, "What happened in Budapest? Why are you home early?"

"*Nagymama*, it is a long story. I need time to explain."

Before I could say more, she said, "We will get some warm water and you'll take a bath, so we can lock the door and talk. It's the only time we can talk privately."

After a quick wash I had a chance to pour my heart out to Grandmother about Slicker, the AVO man - about how he had questioned and followed me, and how he became furious when I refused to sit in his taxi. I was blessed that my cab driver was close by me, and Slicker didn't dare to grab me and force me to go with him. But he had threatened me, if I were to go to see Barni in Debrecen. Sharing the story with Grandmother lightened my burden that I was targeted.

Grandmother listened quietly and intently. She thought for a few minutes, and then said, "It is certain that we have to get rid of Barni. It's the only way you will free yourself from the secret police, and be able to live a fearless life."

"But how? Mother will fight bitterly with me."

"This is a serious matter," Grandmother said gravely. "We have to tell your parents about this threatening situation." She reached for my hand and squeezed it gently saying, "I will figure out how to tell them and when."

Just then Mother called, "We have to hurry with supper. Manci's boyfriend, Jozsi, is coming."

I was happy for Manci; Jozsi seemed to be the right match for her and the family favored him, because he wasn't a Communist. After supper they left to go to a movie.

Later, I told Mother about Jutka's sick mother. I told her I would be looking after Jutka's girls for three days until Andras came home from work. Mother made no attempt to conceal her anger.

"No! You are not going. I forbid you to babysit for her any more."

"But, why, *Anyuka?* I like the children and enjoy being with them."

"I have my reasons," she said. To her, the matter was closed.

Then Grandmother cut in. "What has got into you, Mari? It was all right for her to babysit before, and now it is not? I want to know what your reason is. Why are you so unfair to her?"

Mother, breathing down on Grandmother, rudely stated, "Jutka is a bad influence on Ilona."

"I don't believe that for a second," Grandmother retorted. With that she left the table and walked out of the house. But later, alone with Mother, I questioned her.

"What was Andras doing here with you alone?"

She glared at me. "That's none of your business."

Before I could reply, she said, "I want you to go to the store right now and get some yeast for me. And on your way stop in at Jutka's and tell her that you are not going to babysit for her any more."

Angry at her harsh statement, I wished to harm her with my evil look. Walking to the store, the thought that Mother and Andras were having an affair made me sick. Jutka was shocked by Mother's decision and wanted to know her reason. But I couldn't tell her.

I felt sorry for her, but I couldn't help her. I had problems of my own. One of which was to figure out the true connection between Mother and Andras, and I had no idea how I was going to tell Grandmother about what I'd seen, let alone my poor father. Eventually I decided I would have to talk with Andras first, to ask him what was going on between him and my mother. How could Mother, a married woman, be interested in a much younger man?

As much as I was upset about Mother, I still had the problem with Barni and the secret police to worry about. Completely confused, knowing I had to get away from the house for a while, I got on my bike and went to *Szentkut* without telling anyone.

The church was quiet with only about a dozen pilgrims present reciting the rosary. I knelt down and joined them. The harmonious chanting of the prayers brought such tranquility over me that I momentarily forgot all my troubles. Oh, how I wished I could hold on to that blissful feeling forever.

It was almost dark when I arrived home, and Mother immediately questioned me, "Where have you been?"

"In *Szentkut's* church," I answered calmly.

Her voice rose sharply. "Next time, you have to ask my permission before you go anywhere."

At that moment, I couldn't stand the sight of her, thinking how hurt my dear father will be when he finds out that Mother was cheating on him. I wanted to tell her that I went to church to pray for her to come to her senses about having an affair. Instead, I went into the other room to continue my sketching of *Szentkut's* church, trying to recapture the blissful feelings I had experienced there and infuse them into my picture. But I couldn't. My horrible thoughts for my mother took over again.

Lord, how can I go on like this, keeping these lies and secrets? It is taking over my life. My heart was aching for my dear father. While lying on the bed, Grandmother came in.

"What's wrong, dear?"

"*Nagymama* I can't keep all these secrets. They are taking over my life."

Not realizing I was speaking about more than Barni's situation, Grandmother said, "We will definitely talk to your parents after supper. Yes, definitely, we will talk. This has gone too far and it has to stop!"

The determination in her voice gave me some measure of hope. I knew Grandmother could be harsh if she had to be. Too upset to eat supper with the family I stayed in bed. After supper, Grandmother sent Julika next door to play with her friend. With just the four of us at home, Grandmother called me into the kitchen. She sat me down at the table and handed me a glass of water. With everyone settled, she began addressing my parents.

"Ilona and I have some very serious matters to discuss with both of you. First, about Barni's abusive and terrifying behavior in the garden . . ."

"Oh, that was because he was intoxicated," Mother interrupted.

"Mari, I'm warning you to keep quiet until I'm finished," Grandmother commanded. Father motioned for Mother to hush up. Grandmother continued, "Second, he has revealed to Ilona that he is plotting to be get out of the military early by faking insanity. He made her swear to keep his dangerous secret."

"Oh, that's because," Mother interrupted again, but Father said quickly, "Mari, keep quiet!"

Grandmother continued, "For that reason we were interrogated by the secret police on our way home from church. And believe me, the way they treated us they were worse than the cruel German SS soldiers. One of them pushed me around, even at my old age. I was frightened for myself, but especially for Ilona." She turned to me. "And now, dear tell us what happened on your trip to Budapest."

It was painful for me to tell the story again, but I knew I had to do it. Taking a deep breath I told my parents everything. After reliving this terrible situation, I turned to Father and said, "*Apuka*, I'm scared of the savage AVO men."

"You see Mari? We have to think about Barni's mentality. You are jeopardizing our lives, especially Ilona's."

Mother shrugged. "You're making a big thing out of nothing."

"Because it is a big thing," Father declared strongly. "I wish you would understand that. It is not only a big thing - it is a dangerous thing - for the whole family, especially for Ilona if Barni is arrested.

"There is more," I continued. "I met a lady on the train who was taking her two children to leave them with their grandmother, because she could not look after them. Her husband, who often spoke out against the Communists, just disappeared one day and she doesn't know where he is."

Mother started to say something but Father cut her off.

"*Mama*, take Ilona with you into the other room. Mari and I have to have a serious discussion about this situation." Before we left the room, Father came over to me, put his arms around my shoulder, and gave me a reassuring hug. "Go to bed dear, your mother and I will solve this situation."

From the bedroom, I could hear my parents arguing, but it was still Mother's voice ruling over Father's. I wanted to go out to reveal Mother and Andras' private visit, but I could not hurt my dear father. Instead I prayed. "Dear God, I'm pleading with you, please take away this continuous fear in my life."

CHAPTER 14

The next morning at the breakfast table, I lost my appetite when I saw Mother pampering Father with his favorite potato pancakes. I thought, "Mother you'll have to do more than that to cover up your disloyalty to Father with Andras."

I wondered how I was going to find out the truth of what was going on between him and my mother. I was also upset that my friend had taken my babysitting job at Jutka's. Not only had I lost the enjoyment of spending time with the girls, I also lost my opportunity to escape from Mother - even if it was only for hours at a time.

"Ilona, since you are still on holidays you can dig up the kitchen garden and get it ready for spring seeding." When my mother ordered me around like that, she made me feel like a working slave and a caged bird at the same time.

I dug until my back ached, then, taking a break, went for a walk in the meadow. Along the way I admired the lovely mustard-yellow dandelions covering the meadow like a magic carpet. They looked so beautiful, and I picked a bouquet for Grandmother. Walking through this beauty of nature, enjoying the warm rays of the spring sunshine, it seemed not so long ago in this same meadow that I had carried my terrified baby sister, running for cover to escape the bomber planes.

At the edge of the creek, I stopped by a pussy willow bush, picked one of the soft, furry, silver-gray catkins and swallowed it. It was supposed to prevent sore throats according to Mrs. Orvari. I remembered my friend, Terri, and I following another of Mrs. Orvari's superstitions when we were children. We used to come to the creek before sunrise on Good Friday just to wash our faces, so we would have velvety complexions free from blemishes. We speculated that Mrs. Orvari might be a witch due to her weird predictions.

After a long time pondering about my life, which seemed hopeless and meaningless, I wandered back home. It was beginning to look like the only way I could get away from my mother was to marry Barni. Even if I didn't love him, perhaps I could learn to tolerate him. But knowing marriage involved sex, I wondered how that would be possible if there was no love? Could I submit to a marriage without love? Would it lead to divorce and heartache for the children of such a marriage? On the other hand, I reasoned, marriage to Barni might work if I gave it a chance.

Approaching home, the sight of my cousin, Piri, running towards the house caught my attention. Why was she running? Something must be wrong! As I rushed into the house, I heard the sad news that Grandfather Batta was very sick with pneumonia. Without delay, I ran to his side to find him burning with fever. The doctor had given him some medication, but he was still hallucinating, his voice weak and rasping as he mumbled his favorite story.

> *The rays of the moon beaming down through the window, under the kitchen table two huge, white, shaggy-haired dogs, with scarlet blood, oozing out of their mouths and trickling down on their snow-white ruffles were growling, while munching on human bones …*

And the rest of the story was a mumble from his confused mind. I held his hand, but he didn't recognize me.

He always held our attention with this story, scaring us to the point where we were petrified of the dark, so much so that our trips to the outhouse weren't made alone. He had many stories to entertain us.

Later, Father and I left Grandfather and walked home in silence. I considered the wisdom of telling him about Mother and Andras. At last he broke the silence.

"You know, Ilona, I heard the white dogs story for the first time when I was about six years old, and it's getting scarier every time I hear it. It is still as vivid in my mind now as it was when I was a youngster."

He turned his face away from me, but not before I saw the trickle of tears on his cheeks. I suggested we pray for Grandfather's recovery, and Father started praying as we continued to walk home.

The next morning, Mother came home from Grandfather's and sat down at the kitchen table. She wrote a note and stuffed it into an envelope. She asked me to take it to *Szentkut* to our priest, and wait for his answer. When I handed him the note he read it quickly and said, "Ilona, tell your mother I'll be there tomorrow morning at ten." I was beside myself with grief, because I knew that when the priest was called to give the last sacrament there was no hope of recovery.

The next day, we prepared to go to Grandfather's. All the family left ahead of Grandmother and me. She had to walk slowly due to her sore leg, so I stayed behind to keep her company.

At the house, I ran inside to see Grandfather. He recognized me and asked if I had finished my drawing of *Szentkut's* church. I was shocked to see how pale he looked. His eyes were glassy and his lips were blue, but he was alert. Before I left I kissed his cheeks and whispered, "I will be back, *Nagyapa*."

His frail voice whispered back, "Promise you will finish the drawing of the church for me."

"Yes, *Nagyapa*, the picture is yours," I answered through my tears. After gently squeezing his hand to assure him, I left his bedside. Passing through the living room, I noticed the ladies in black, with several burning candles in front of them on the table, silently reciting the rosary.

When I got outside, Mother was there with Julika and said, "Take her home and take care of her."

Desperately I wanted to work on my picture for Grandfather. I quickly took Julika home, gave her some colouring to do, and hurried to put the finishing touches on the picture. It was hard to see in the dim light of the petroleum lamp; the colours didn't look the same as in the daylight. When I was finished I wrote on the back: *To my dear Nagyapa Batta, with my everlasting love, Iluska* (his nickname for me).

The next morning, I rolled up the picture, tied it with a ribbon, and hurried to see Grandfather. I rushed into the house, ignoring the people praying in the living room, and ran into the bedroom where Grandfather was sleeping. "*Nagyapa, Nagyapa!* Wake up and see I finished the picture for you," I said excitedly, gently touching his face to wake him. But his face was cold and motionless. Grandmother Batta rushed into the room behind me and pulled me back, putting her hand on my mouth to stop my rush of words. Then I saw the tears in her eyes.

"Grandfather passed away last night," she said softly.

I was startled. Then I cried out, "*Nagyapa*, I finished the picture just for you. And now you can't see it!"

Grandmother held me in her arms for a moment, then she led me out of the room.

"Don't worry, darling he is seeing your picture. Don't worry, he is seeing it." Then she led me into the kitchen and asked me to help her serve coffee to our praying guests. It was then I noticed a ring on her finger and asked her about it, but she hushed me, putting her finger to her lips. "I will tell you tomorrow. For now, please just serve coffee."

Finally, Grandfather's five children, including my father, arrived to arrange the funeral. There were funeral homes in the cities, but in the country the deceased stayed in the family home for two days until the burial. I wanted to stay and help, but children weren't allowed to take part. At home I asked Grandmother Usak about Grandmother Batta's ring. All she would say was, "Ilona, ask her yourself."

I told her that I had asked Grandmother Batta already, but she didn't tell me.

"Well then, you will have to wait until the funeral is over."

That night when we were changing into our nightclothes, before getting into bed, I had to go to the outhouse. I wanted badly to ask Grandmother to go with me. Then I remembered Grandfather Batta had always told me not to be afraid in the dark, as God is always with you. I tried to build up my courage by telling myself it is only a short distance to go, and nothing would happen. I wasn't convinced, but I went out anyway.

Rushing back to the house, in the radiant moonlit night, I noticed a huge, gray owl sitting on the *patka* (a long narrow extension in front of the house) calmly looking at me with his large, shining eyes. I froze. My legs refused to move, but I had to pass him to get into the house. I tried to call Grandmother, but no sound came out of my mouth. I could only whisper, "Shoo . . . shoo." The owl moved a little sideways, obviously not afraid of me. I gathered up my courage and went a few steps closer, facing him in case he tried to attack me. Finally Grandmother came out.

"What are you shooing, Ilona?"

I pointed at the owl. The sight of the owl startled her, but only for a moment. She bravely came to me and reached for my hand. Together, we walked slowly to the door; the owl bravely hopped closer to us, instead of away from us. He let out a couple of hoots and then flew away toward the radiant moon.

In the kitchen we sat down, but neither of us was able to speak about our strange encounter. At last Grandmother said, "Let's go to bed, Ilona." Still confused and frightened about what had happened, I wanted very much to sleep with Grandmother, but I didn't want to say so. Just before I got into bed she said, "Ilona, would you like to sleep with me tonight?"

I nearly knocked her off her feet as she stood beside the bed putting on her bed-jacket. Before saying yes, I was in her bed. Afraid to close my eyes, I could still see the owl's own radiant ones. I asked, "Why wasn't the owl afraid of us Grandmother?"

She posed, "Ilona, dear, I think the owl was your grandfather's spirit, giving you a message not to be afraid any more."

And I surely believed it, having never seen an owl so close and so still. We said a prayer for Grandfather before saying goodnight. I fell asleep thinking about the stillness of the mysterious, beaming-eyed owl.

The following day, before the funeral, I rolled up my picture and put it in my duffel bag. I carried it with me to Grandfather's house. When we arrived, I went into the bedroom and quickly put the painting under the white cover beside Grandfather's body. Just as I rearranged the cover, four men came to take the casket out.

The funeral was very sad for everyone, especially for me. I was broken-hearted as I watched him being lowered into the ground of *Szentkut's* cemetery. One by one, into the grave, people threw a piece of dirt, which landed on the wood coffin and echoed back with the unpleasant sound of knock-knock-knock. Tradition or not, I didn't like it.

While the priest conducted his ritual, the sweet aroma of the burning incense mingled with the flickering candle smoke and swirled around the cemetery, carried by the sudden breeze. Standing close, I inhaled and tasted the incense and the waxy candle smoke on my lips, fully aware of the reality of my grandfather's funeral.

A few days later I visited Grandmother Batta with a bouquet of flowers. She was glad to see me, and as we talked over tea her ring caught my eye again. Still curious, I asked her about it. She looked down at the ring and a small secret smile crossed her face.

"Ilona," she began "your grandfather and I were never legally married. We loved each other for sixty-two years and had five children together. In our hearts we were married and for us that was official enough. Grandfather was eighty-two and I'm eighty, and I have no regrets. He was a wonderful man."

I nodded and was speechless. I had always admired them. Never in my life had I ever heard an argument or a harsh word spoken between them.

Grandmother continued, "Your mother arranged with the priest, just before Grandfather passed on, for us to be married." Tears trickled down on her cheeks as she was rolling the ring on her finger. I was curious about what she was thinking. But, she didn't say, and I didn't ask.

On my way home I prayed for my dear, wise, and noble *nagyapa*. Thinking about the beautiful life they had spent together, I realized it was their true love that had kept them together so faithfully for all those years. Thinking of their love, I knew this was the kind of love I would have had with my cadet, but not with Barni.

Grandfather's human journey had ended; now he was on a journey to an everlasting spiritual life, leaving me behind with an aching heart.

CHAPTER 15

"Jozsi, Jozsi wake up! I have disturbing news to tell you!" My mother's voice woke me up as it did my father.

"Mari, it is four a.m. What are you doing all dressed up?"

"I just came home from next door, where I was listening to *Free Europe* radio with the neighbors. This is what we heard: *Joseph Stalin has targeted Marshal Tito for elimination.*"

Josip Broz (code name Tito), President of Yugoslavia, was determined to direct the destiny of Communist Yugoslavia, without interference or domination from Moscow's leader, Joseph Stalin. Marshal Tito had a strong grasp on his own party and fellow countrymen, so he was able to defy Stalin. For this reason, Stalin targeted him for elimination.

Father was shocked. Since Yugoslavia bordered Hungary, he was terrified Stalin would fight Tito from Hungary. Being only sixteen, I didn't fully grasp the world's political situation, but I knew Father would be worried about being drafted into the army. Our already heavily burdened lives seemed to worsen day by day.

The next day at work there was an undertone as to what would happen next. I tried to put it out of my mind, but I worried about my dear father. When my shift ended, Iren came to relieve me and said, "Ilona, someone is waiting for you outside. Come and see." To my amazement there was Barni in civilian clothes, talking to our Communist leader.

I hurried outside and Barni waved to me to come over. As I approached them, they stopped talking. "What is going on?" I asked.

"Nothing," Barni answered rudely. He gave me a hug and whispered in my ear, "Let's go right now!" He grabbed my hand and pulled me away without saying goodbye to the leader, whose voice echoed, "Keep in touch, Barni. I will be keeping an eye on you."

Once away, apprehensive and curious, I asked, "Barni, why did he say that?"

His eyes glittered defiantly. "I hate the Communist bastard! I could kill him without mercy!"

I gasped, "What are you talking about, that you could kill him? You're insane!" I was troubled by his outrage and cried out as his steel fingers crushed my hand.

Controlling his rage, he quickly apologized, "I'm sorry if I hurt you. Let's walk to the meadow. I want to talk to you before we get to your house."

Absorbed in our own thoughts, we did not speak until we reached the bridge and sat on the edge. Breaking the silence, I said, "Barni I have so many questions to ask you. First of all, how is that you are home in civilian clothes, before your time is up in the military?"

A devious smile crossed his face. "I got out of the military with a paper saying that I'm mentally incompetent."

"Does that mean something is wrong with your brain?"

"Nothing is wrong with my brain, Ilona. I just fooled the Communist morons."

By this time I was completely puzzled. "If nothing is wrong with your brain, how could you fool so many intelligent people in the military?"

He grunted. "I fooled them didn't I?"

"Barni, may I see your discharge papers?"

"No, you can't!" he answered with anger and he changed the subject.

"I'm home now. I will find a job, and we can get engaged and married. This is what I want." He moved close to me and wanted to put his arms around me. I was frightened of him and quickly moved away. He said firmly, "Ilona, I always get what I want."

The dictatorial tone of his voice completely infuriated me. I sprang to my feet. "Let's go home, and you will have to tell all this to my parents. If you don't, I will."

"Yes, Ilona. I will tell them when I find the right time and when I am alone with them. In the meantime I will just say jokingly that the military couldn't put up with me." I stared at him furiously. "Ilona, let me handle it," he demanded.

When we reached home, everyone was surprised to see him in civilian clothes. Of course, Mother asked him to stay for supper. I was glad she did, because it would give him a chance to confess his stupidity, which didn't make sense to me; on the contrary, it frightened me to death given my brutal encounter with the AVO. During supper, Father looked gravely at him and asked, "Why have you been discharged early Barni?"

With a grin, he answered, "They just couldn't put up with me." He warned me with his piercing eyes to say nothing. Grandmother stared at him suspiciously. But Mother was ecstatic about his early discharge. Julika cuddled up to him and called him her big brother - which was literally true as he was 190 cm tall. I was perplexed. I wanted to reveal everything that he had told me, especially that he always got what he wanted in life. He had made it clear that meant me as well. I despised his statement.

After supper, I offered to do the dishes to avoid talking to anyone. Later, Julika asked me to check her homework and we went into the other room. Shortly, Mother called me saying Barni was leaving. He said goodnight to the family and I walked out with him.

When we were outside he hugged me and held me tightly, as if he owned me. But I freed myself from his embrace. At that, he said goodnight and left. Feeling helpless and victimized, I sat down on the bench outside. His harsh words flashed through my mind: "I could kill him without mercy" and "I always get what I want." I sat outside for a long time, deep in thought about the possibility of marrying him. He was tall and handsome on the outside, but cruelty, selfishness, and arrogance reflected from the inside. What was the real reason for his discharge? The brutal Communist party did not discharge a soldier without a valid reason. They'd rather kill him first. Is he really mentally unstable? No matter how desperately I wanted to get away from my mother, I had to consider if I could cope with his strange mental attitude. Thinking of the crossroad, I prayed, "Lord, I don't know what to do. Please help me as you always do. Amen."

The door opened and Grandmother walked out. She sat next to me and gently put her arm around my shoulder. "My dear, do you want to talk about it?" She stayed silent. She always knew when I needed help, and by her reaction I knew she was feeling my troubles and pain. Then, Father came out. Grandmother thoughtfully left us alone. I started to tell him about Barni, but not for long. Soon Mother was right there, praising him, saying what a handsome, intelligent, good man he was, and how happy she will be to call him her son-in-law. I answered furiously, "Mother, if you are convinced that Barni is that good, then let Manci marry him!" Running into the house, I immediately went to bed before anyone could say anything more. Perplexed about the situation, I cried myself to sleep.

A few days later, Barni showed up, again greatly excited. He had been hired to work for a petroleum company in Salgotarjan. I was glad that he had a job and wouldn't have any time to see me. But that didn't stop him. The following Saturday was my turn to work the afternoon shift. Barni was disappointed but I was glad, hoping by the time I came home at ten p.m. that he would be gone.

I arrived at work early and went into the lunchroom, where we all congregated before starting our shifts. Suddenly, the shrieking sound of the emergency alarm broke into our conversation. There had been an accident in the mine! Thinking this could only mean that either water or gas had seeped into the mine, putting the men in extreme danger, I ran to the office where we were instantly very busy on the switchboard.

From the tower, Andras asked me to connect him with the Nagybatony emergency crew. After connecting him, I glanced out the window and saw all the outside workers gathered at the mine's opening. Just then Comrade Makos ran in and asked me to connect him to the mine head office in Salgotarjan. Listening to his conversation, I discovered that the mine elevator cable had snapped and ten miners were trapped about half way up the 380-meter mineshaft. Fortunately, the emergency mechanism had stopped the elevator within two meters of where the cable had broken, otherwise it would have crashed 190 meters, killing the miners trapped inside. Keeping the elevator emergency stop in working order was Andras' specialty. Every Sunday, when the miners were not working, he and his special crew deliberately dropped the elevator for a safety check.

I was frantic with worry, as I knew my cousins were both working that shift. The emergency crew arrived and set to work to free the frightened workers. Everyone knew the emergency mechanism could only hold the elevator for a short time. If the cables were not repaired quickly, the workers would fall to their deaths.

Standing in the doorway of the office, I overheard the miners talking. They were upset and complaining, muttering amongst themselves about their low wages and the dangerous working conditions. They became increasingly agitated, since most of them hated the dictatorial Communist system that owned the mine.

Watching the tense crowd that had gathered outside, one of our Communist leaders turned to me and commanded, "Ilona, no one is allowed in here to use the phone without my permission. Someone will be here to stay with you until this is over." To my surprise two young men dashed in and asked, "Where is Barni and when did you see him last?"

"I left him at our house," I replied.

He looked at me and said, "Don't tell me you date that mentally unstable idiot?"

Before I could respond, the other man turned around, and I was startled to see Frank, one of the AVO men who had been involved in the incident with Grandmother and me on the *Szentkut* road. Seeing him convinced me that the Communists were afraid of the emotionally charged crowd outside. And they were definitely keeping an eye on Barni. That just reinforced how dangerous a relationship with Barni could be for me.

The crowd waited impatiently as the emergency crew worked quickly and efficiently to fix the cable. At last, Andras slowly raised the elevator. At the sight of the rescued miners, people cheered and ran to embrace their loved ones. Finally, around eleven, all the miners were rescued, and I went home.

As usual, Grandmother was crocheting while she waited for me. With tears in my eyes, I embraced her to show her how happy I was to see her waiting up for me. She patted me gently. "Now, now. Hush, dear. I know it was a hard shift for you. But thank the Lord everyone is safe. I'm glad you were a part of it, dear, and now just eat your cornmeal and get ready for bed. I will come and pray with you." She looked more closely at me and asked, "You look so distraught, has anything else happened?" I could not tell her that I was questioned again about Barni's whereabouts. I just answered, "No, *Nagymama,*" I'm just tired."

CHAPTER 16

On Sunday, I went alone to early Mass at the *Szentkut* church, trying to sort out my troubled life. Our kind, wise, old priest conducted the Mass. I reasoned that perhaps I should talk to him about my tormented life, but I was fearful that my mother would do some dreadful thing to me, if she discovered I had revealed our secrets to him. The Father's message was clear to me when he said, "If you have a problem you cannot solve, take it to your Creator with prayer. He will surely help you; His specialty is to help troubled people, and heal broken hearts."

I prayed deeply from my heart, especially that Mother would see the truth about Barni. After the Mass, walking home alone, I felt at peace within and began to sing my favorite hymn. On the way, I passed Manci and her friends going to the later Mass.

Manci said, "Ilona, Mother is angry with you for some reason; she wants you to hurry home."

As I continued walking, I wondered what Mother was angry about now. Arriving home, I found Mother, Father, and Grandmother waiting for me. Mother looked at me with her narrowed eyes; it was obvious that she was very angry. Grandmother sensed her hostility and offered, "Ilona, you must be hungry. Come and eat breakfast." I sat beside her, and Father passed me some of Grandmother's fresh *langos*, flat yeast dough fried in fat to a crisp.

Mother continued to eye me nervously. Finally, she said, "Ilona, hurry up with your breakfast. I want to talk to you privately in the other room."

Even though I was afraid of her, I said firmly, "Why can't we talk here with Father and Grandmother present?"

"This concerns only *you* and *me!*" she said, frowning at me to stress her point.

I looked at her cautiously. Asserting myself more strongly, I asked, "What do you want to talk about, Mother?"

She glared at me and hesitated for a moment. Grandmother, glancing at Father, interjected, "Yes, Mari, Jozsi and I want to know what Ilona has done that you are so furious about."

"Ilona disobeyed me again. I forbade her to go to Jutka's, but she went and only the children and Andras were at home."

"Listen, Mother I am glad that you brought Andras up. I found you two alone several times. What are you doing with him alone?" That aroused Father's curiosity.

"Yes Mari, I want to know."

"I have my reason," she answered nervously.

"Mari, that is not an answer. We want to know, " Grandmother pressed.

Mother turned away from us and answered, "Andras has been pleading with me to date Ilona, with the intention of marrying her."

"What are you talking about?" Grandmother yelled with amazement.

Mother pressed on. "Andras is divorced and he is too old for Ilona."

I answered quickly, "But he is mature and sensible, and not a Communist."

Mother made her position clear. "Regardless, you can't marry him. You are underage and you need your parents' consent for marriage. And I will not give you mine."

Father put his hand on my shoulder and said, "Ilona, dear, I agree with you that Andras is a very fine, sensible man, but he is too old for you. You are only in your teens and he is in his thirties. This time I have to agree with your mother."

I replied furiously, "I will marry anyone except that tyrant, Barni!" No one made any comment to that.

I felt I had to go somewhere to get away from Mother. I turned to Father, "Since I don't have to work on Sunday and I have Monday off, can I please go to see Grandmother Batta and stay with her overnight?"

Father quickly agreed, "That is a good idea and she would love to have you."

Mother cut in, "No, you can't. Today is Sunday and Barni will be here this afternoon."

Enraged, I jumped up. "I'm going right now and you can't stop me!" I ran into the other room and threw my nightclothes into a bag. As I rushed out of the house, Mother tried to stop me, but Father held her back saying, "Mari, let her go."

I was out of the house and on my bike in seconds. Having escaped from Mother, I began to feel a little more placid. Riding down the rugged country road, the beauty of the wild flowers spread over the roadside captivated me. The red poppies (*piros pipacs*), blue cupid's dart (*kek buzavirag*), and white daisies (*feher margarita*) brought me towards complete serenity. I sat down and played with the daisies' velvety white petals: "He loves me, he loves me not, he loves, he loves me not," I thought. Remembering Grandmother Batta's usual plea, "Ilona, please don't mutilate those poor daisies," I eventually stopped fantasizing, picked a bouquet for Grandmother, and proceeded to her house. She was in the garden and spotted me coming down the road.

She called to me while I was still some distance away. "Ilona, I was just thinking of you. How nice of you to come." She was so thrilled to see me that even though she was quite elderly, she ran to meet me and greeted me with a warm hug and kiss.

She ushered me into her unique, country kitchen, which lingered with the scent of all spice. Great-grandmother's hand painted plates and mugs decorated the main wall. The table was covered with Grandmother's hand-loomed, white, embroidered tablecloth with red and green thread. Her chipped, noble, antique, ceramic teapot dominated the center of the table with a dried, floral arrangement, which she replaced with my wild flowers.

Later, we made vegetable soup with flour dough (*csipetke*), which we dropped in the soup pinch-by-pinch. As the soup simmered, the sweet and savory aroma was overpowering and I could hardly wait for it to be finished. Grandmother, who knew I was always hungry, put the whole pot of soup on the table and encouraged me to help myself.

While I gobbled my food, she kept saying, "Slow down, child. Slow down. No one is going to take it away from you." I happily savored three bowls full of the delicious soup.

After the kitchen was cleaned up, Grandmother suggested we go to the forest to pick some mushrooms. This was one of my favorite pastimes and I gladly agreed to her suggestion. In the forest I had to stay close to her, as she knew which mushrooms were edible and which were poisonous. I loved the forest's quietness and its pine-scented, gentle, cool breeze. Searching for mushrooms peeping out from under the rusty leaves, I excitedly shouted, "Here is one, there is one… and there is another one." I ran to Grandmother with a handful for inspection. Before we realized it, our big basket was full.

As we rested our heavy basket by the roadside, Grandmother said, "Ilona, we have lots of mushrooms, so we will make mushroom paprikas for supper, and you can take some home with you. The rest we will slice and I will dry them for winter." During those hard times we learned to share whatever we had.

After supper, I cut Grandmother's toenails and washed and braided her long hair, which she wore in a bun on the top of her head. Later in bed, we said a special prayer for Grandfather Batta, and we thanked God for the divine day that we had had together. Having been in the fresh air of the forest, I felt peaceful and fell asleep quickly.

The next morning I helped Grandmother with her strenuous Monday wash, by carrying water from the well. After the clothes were on the line, we said goodbye. On my way home, I thought of the peaceful, happy time I had with Grandmother Batta and how wonderful it had been to live without fear and anger. Fantasizing about how desirable it would be to always live that way, I picked a bouquet of wild flowers for Grandmother Usak - and this time I didn't mutilate the daisies. I walked slowly beside my bike, dreading the thought of reaching home.

Julika was playing in the yard when I arrived and eagerly reported, "Ilona, Barni was here Sunday and Manci played cards with him all afternoon." I was glad to hear this and hoped they would become friends and he would leave me alone.

Mother was shelling peas on the porch and stopped me before I could get into the house. "Barni was upset that you weren't home," she reported.

"Mother, I don't care," I replied.

"From now on I will tell you where and when you can go away from home," she said menacingly. When I saw the look on her face, I knew she meant what she said. I also knew she was trying to provoke me. I left her without any further discussion. I knew she wanted to marry me off to get rid of me.

When I went into the kitchen, Grandmother Usak was starching the doilies she had crocheted for my dowry. "Hello, dear," she greeted me. "I'm glad you are home. I missed you."

Her soothing words showed her radiating love for me. Grandmother was thrilled at the sight of the mushrooms and got out her recipe for mushroom soup. As we were cutting up the mushrooms, she asked me what kind of a cake I would like her to bake for my name day. We decided on cheesecake, as it was my favorite. In Hungary we celebrate name days instead of birthdays. August eighteenth is the name day for all females named Ilona. It is easy to remember, as each name day is printed on the calendar.

Suddenly, there was a knock on the door and Mrs. Orvari walked in bringing chamomile for Grandmother to soothe her ulcerated leg. She had hardly sat down when she asked, "Ilona, where were you yesterday? I didn't see you around."

I was immediately angry and didn't answer. When Grandmother noticed that I was upset, she winked at me and asked me to go to the store for icing sugar. I knew she would question Mrs. Orvari to see if she were our informer. When I got to the store, Ilcsa and Klari were there debating on some hand-made choker beads. They called me over and asked me which one I liked. I said that I didn't like any, because I didn't have any money to buy them. When I arrived back at the house, to my surprise Mrs. Orvari was gone.

"How come the stool pigeon left so soon?" I asked.

Grandmother smiled. "She wasn't pleased when I told her if she is squealing on us, she wouldn't be welcome in our house. That offended her and she left."

"I hope she never comes back. But most likely Mother will call her in to hear more gossip, which she loves to listen to."

"Try to forget about your problems and think about celebrating your name day," Grandmother advised.

The next day at work, Laci gave me a package and said, "This is for you Ilona, from an admirer of yours who asked me to give it to you."

"Who is it Laci?" But he just shook his head and didn't answer. Since I couldn't open it at work, I decided to hide it in my locker and wait until the next night, when I was in church, to open my precious gift in peace. Thinking that Laci was working with Andras and chumming with some of the cadets, it puzzled me, as to which of them gave me the present.

When I arrived home, I noticed Mother and Barni talking in the garden. When I saw their rapid hand movements, I knew they were engaged in a serious discussion. Wondering what they were discussing, I reasoned they didn't want anyone in the house to hear what they were talking about. When Barni noticed me, he rushed to meet me.

"What were you discussing with Mother?" I asked.

"Never mind that. There is going to be a big soccer game on Sunday with the mighty Salgotarjan team versus the underdog Kisterenye. Two of my friends are playing and I bet on Kisterenye. How about you?"

"Sorry, Barni. What did you say?"

"Ilona, you are a thousand miles away. What are you dreaming about?"

"Oh, nothing really. Just about my name day party." Actually, I was dreaming about Andras. I realized that the more I talked to him, the more I liked him. I was touched that he was concerned enough about me to maybe give me a gift. It seemed to me that our difference in age wasn't as important as my growing feelings for him.

I was sure the gift was from him. Finally Barni said goodbye and left. The next day I went to church. During the summer we had evening prayers and hymn singing on Wednesdays. Inside the church I sat in the last row by myself and excitedly tore the box open. When I saw what was inside I forgot where I was and let out a loud, "Oh my!" People close by turned around and someone said quietly, "Shhhh." I was embarrassed and lowered my head trying to hide. Admiring the lovely gift, an engraved glittering heart-shaped locket on a gorgeous silver chain, I put it around my neck. I was so overjoyed I didn't realize they had begun singing the closing hymn. I joined in from the innermost part of my heart. On my way home, I tried to figure out what I was going to say about the locket. I couldn't tell the truth, as Mother would antagonize me and take it away from me. If I wanted to keep the locket I would have to lie about it.

I still hadn't come up with a believable lie by the time I reached home, so I buttoned my shirt blouse up to my neck to hide my precious locket. When I went into the kitchen for a glass of water, Mother glanced at me and said, "Ilona, it is summer. Why do you have your blouse buttoned up to your neck?"

I turned away from her. "I like it this way," I said quickly and hurried into the bedroom. I lay on the bed dreaming of choosing Andras over Barni for a husband, as I tried to think of an acceptable lie that Mother would believe, so I could keep my precious gift.

CHAPTER 17

"Ilona, wake up. It is 6 a.m. Godmother and Auntie Anna are here from Kisterenye to help us cultivate the cornfield." Hearing Mother's voice, I instantly reached for my locket. It was still around my neck, covered by the blanket. Thank God, Mother didn't see it or she would have ripped it off my neck without any questions asked.

"I'll be there shortly," I answered. Sitting at the edge of the bed, I wondered where I could hide my locket. Then Grandmother came in to rush me along.

"Come on, dear, they are waiting for you."

I handed her the box with the locket. "*Nagymama*, please keep this for me. I'll explain later."

She opened the box, and exclaimed, "Oh my, this locket is gorgeous. Who gave it to you?"

"Just hide it and I will explain tonight," I replied as I rushed out.

In the kitchen my aunt, godmother, and mother were having breakfast. After greeting our guests with a hug, I quickly ate my cream of wheat. Then, the four of us walked to *Szentkut* hill, *Gorzsas,* to hoe the cornfield. Grandmother stayed home to cook for us, and Julika would bring our lunch later. Manci was lucky to have a nanny job; she didn't have to labor under the hot sun.

During the half-hour walk to *Gorzsas,* I vaguely listened as Mother and Godmother discussed our destitute country's political situation under the Stalinist dictatorship. Even our Hungarian Communist leaders greatly feared Stalin and his brutal rule. First, they had denied us our human rights and freedom of speech. Then, they allowed Russian families to move to Hungary to live in the most prestigious district of Budapest, form a community, and claim it as their own. I wasn't interested in politics. My mind was on the locket as I tried to figure out who sent it to me.

By eleven o'clock, the heat was unbearable. Nevertheless we continued to hoe. Finally, Julika arrived with our lunch. Grandmother had prepared a three-liter bucket of chicken paprikas, with sauce and noodles, for the four of us. I was starving and when Mother uncovered the bucket, the tantalizing aroma was mouth-watering. I imagined that everyone had disappeared and the whole bucket was mine. But it was only a momentary dream. Mother dished out the food to the others first, while I silently implored, "Mother, hurry up."

Finally, she handed me my bowl and said, "We only had one chicken. We have to share it between the four of us here and the three at home. We just have to be satisfied with what we get." I couldn't believe the meat portion she had given to me: the two tips of the wings and about five cm of the neck. Mother's need to impress the relatives was more important than my hunger. And this worked out well for Mother's scheming: feed them well and they would volunteer regularly to work, since food was scarce in the country.

Mother's piercing eyes warned me not to say a word, and I didn't. Finally, she let go of my bowl, which I was impatiently holding on to. Hunger and fury warped my mind, and I wished them all in hell. I looked at the others' generous portions of the juicy, brown drumstick and the tender creamy, white, breast meat they were sucking on. Aunty and Godmother were fat and obviously well fed. Suddenly Godmother threw a piece of white meat on my plate, while Mother was turned away, reaching for the water jug. Quickly, I shoved the meat in my mouth without Mother noticing. I thought of how caring and loving Godmother was; it was too bad she didn't have a child of her own.

After lunch, while everyone was napping in the shade of an acacia tree, I sneaked away to a nearby orchard and stole some crabapples, because I was still hungry. While eating them my mouth puckered from the sour and bitter taste. When I came back, everyone was awake.

"Where were you, Ilona?" Mother asked. I couldn't tell her that I had stolen apples because I was still hungry, so I ignored her question. We started working again. There was still half of the field to hoe and by afternoon the heat was extreme. Later, Mother sent me to *Szentkut* to get some drinking water. When I hoisted the bucket up from the well the cold water smelled like ice and tasted so refreshing, I had two big dippers full. When I got back with the water, my elders almost emptied the whole bucket, but I didn't feel like walking back for more in that heat. I went back to work. All of a sudden, as I was bending over my hoe, I had an excruciating stomach cramp. Despite my obvious pain, Mother refused to let me go home.

"Ilona, you can't go home until we are finished. Besides, I don't believe you are sick."

As the pain worsened, I doubled up, fell to my knees, and vomited. I thought I would die. Godmother came over to comfort me, and said, "Mari, she is so pale and vomiting some green stuff. Something is really wrong with her."

"While we were sleeping she went and stole some green apples and ate them. That's what's wrong with her. I saw her from a distance. It serves her right," Mother said.

"Mari, how can you be so cruel to her?" Godmother protested. Mother ignored her and continued hoeing.

Godmother helped me to lie down and covered me with her sweater as I was shivering in spite of the heat. "Now you will be fine, dear, since you expelled the green apples." She comforted me. But Mother was unhappy that I wasn't able to work for the rest of the afternoon.

When we reached home I went straight to bed and Grandmother brought me chamomile tea to soothe my aching stomach. The next morning I was still nauseated, but it was Sunday, August 18th, my name day and that lifted my spirits. Grandmother came into the room and sat beside me on the bed, opened the box, and admired the locket again.

"Ilona, I want you to tell me the truth. Who gave you this expensive locket? Was it Janos or Andras?"

"*Nagymama* I don't know for sure. Laci give it to me and he couldn't tell because he had to swear to it. But in my heart I feel it is from Andras. And, you know *Nagymama*, I'm not only touched by his attentive gift, but I have feelings for him. I think I'm in love with him."

Her eyes widened. "I-I-I like him too," she stuttered shocked by my statement, "and I wish you could marry him instead of that arrogant Barni. Just leave the locket with me, dear, and I will think of something to deceive your mother." Sometimes it felt like Mother and Grandmother were fighting their own battles, and I was caught right in the middle of it.

The afternoon of my name day with my friends was delightful. We enjoyed the cheesecake, and raspberry drink, fantasizing about boys and romance, and giggling endlessly. Opening my few gifts was thrilling, especially the green and white beaded choker from Ilcsa and Klari, about which they asked my opinion the other day in the store. My party had to end as Mother rushed us to get ready for the soccer game. Then Grandmother walked in, "Just a minute. I have a gift for Ilona." She handed me a folded, hand-embroidered handkerchief. Unfolding it to admire her lovely handwork, to my astonishment the silver locket fell out. I glanced at Grandmother with a secretive smile. Everyone admired the uniqueness of my heart-shaped locket.

Mother's face froze into a scowl. "Where and when did you get that?" she asked.

"That isn't important," Grandmother said. She took the locket from me and put it around my neck. Mother wasn't satisfied with the answer, but there was no time for discussion. She rushed us out the door as Barni was waiting for us. When we arrived, he was angry with me because I was late. The next minute he put his arm around my shoulder and shouted, "Bravo, Bravo!" as Jancsi, one of his friends, scored the winning goal for Kisterenye. After the game, we all went to an ice cream stand for a cone to quench our thirst. It was then Barni noticed my locket and exclaimed, "Ilona, that is an expensive locket. Who gave it to you?"

Ilcsa answered, "Her grandmother gave it to her for her name day. I never got such an expensive gift in my life," she mumbled with resentment.

I thought to myself, "Ilcsa, you don't know the whole story."

As we were sitting on the grass in a big circle, Barni moved close to me and pointed to his pocket, indicating that he also had a gift for me. He would give it to me when we were alone. While we were strolling around Kisterenye's well-landscaped park, we met Laci and his friends. He congratulated me on my name day and gave me a celebratory hug, and I whispered, "but you still have to tell me who sent it to me." Instead he said, "I like your locket Ilona. It looks nice on you," looking into my eyes with a sincere smile. I returned his smile. "I like it too," I replied, stroking the locket.

Barni must have noticed the glance that passed between us. He reached for my hand and quickly pulled me away. "We have to hurry to catch up with the others," he said in a dictatorial voice. A short distance away, he said angrily, "I don't like it when other men smile at you that way."

"I resent that Barni," I replied.

"You are mine!" he said possessively.

I resented his words even more, but I didn't press the issue because he was already angry. But, I thought, "Barni you don't own me. Maybe I could like you if you weren't so domineering and rude."

When we arrived home, like a sports reporter, he described the whole soccer game to my parents. He liked to be the center of attention. I went into the bedroom to see Grandmother. When I came in she was reading in bed.

She looked at me solemnly and asked me to shut the door. When I came back and sat on the bed, she told me about the bitter discussion she had had with Mother about the locket. Mother told her she was going to take the locket away from me, and she will return it to the rightful owner.

"*Nagymama*, what are we going to do?" I asked.

"I'm afraid, dear, we are going to have more arguments about the locket, because your mother is not going to rest until she finds out where it came from. We could tell her the truth, but we don't know it. She wouldn't believe us anyway."

Just then Mother came in and said, "Ilona, you should be in the kitchen. Barni is asking for you."

He was still discussing the soccer game with Father when I went back into the kitchen. I listened to him for a while, but my mind wandered. Finally, when he decided to leave I went outside with him. He sat down on the bench and asked me to sit beside him. He handed me a box and asked me to open it. To my amazement, it contained a gold ring. Quickly he took the ring out of the box, put it on my right hand ring finger, and declared, "Now we are engaged."

In our destitute country, diamond engagement rings were only a dream. Most people just wore a wedding band, as an engagement ring, on the right hand. After the marriage ceremony it was worn on the left hand. Barni held my hand and viewed the ring approvingly.

"It fits perfectly," he said.

"Barni, you didn't ask me, nor did we even discuss an engagement," I said resentfully.

"I discussed it with your mother and she approved," he replied.

"But Barni, you are not marrying my mother."

"Ilona, nevertheless, she rules," he said confidently. It was true. I lost. I gave up. It was hopeless.

"But how did you know my ring size?"

"Your mother measured your finger while you were asleep."

By this time I was furious with both of them. Sensing my distress, he said, "Don't be frightened, Ilona. We are going to have a good life together. I will take care of you." His words frightened me.

"I have to go inside, think about this, and discuss it with my parents."

"There is nothing to think about, Ilona," he pressed. "We are engaged." When I stood up, my knees were shaking and I felt numb. He gave me a hug and announced, "You are mine!" Then, he left.

I walked into the house still shaken with fear. Mother asked me impatiently, "What did Barni give you for your name day gift?"

"Mother don't act innocent. You know all about this ring; you arranged this with him." Father looked surprised and asked, "Show me your ring Ilona." Looking at my ring he said, "That looks lovely dear. I wish that would radiate from your heart." He gave me a quick hug, released a big sigh, picked up the water pail, and rushed out for water.

With a devious smile, Mother said, "Isn't that wonderful? Now you are engaged."

"But, Mother, I don't love him, and I don't want to marry him."

"Too late; now you are engaged," she answered with a smirk.

Without thinking, I blurted out, "I'm in love with Andras, and he wants to marry me!"

Mother looked shocked and abbreviated her response to six words: "Not if I can help it."

I knew I couldn't reason with her about Andras because she had Father's support. Defeated and distraught, I dragged myself to bed. I cried out to Grandmother, but she was sound asleep. Lying in bed, feeling tormented and lonely, I touched the locket on my neck, given to me by a man I had a *passion* for. Then I glanced at the engagement ring on my finger, given to me by a man I *detested*. What can I do, run away? I'm still under age. And under Communism you couldn't hide, they knew very well where everyone was.

Hopelessly, I turned to God. "Dear God, please help me. You are the only one who can help me."

CHAPTER 18

"What on earth are you doing, Ilona, tearing the bed apart so early in the morning?"

"*Nagymama*, I lost my locket and I can't find it," I said as I threw the pillows on the floor and turned the mattress over.

"I had it last night in bed. I'm sure I touched it before I fell asleep. I'm sure I did." I crawled under the bed and we searched every part of the bed, but there was no locket.

"*Nagymama*, this is a mystery."

"Ilona, come and sit down, dear. This is not a mystery." Grandmother comforted me.

"What do you mean?"

"Just think. Who could have done it?"

"*Nagymama*, this isn't Mother's doing, is it?"

"I think so, dear. Now you just listen to me and don't confront your mother about the locket under any circumstances. Pretend nothing has happened. Just leave it to me. You go into the kitchen and have breakfast."

As I sat at the table, Mother asked, "Ilona, you're not wearing your locket. Where is it?" Grandmother stood at the door holding her breath, waiting to hear what I would say.

"I don't want to wear the locket to work, so I gave it to Grandmother to keep it for me."

Utterly flabbergasted, Mother shrieked, "What?"

She stared at Grandmother, who replied, "Yes, Mari, I'm keeping it for her."

To avoid any further discussion I quickly left for work. On the way I decided that it could have been Mother who took the locket from my neck while I was asleep. Yes, yes, Grandmother is right. The locket disappeared just like the beaded bracelet my cadet gave me. What a cruel thing to do to your own child. It was beyond me why she couldn't be as reasonable to me as she was to my sisters. I thought, maybe, I should learn to love Barni just to get away from her. But how could I, when he was so possessive and domineering. Maybe I could learn to *pretend* that I loved him.

As usual before work, our gang sat together in the cafeteria. When Andras came to us he noticed my ring, gazed in my eyes for a moment, and then quickly rushed away. The others at the table were in a deep discussion and didn't notice our sentimental moment. When I lifted my cup to have a sip of tea, to ease my heartache, Iren also noticed my ring. Everyone congratulated me and asked when the big day would be. "We haven't set a date yet," I told them.

"Don't forget to invite us. We like a good wedding with wine and Gypsy music," Karcsi said.

"I promise you are all invited," I assured him.

Now Barni came to our house regularly; he became almost a part of the family. Mother was delighted and catered to him in every which way. Shortly after, Andras left Kanyas and a part of my heart went with him. But, being under age, I had to accept the situation in spite of my heartache.

The following Friday, Barni arrived with an invitation. "Ilona, my parents are inviting you for dinner on Sunday. Since we are engaged, my family wants to meet you." I had met his mother, older brother and sister at the harvest dance, but I hadn't met his father, grandmother or his other four brothers. I was nervous about meeting the family, but he insisted that I had to meet them and my mother gladly agreed. Father just looked at me with his reassuring smile. I saw jealousy on Manci's face. She was the oldest and she should get married first, according to Hungarian custom. Julika was happy for me and bragged that she would be my flower girl. Grandmother, who disapproved of Barni because of his oppressive behaviour, sadly turned and walked into the other room and closed the door. Desperately wanting to be free from Mother's control, I reasoned that if I tried very hard to be a friend to Barni, perhaps I could even change his behaviour.

At work, it wasn't the same without Andras there, which made me realize how deeply I felt about him. Yet I had to accept that he had gone out of my life, regardless of how much it hurt. I hoped for both of us to find love and happiness as we went our separate ways.

Sunday came and Barni arrived to take me to his home for dinner. Later, we would go to the movies. He visited with my parents on the porch while Grandmother French braided my hair. The window was open and I overheard the discussion outside about our harsh political situation.

"The Soviet leaders of our country blame Matyas Rakosi, the Prime Minister, for Hungary's dreadful economic situation. Now they have begun a more flexible policy called *The New Course*."

"Yes, they are squeezing the people more and more for their own benefit," I heard Barni say.

Father tried to calm him down. "Barni, why can't you just tolerate the Communist system like the rest of us?"

He replied with anger, "I can't. It infuriates me that they take over the country and dominate and suffocate us. I hope the revolution, which everyone is predicting, will come soon."

Mother came into the bedroom and closed the window, then began to lecture me on behaviour at Barni's house. "Ilona, don't talk about politics or what we discuss at home. Just eat a small amount of food, and if they offer you more just say no thank you, regardless of how hungry you are." Thinking, yes Mother, I know what hunger pangs are, remembering how disappointed I was with my small portion in the cornfield.

"Mari," Grandmother interrupted, "you are making her nervous. "You just go out. Go, go, go!" Grandmother pushed her out and closed the door.

"Ilona, don't be fearful. Just be yourself, like you are with me, and you will do fine, dear."

I wore my green, floral print, bell-shaped skirt with a white cotton blouse. I wished that I had my silver locket, which had vanished so mysteriously. Instead, I wore my green and white, braided, choker beads that matched nicely with my skirt and braided hair. When I was ready to go, Mother handed me a small parcel to drop off at Godmother's. She said Manci and her friends would meet us at the movies and we were to come home together. I was just about out of the door when Mother came and buttoned up my blouse to the last button saying, "Don't show your chest."

"Mother, it is a shirt blouse and it is too hot," I protested. "The other day you told me to open my blouse because it was too hot. Why do I have to close it now?"

"Just leave it closed and go," Mother insisted. "Barni is waiting." Of course, I unbuttoned my blouse as soon as I was away from the house.

On our way, Barni held my hand and discussed our marriage and where we were going to live. After a long, unsuccessful search for an apartment, his resentment against the Russian families who had moved to Hungary surfaced. His voice rose. "Because of them and our Communist system we have a severe housing shortage, without any construction in our area. Therefore, we have no choice but to renovate my parents' downstairs storage room for our living

114

quarters." Then he went on to say that he wanted a big family like his parents. Hearing that, I was completely terrified. Being a teenager and not sexually involved, it was impossible to comprehend being pregnant, nonetheless bearing six children.

I said, "Barni, I don't even know if I really love you or not. I'm not even used to our engagement yet, never mind marriage and six children."

"You will get used to it, Ilona," he said casually.

"Barni, you are not listening to me. I don't want to get married yet, and I don't want six children." I was glad we had reached Godmother's place, before I lost control and screamed at him to understand my feelings about the whole situation. Godmother was sitting outside and she immediately offered us refreshments. Auntie noticed my ring and gave me a hug and shook Barni's hand. Godmother did the same. Godfather, clasping Barni's hand, wished him happiness. But I was shocked that he didn't say a word to me. I wondered why. Godmother called me inside.

"Ilona, we have to get together and look for patterns and material for your wedding dress and a nice suit for your civil wedding." It was customary in Hungary that the godparents bought the bridal outfit.

"Hold on, *Keresztmama*. We haven't even set a date yet," I said quickly.

"But we have to look, dear. It takes time to find the right material and pattern, and the tailoring takes time."

Barni called, "Ilona, we have to go. Mother is waiting for us with dinner." We said goodbye and left.

As we reached Barni's house, I was impressed by the variety of flowers in the garden. Some of the family were sitting on the veranda and I was greeted with a warm welcome. Barni introduced the rest of the family whom I hadn't met yet. His mother and grandmother came out of the house to meet me. As we greeted each other I noticed the trickles of perspiration on Barni's mother's face. She had been cooking on a wood stove in the hot kitchen for twelve people, including Barni's older brother and his wife. It was quite an experience to meet all of them together.

They were a good-looking family, especially his mother who was almost 180 cm tall and had pretty blue eyes, which most of the children had inherited. He had only one sister, who was tall and pretty, but conceited. His father was well over 180 cm tall with brown eyes and an authoritative personality, which I noticed especially when he talked to the younger children. He made me feel uneasy with his sharp eyes. He had the habit of answering a question with a question, just to disturb the flow of the conversation. It didn't take me long to realize where Barni's attitude came from.

The chicken soup was delicious with yellow, hair-string, home-made noodles, which Barni praised his grandmother for making. His mother had made cabbage rolls for the main course and *turos lepeny,* sweet yeast dough topped with sweet cottage cheese and fresh dill, for dessert. It was so scrumptious I ignored Mother's instruction and I had two pieces. Since I didn't drink espresso, I went into the kitchen for some water. When I saw dishes piled up almost to the ceiling, I offered to help Barni's mother and grandmother. While we were cleaning up, we had a nice visit talking about our families. Listening to them, I perceived that the two ladies wanted to marry the boys off as fast as they could. I sympathized with them. Cooking for ten people day after day can be very stressful. Without meat, or refrigeration and only a wood stove to cook on, it was difficult to prepare meals from scratch.

Barni called for me to come so he could show me our future home downstairs. We would have to clean it up, paint it with white lime, and level the dirt floor. It would be hard work, but it was rent-free. For me, it sounded like a relief to get away from my mother's dictatorship for good. Barni became so excited that he started to hug and kiss me. I had a hard time to fight my way out of his arms. I was glad I did, as his father walked in; it was considered improper to kiss in front of our parents. Barni and his father discussed how they would quickly put in a chimney for a wood stove, so it could be finished soon before the wedding.

Shortly, we had to say goodbye. I thanked Barni's parents for their hospitality as Grandmother had told me to do. When we arrived at the movies, Manci and her friends were there. While waiting in the courtyard, my school friends came over and congratulated me on my engagement. In a small town, news travels quickly. Everyone looked happy for me, but they didn't know Barni the way I did.

During the intermission, Barni bought a bag of candy. He took one, and then offered me one. The rest he put in his shirt pocket. Shortly after the movie started he slowly took out one, then another. I waited for him to give me one, but he didn't. Later, he sneaked another one without offering me any. I thought, even if I died, I wouldn't ask him for one. How, I reasoned, if you really loved someone, could you not share even a bite? Oh, I told myself, maybe I'm just being childish. Maybe he forgot to give me one. A little while later, he slipped another candy in his mouth. This time I knew it was deliberate. Analysing the situation, I didn't see how I could learn to love such a greedy man.

Walking home, he wanted to put his arm around my shoulder. To avoid his embrace, I pretended that I had to take a pebble out of my sandal. I bent down to do so and that kept him from cuddling me. He was deep in thought for a moment, and then he unexpectedly asked, "Ilona, next Sunday a group of my friends are going to hike up to the Kekes-teto. Would you like to go?" The Kekes-teto is a summit in the Matra Mountains, which is 1,015 meters high.

"I would love to go Barni. I have never been up there and I bet the view is breathtaking. But you have to ask Mother. I hope she will say yes."

"Don't worry. I will ask her in a way she can't refuse." Shortly after we arrived home, while we were having coffee, Barni asked Mother if I could go on the hike with him.

"Of course she can. She is your fiancée, so she can go," Mother agreed.

To my shocking surprise, Father spoke up harshly. "Under some conditions, Barni. Since Ilona will be with you all day, there's to be no drinking and certainly nothing like the garden episode before you were drafted. Do you understand me, Barni?"

"Certainly he understands, Jozsi," Mother answered, wanting to lighten Father's harsh command. Barni looked astounded, but I was proud of my father. He had showed that he truly cared for me.

Mother broke the silence, "Anyone for more coffee?"

"I would like to have one more before I leave," Barni answered.

Early the next Saturday morning, Grandmother helped me to pack a lunch and get ready to meet Barni and his friends at the Nagybatony train station. We had to take a train to Tar, the closest town to the foot of the mountain. From there we would hike up to the Kekes summit. Three couples and Barni were waiting for me at the platform.

He spotted me and called, "Ilona, we are over here." I didn't feel comfortable with the city girls, who wore heavy makeup, had painted nails, and conceited attitudes. They made me feel like a country bumpkin again.

After our greetings, Barni called me aside and informed me that there was a change in plans, and we would be going to Bukszek hot springs instead of the Kekes summit.

"But I have no bathing suit," I exclaimed.

"Don't worry. I brought you one. Don't say anything to the others. Just come." He dragged me by the hand and we joined the others. I was puzzled that he had brought me a bathing suit and had a ticket to Bukszek, not Tar. It looked like he had this all planned. Well, I had never been to Bukszek, so I decided I was going to enjoy it. On the train we played games and the time went quickly. When we arrived, I noticed the beautiful flowers, especially the red and white stripy petunias. There were three pools to enjoy: two small, and one Olympic size.

When we walked into the swimming area, Barni handed me a bag and said, "Here is your bathing suit. Go with the girls and change." In the changing cubicle I had the shock of my life... I pulled out of the bag a satin, forest green and white small polka-dot bikini. I was reluctant to put it on knowing that Mother would kill me if someone told her about it. I just sat and stared at the garment on my lap.

"Ilona," Zsuzsi called. "We are waiting for you."

"You girls go. I will be there shortly." I tried to figure out what I was going to do. I had never been out in public with such little clothes on. I owned a two-piece bathing suit, but the bottom looked like shorts, not like this skimpy bikini. At last, I put it on and scarcely glanced in the mirror. It looked very nice on my small body; nevertheless it covered very little of it. I was too shy to go out. I just sat there for a while. I finally built up enough courage to join the others where Barni was waiting for me.

He eyed me from head to toe, and then said, "It fits you perfectly. Please turn around."

I ignored his request and rushed into the pool. The girls wore bikinis also and seemed comfortable in them. But I couldn't help feeling that if Mother could see me, she would erase me from the face of the earth. Since I wasn't a good swimmer, I stayed where I could touch the bottom of the pool. The others were diving, playing and swimming under water, which terrified me. I paddled only where I felt safe. When I got out of the pool, Barni brought over some suntan lotion, which he enjoyed smearing on my back while we were lying in the sun. It dawned on me again that he had planned all this. I asked him about it, and he admitted that he dreamed of seeing me in a bikini.

"Barni, that was dishonest and I don't like it. Wait until Mother finds out."

"She won't, Ilona, because we are not going to tell her."

We went back into the water and the girls coaxed me to the deep end of the pool. I pleaded with them that I feared deep water ever since I had nearly drowned with my baby sister in my arms. But they insisted and called me a coward; they didn't understand the horrible feeling of drowning, which I had experienced. Barni came to me and told me to show them that I was not a coward. He tried to coax me to the deep end, telling me I was missing all the fun. Suddenly, he grabbed my head and pushed me under the water. I was suffocating, fighting with him, but he didn't let go of my head.

When I regained consciousness I was lying by the side of the pool, in the recovery position, gagging and coughing up water. I heard the lifeguard warn Barni that he was playing a dangerous game, and he could have drowned me. He added harshly, that this was not the way to teach someone to overcome fear of deep water and drowning. Barni apologized, but it didn't help. I just wanted to be alone with God like I always did when I was frightened. I sat alone for the rest of the day, even though the girls came to cheer me up. They realized it was useless and left me alone.

On the way home, I was withdrawn and hoping that the pain in my chest would ease. Barni joked with the others as if nothing had happened. Just before we arrived home he told me, "Ilona, don't say anything at home about where we were and what happened."

"I will see Barni, but I won't promise with this pain in my chest."

I could hardly wait to share my anxiety with Grandmother. I was glad he stayed at the house for only a short time, as I was exhausted. I pretended that I was fine and said very little to my parents. I was so worried about the pain in my chest; I didn't even have the energy to tell Grandmother what had happened. I just wanted to go to bed. In my thoughts I was at the crossroad, down on my knees praying, appealing to God to help me with my tormented life.

CHAPTER 19

"Mother, what are you doing?" I was startled to see her unpacking my hiking bag, where I had hidden the bikini Barni had bought for me.

Shocked for a moment, she asked, "What are you hiding Ilona?"

"Nothing," Grandmother answered nonchalantly, and called me to the breakfast table as she was dishing out hot cornmeal, covered with Mother's organic honey. I watched her anxiously as she searched through my bag, but to my great relief, there was no bikini. Grandmother's secret smile assured me that my life was safe; she had hidden it.

I left for work feeling I had escaped a crisis with Mother. But Barni's scheming troubled me. I was sure he had planned to go to Bukszek, instead of the Kekes summit, before he had talked to my parents. That's why he had brought the bikini and suntan lotion and had the train ticket in his pocket. Yes, he had definitely arranged all this beforehand.

When I came home from work I heard loud voices. I thought for a moment that we had visitors, but as I got closer I heard Mother's raging. "They have to get married. That is all there is to it. It is disgusting wearing such a small thing on her body. She has no shame at all. I wonder what Barni was thinking of her."

"Mari don't blow things out of proportion; in Budapest young people wear that kind of bathing suit," Grandmother pleaded.

"I don't care. Ilona is not going to wear it, until they get married. After that, it is up to Barni. I don't want a child out of wedlock."

"I don't either, Mari. That is why Ilona should know more about dating and marriage," Grandmother suggested.

"They just have to get married and my worries will be over. Barni is coming tonight, and I will talk to him about setting a wedding date. The sooner, the better."

"No, you don't Mari," Grandmother insisted. "We should discuss this together, especially with Ilona present, because this is all about her life, not yours Mari."

I was completely perplexed about Mother's accusation and decision about my life. In my confused state, I didn't know what to do. Should I run away, or go inside and plead with Mother that she had to listen to me and try to understand what had really happened? When I stepped into the house there was a dead silence.

Mother, breathing heavily, yelled, "Ilona, sit!" Her look was sharp enough to kill. She threw the bikini in my face and began humiliating me, using foul words and calling me names.

"Where did you find that?" I cried out.

"Where you hid it under your mattress."

I tried to explain to Mother that Barni bought the bikini, to which she replied that if Barni wanted to see me nude, he would have to marry me first. Nude!! That harsh statement made my flesh crawl. Unexpectedly Barni walked in, overhearing Mother's last words.

"Who is marrying whom, Mrs. Padar?" he asked. Noticing that I was crying, he sat beside me and gently wiped the tears off my face with his handkerchief. He looked at Mother, and asked, "What's wrong?"

Mother pushed the bikini in front of him. "This is what's wrong." He hesitated for a moment, frowned, then sat up straight and told Mother the truth about the Bukszek trip and the bikini. He kept his arm around my shoulder and said, "Ilona please don't cry. This is all my fault."

He turned to Mother. "Mrs. Padar, I'm serious about marrying Ilona as soon as we finish renovating the downstairs storage area at my home."

"When will it be done Barni?"

"In about a month," he answered.

"That is settled then. Oct. 4th will be the wedding date."

"That is fine with me," Barni answered joyfully.

I sat there dazed. They were arranging my life just as if I wasn't there or didn't even exist. I wished Father were there. I needed his support more than ever.

Finally Grandmother asked me, "What do you think about that, dear?"

"I don't know, *Nagymama*. I don't feel ready in my heart to get married. As a matter of fact, I'm dreading the thought of being his wife."

"That's all right Ilona. You will learn to love me in time," Barni stated.

"Yes, you will," Mother agreed.

I wanted to scream: "Will any one of you listen to me and understand my feelings?" But I knew it was useless. I looked at Grandmother, whose eyes were misty.

"This marriage will never work," she stated furiously and walked out of the room.

Julika came home and childishly started chatting with Barni. I rose and, with shaking legs, started to walk out. Then Mother asked in a dominating voice, "Ilona where are you going?"

Ignoring her, I walked out into the garden and sat there in a daze. Barni came and tried to reassure me, "Ilona, dear, everything will be fine. You'll see."

But his words weren't assuring to me. I tried to reason with him. "Barni, I don't want to get married yet; I'm not ready to make a commitment."

"Ilona, we have about a month to get ready before the house is renovated. My father is working on it already. You will love it and it will be our home."

Regardless of what I said, he didn't hear me. No one did. Echoing from the house I could hear Mother and Grandmother arguing. I was curious as to what they were arguing about and wanted to go inside, but Barni was still with me, so I asked, "Barni I'm tired; would you mind leaving?"

Feeling the tension in the family he agreed. Without hesitation he gave me a hug and a kiss. "I love you so much," he mumbled.

Finally, he let go of me and left. I ran in the house, to find complete silence. Seeing my dear grandmother crying, I became furious. "What happened? Why are you crying?" With a deep sigh, she answered, "I warned your mother not to force you into this marriage, against your will, because you are not ready. You don't love Barni enough to live a happy married life. For her to force you into this marriage is cruel. For that she cursed me." Grandmother continued to pour her heart out. "She was only four when her father died. Raising her alone, I tried to be both a mother and father to her. I gave her everything I could. But she rejected me, even to this day. I just want her to face reality and see what she is doing to you and your life. She knows how much I love you, and by controlling and hurting you, she knows it hurts me."

Seeing my dear *nagymama* sobbing, I felt like a knife had been twisted in my heart. I ran up to Mother, screamed in her face, "You're wicked!"

Without hesitation she slapped me across the face. With Grandmother's help I restrained myself from slapping her back. I yelled at her, "I'm not a child any more. I'm too old to be slapped around."

Seeing how enraged I was, Grandmother gently led me to the bedroom and made me sit down.

"You change into your nightgown, and I will go and make us some chamomile tea. I'll be back shortly."

Quietly sitting in the bedroom, I glanced at Julika. I was glad that she was sleeping peacefully in her bed. I heard Mother in the kitchen, apologizing to Grandmother for using cuss words. Hearing her, I thought maybe I should do the same and apologize to Mother for nearly hitting her. But I couldn't bring myself to do it.

Grandmother brought in the tea. "After all this anxiety, we need this nice chamomile tea to relax." As she slurped her tea, she continued, "I put extra honey in yours dear."

"Thank you *Nagymama*. I don't know how I could live without you." God bless her soul. Everything she did for me showed her devoted love.

She was sipping her tea, deep in thought. Finally she said, "Ilona sweetheart, listen to me carefully. Hear me out; before you say a word . . . You have to marry Barni now to get free from your mother. With Barni, you might have a chance to live. After today's episode, I'm not sure if you would survive here with your mother."

I looked at her deeply distraught. "*Nagymama*, what are you talking about?"

"I'm sorry to say this dear, but this is the way I feel. This will be the best for you. And you know I'll always be here for you."

We embraced and wept together. I thought, maybe Grandmother was right. I would have to marry Barni. I couldn't live with Mother. Just moments ago we could have harmed each other physically. And yes, my life would always be in turmoil under Mother's continuous domination.

Grandmother motioned me to kneel down beside her and she led us into the prayer of "Our Father." After that she suggested, "Now dear you have to say your own pleading with the Lord."

I prayed from my innermost feeling:

Dear Creator, I thank you for granting me the privilege to bring every trouble of my soul to you. Every hidden grief, every sorrow - with the assurance, trust, and hope that you will help me. Guide me, by your spirit, with my tormented life. May I build the frail shelter of my life beneath the shadow of your Almighty, that in the days of my desperate need I find my way into the secret of your presence through my Lord. Amen.

I crawled into bed, exhausted, but with hope.

CHAPTER 20

When I awoke, an idea came to me. I would go and see Judit, my friend in Paszto. I could talk to her; she was nine years older and married. I could ask her about menstruation, sex and marriage. I wasn't shy with her, as we had developed a strong friendship during the Budapest seminar. But what lies would I have to make up to be able to see her? I could say that I had a dentist appointment in Paszto. I could not tell anyone about my plan, not even Grandmother. I decided to take Tuesday off from work and go to Paszto. Yes, this was a good idea and Judit could answer all my questions.

Tuesday, I pretended to go to work as usual. On the bus some workers asked me where I was going. Because of the circumstances with my mother, I had become a natural liar and answered without hesitation, "I am going to see my dentist in Paszto."

While I was waiting at the train station, to my delight I spotted Janos in the crowd. I got so exhilarated I wanted to run to him, give him a hug and kiss, and tell him all my problems. But I couldn't. To my shock a girl was clinging very closely to him. I felt jealous and tormented; instantly from the height of ecstasy I was in the depth of despair. Turning away, I tried very hard to hold back my tears, but they still escaped and rolled down my face. I sadly boarded the train, and closed my eyes, trying to erase the agonizing sight of Janos with a girl.

Finally, I reached Paszto. Traveling in the taxi to Judit's place, I reflected on the frightful encounter I had with the AVO man in Budapest. I wondered if they were still keeping an eye on Barni. Fortunately, I found Judit home alone. For a moment she was surprised to see me, however, she welcomed me with open arms. Seizing my hand, she led me into the house, and pulled me to sit beside her.

"How are you my darling? What brings you to Paszto?" she asked.

"I came to see you especially." She was still holding my hand when she noticed my ring. She gave me a hug and wished me good luck with my marriage.

"That is why I have come to see you. I need your help."

"What is the problem?"

Comfortable, but still shy, I told her, "I am past seventeen and I have had only three menstruations, about four to six months apart. I know it's not normal, but I have no one I feel comfortable with to talk about it, except you."

"Ilona, I feel honored that you came to me. My advice to you is that you should see a doctor."

"I would never see our doctor because I am not comfortable with him, for that kind of examination."

She hesitated for a moment, rushed into the other room, brought back a book, and handed it to me. "Read this book. It can explain everything to you better than I can." The title was *Sex and Marriage.*

"Ilona, you definitely need help," she continued. "Get your purse and we are going right now to see my doctor. I have to take you because I know your mother wouldn't. And with you getting married, you need help." I did not object and we were on our way.

I sat nervously in the doctor's waiting room, not knowing what to expect. I had never had an examination by a gynecologist before. Judit noticed how fearful I was and sat close to me, reached for my hand and whispered, "Don't be frightened, darling; I'm here with you," and squeezed my hand gently to calm me.

Soon the nurse called, "Ilona Padar next." She led me into the doctor's office. He extended his right hand saying, "I am Dr. Sarosi. Please sit down, Miss Padar," and he motioned me to a chair. "How can I help you?" Being nervous, I hesitated for a second. "Don't be frightened, Ilona. I am here to help you." He handed me a gown to change into and continued, "After that come into the examination room."

My lengthy examination was easier than I had thought it would be, due to the doctor's sincere talk and maturity. I had just finished dressing when he returned with the diagnosis.

"Miss Padar, you have secondary *amenorrhea.* As we discussed, this is caused due to excessive stress, which is disrupting your hormone balance and interrupting your normal menstrual cycle. Also, you are anemic due to a nutritional deficiency. Mainly, you are lacking iron. I will give you prescriptions to help and I want to see you in a month. We hope to have it under control before you get married. And remember, we can endure only so much stress in a given period of time. Next time when you come, please bring your mother or tell her to come and see me anytime. I would like to talk to her."

When I came out of the doctor's office, Judit was waiting patiently for me and asked, "Ilona, what did the doctor have to say?" And I told her about my diagnosis.

"Ilona, dear, just have faith. He is a good doctor, and with his help you will be fine." It was good to hear her reassuring words.

As we walked, in deep discussion, I completely lost track of the time. Glancing at the city hall tower clock, I saw that it was 3:45 p.m.

"Oh, no! I am late! I have to go. I still have to get my prescriptions and catch my train in twenty minutes. Thank you, Judit, for your sincere help. It meant the world to me that I could confide in you with my personal problems."

As I started to run for the drugstore she said, "I'm glad that I could help you. Keep in touch, Ilona."

"I will. Definitely, I will. I'll write to you, but now I have to hurry to catch my train."

At the pharmacy, I was further delayed, waiting for my prescription. I had to sprint the short distance in the pouring rain to catch my train, which was already standing in the station. Just as I reached the station, the train pulled out, leaving me behind. I was furious, yet relieved to sit down before I collapsed. After resting on the bench for a while, I had to wring out my drenched sweater from the cloudburst, then quickly inquired at the ticket office for the next train to Nagybatony. The answer was "in two hours."

It gave me plenty of time to think about how I could cover up the two hours difference between when I should have arrived home from work and when I would actually get home. Feeling dizzy, I realized I hadn't had lunch, and now it was late afternoon. I went to the cafeteria and bought a big, red apple. Crunching on the sweet, fresh, fragrant apple, I wished I could afford another one, but after paying for my prescriptions, I did not have enough money left.

While waiting for the train I started to read my book, *Sex and Marriage*. As I looked up, I realized that an elderly lady sitting across from me was staring in my direction with squinting eyes, trying to read the title of my book. Embarrassed, I slowly lowered my book so she couldn't read the title. I blushed and continued reading by holding the book down on my lap.

Boarding the train, I was fortunate that no one sat close to me so I could continue to learn more about sex and married life. It was so absorbing that it seemed that I reached Nagybatony in no time. I still hadn't come up with a believable lie by the time I had reached home. Suddenly, it occurred to me that I would not lie. I had a health problem and we had to be honest and open about it. It had to be dealt with, regardless of what Mother said. This time, I was determined that I would face up to her and not be intimidated. The doctor had advised me, "Ilona you are a young adult and it is time to get assertive with your mother, for the sake of your health." I walked into the house without fear. I found Mother alone.

Outraged, she instantly asked, "Ilona, where were you? I found out that you weren't at work today. What lies are you going to tell me this time?"

"Where is Grandmother?" I asked.

"Never mind that. Where were you all day? Meeting Janos or Andras, planning to runaway with one of them? I want to know right now," she insisted.

"Not until Grandmother is present," I replied and I walked out to look for her. I noticed her way back in the garden digging potatoes. I called to her, "Grandmother, please come in. I have something very important to share with you."

"I am coming, darling." She dropped her hoe and strolled in behind me. In the kitchen we sat down at the table where Mother was peeling cucumbers.

"Tell me where were you today," Grandmother requested.

"That's what I want to know. Without lies," Mother insisted.

"I went to see a doctor in Paszto," I said. I put the prescriptions on the table and told them everything that had happened.

"That was a very good idea, dear," Grandmother said as she picked up the prescription bottles and continued, "this one is for hormone imbalance, and this one is for stress. I agree with the doctor, Ilona. You have too much stress in your life. Don't you agree, Mari? The third one is for anemia. I will make sure you take them as prescribed, and you will be fine, dear."

Mother continued to peel the cucumbers. She looked at me and said, "Nothing is wrong with you."

By this time I was infuriated. "Mother, I am seventeen and I have a menstrual problem. That is a problem according to the doctor. And another thing Mother, I had a long discussion with the doctor about how you and I are not getting along."

Enraged, she replied, "How dare you tell a stranger about our family life!"

I did not back down. "By the way, Mother, he wants to see you and talk to you as soon as possible."

"I don't have to see anyone," she said and left to go to the store to get vinegar for the salad. I was absolutely furious with her. She wouldn't even listen to the doctor's advice.

"*Nagymama*, please help me. I don't know what to do any more."

"My darling, I told you already that you have to get married to flee from your mother." She picked up the prescription bottles. "I hope these will help you," she added.

I thought that while Mother was away I would show Grandmother the book that Judit had given me, but I was apprehensive about her reaction. Yet I had to show it to her, if I wanted to ask her to hide it for me, by locking it in her chest so that it wouldn't get into Julika's hands.

"Ilona, what are you thinking about. You are so quiet," Grandmother inquired.

"*Nagymama*, you have to lock this up for me," I said nervously, as with head bowed I handed her the book. I waited silently for her reaction to the title.

"Oh," she paused for a second, "*Sex and Marriage*. I am glad you are reading it and I will hide it for you before your mother gets hold of it." Just then, Mother walked in.

"What am I getting hold of, Mother?"

"Nothing, Mari, nothing," said Grandmother as I slid the book back into my purse.

Later I settled in bed and continued reading my book. I put another book beside me to switch to in case Mother came into the bedroom. I decided to peel the book jacket off for safety, since there was no title on the hard cover.

Afterwards, Grandmother brought some tea and my prescription pills, which she had also kept for safekeeping. While drinking our tea we reflected on our good times together in Budapest.

"Do you remember, dear, the beautiful Margit Island where you contentedly played on the Danube shore? Later, we visited the zoo where I hoped you would run out of questions about the animals - but you didn't. My favorite time with you as a little girl was holding your hand as we walked to church. And look at you now. All grown up and preparing for marriage, and before long you will have children of your own. And I will be there to babysit for you."

"I would like that, *Nagymama,*" I answered with my misty eyes half closed.

Then she covered me, kissed me gently, and traced the sign of the cross on my forehead saying, "Go to sleep, dear and I will pray the rosary for you."

"*Nagymama*, I love you dearly."

"I love you too darling. Goodnight now. And may God bless."

CHAPTER 21

On Saturday, Godmother and I took the train to Salgotarjan to buy material for my wedding gown, as well as material for a suit to wear at our civil wedding at City Hall. On the train, Godmother was visiting with the lady sitting next to her. I sat back, closed my eyes, and visualized my dream wedding dress made of fine white crepe fabric, fitted at the waist. It would be sleeveless with a low neckline and a closely gathered skirt with a long white veil trailing behind. I'd have my hair styled back and up with a pearl beaded headpiece. I pictured myself walking down the aisle carrying a white calla lily bouquet. Suddenly Barni's selfish domineering attitude seeped into my mind. How will I cope with him for a lifetime? A lifetime is a long time. Instantly a cold dreadful sensation permeated my whole being.

"Ilona wake up. We are in Salgotarjan," Godmother called. Oh, I was relieved that she had wakened me from my worrisome thoughts.

We searched several stores before we found the fine, navy, gabardine material for my suit. The material for the wedding gown was more difficult. First, we had to choose a pattern, and we debated about the style. As we talked, I discovered that it wasn't my choice or Godmother's - it was Mother who would decide on the style of my wedding dress. She had told Godmother my dress was to be taffeta with long sleeves and a high neck with a round collar. Hearing this, I was shocked and furious. "Godmother, you are describing a style for a child's dress."

"Sorry dear, but you know your mother. I can't go against her decision."

"But, *Keresztmama,* you are paying for everything. You should have a say in the matter."

"Not if I want to keep my friendship with your mother," she said, as she picked up a pattern that fit Mother's description.

Raging, I said, "You know what, *Keresztmama,* I believe even when Mother ceases to be, she will still dominate me from the other side."

Godmother just raised her shoulders and walked away. She picked up some taffeta material and the pattern for my wedding gown, leaving me standing there. The clerk gave me a startled look and said, "Ilona, it should be your choice not your mother's. This is your wedding day, your memorable day. Don't give in; fight for it."

Embarrassed to be seen shedding tears at my age, I rushed out of the store. Godmother came outside and apologized. She was unable to do anything about it; she had received her orders from Mother.

"This is my wedding day. How far will she go to torment me?"

Godmother apologized again. "It is very hard for me to hurt your feelings, when I love you so much, but there is nothing I can do - just like when you lived with us."

Quickly, I apologized to her. "*Keresztmama,* I am sorry to be angry with you. It is not your fault and I understand your situation with Mother." Seeing her troubled face, I gave her a hug to assure her that I was not upset with her. Then we went back inside to pick up the rest of the bridal accessories.

On our way home we stopped at the seamstress to take my measurements. While she was doing that she tried to start a conversation, but I answered her only briefly. Before we left she remarked, "Ilona think before you commit to this marriage, because I have never seen such a distraught, unhappy bride to be as you are."

I only gave her a quick smile and left the room. I didn't want to share my heartache about my wedding gown.

"Come for a fitting in two weeks time," she called after us.

On our way home Godmother was still apologizing about not being able to comply with my wishes. When we reached her place she invited me in for supper.

"Thank you, *Keresztmama* for your help, generosity, and kindness, but I can't stay for supper. I still have a long way to walk home."

We hugged and said goodbye. I was hungry, but to stay for supper and face my arrogant godfather, in my frame of mind, would have been dangerous. If he would pick on me, like he had done when I was boarding at their house, I would probably have slugged him. I did have a long way to walk home, and I was looking forward to it, to being alone. Alone with God. And alone with my thoughts for how to deal with Mother.

On my arrival I was still upset, but in control of my feelings. I confronted Mother about the style of my wedding dress: the high neck, round collar, and long sleeves. She wanted to walk away, but I said, "Mother, please listen. That style is like a ten-year-old child's dress."

She turned around giving me an angry look, "You will wear what I tell you to wear and no further discussion."

"But Mother, it is my wedding!"

"Ilona," she said harshly, "you should know by now I will never give in to you."

Enraged, I blurted out, "Mother you are wicked and heartless to do this to me."

"Don't you dare say another word." She looked at me with piercing eyes, and a motionless face. The anger raging inside of me made me feel dizzy. I had a throbbing headache and my stomach churned, causing me to vomit. I swayed toward a chair to sit down. While sitting on the chair, with my head bowed, Father and Grandmother walked in carrying some firewood.

"What's wrong?" Grandmother yelled, dropping her armful of wood. She touched my shoulder as I was bent over holding my stomach.

"What is the matter dear?" Grandmother asked again as she stroked my back.

"Mari what's wrong with Ilona?" Father raised his voice.

"Ask her yourself, Jozsi. She is dizzy and vomiting. I am curious as to why?" Mother stressed, the humiliating words. Refusing to hear her mortifying words any further I asked Grandmother to help me to bed.

"Ilona, as soon as I am finished talking to your mother, I will come and talk to you."

"I'll wait for you *Apuka*; I want to talk to you too."

Just as I climbed into bed, Grandmother left me to make some chamomile tea. Shortly I heard Barni's voice inquiring in the kitchen.

"Where is Ilona?"

"She is not feeling well, Barni. Go in and cheer her up," Grandmother encouraged him.

Shortly after, a knock on the door, and with my permission, the door slowly opened and a hand holding a bouquet of flowers appeared, with my favorite flower, a calla lily, in the center. Barni entered smiling and saying, "Cheers, cheers."

Seeing the flowers brought a smile to my face. He rushed to me, gave me a lengthy kiss, and handed me a package, saying, "This is for you from my mother," and he urged me to open it. To my amazement there were four pieces of *turos lepeny,* my favorite pastry.

"Mother sent it to you, since you enjoyed it so much at our house," Barni explained.

Even though my stomach was still unsettled, I deeply inhaled the pastry's sweet smelling aroma, and had a bite, savoring the blend of sweet cottage cheese and dill filling. Barni gently stroked my face and whispered, "I love you so much, and I hardly can wait for you to be my wife."

Admiring the flowers I asked, "Barni where did you get these flowers? They are so lovely."

"From our garden," he replied.

"You cut down your mother's pride calla lily for me?"

"Ilona, my mother likes you a lot, and that is why she cut down the pride of her garden and sent it to you with your favorite pastry."

"I am deeply touched. Please thank her for me, until I see her again, and I can do it personally." This act of kindness assured me that there was an Almighty who had arranged this kind of happiness for me, from another mother at just the right time.

"By the way, Ilona," Barni asked, "what's wrong with you, that you are in bed so early?"

"Barni I had an upsetting fight with Mother about the style of my wedding gown. I got so angry with her that I got dizzy and sick to my stomach."

"Ilona, just let her have her way. She will never compromise with you. But, you know what? When we are married I will allow you to wear whatever you want."

"Barni I don't like that phrase *I allow you*; I want to be free from anyone's control. I have been dominated all my life. I just want to be free. I can think for myself. Do you hear me Barni?" I felt my stomach churning again with anger.

"We'll see Ilona, we'll see, when we get married," he replied, glancing back at me with a sarcastic smile, on his way to the kitchen for coffee. I asked myself how I would be able to tolerate being married to him with that kind of attitude.

Suddenly, I felt a warm dampness in my bed. I was glad to get my menstrual cycle, after the absence of five months. My hormone pills had worked. When Grandmother and Julika brought me fresh tea, Julika hopped up on my bed saying, "Ilona I want to come into bed with you," and she flipped up the blanket to crawl beside me.

"No you can't!" I yelled and roughly grabbed the blanket away from her and covered myself.

"Ilona, what's with you? You have always welcomed Julika into your bed," Grandmother questioned.

"Later, *Nagymama,* later she can come." I tried to apologize to Julika, but with tears in her sad little eyes she ran out to Mother.

"*Nagymama!* Finally we are alone. Please lock the door."

"But, Ilona why?" she inquired.

"We have to change the sheets before Barni comes back."

While we were changing the linen, Grandmother muttered with delight, "I knew you weren't. I knew it, I knew it," and she gave me a powerful hug suffocating me.

"What was that special hug about Grandmother?"

"Because you were dizzy and vomiting your mother said for sure you were pregnant."

"Pregnant?" I was shocked. If Mother had listened to the doctor and me, she would have known I wasn't.

Just as I settled back in bed again, Barni came back.

"Ilona, your mother wants to talk to both of us alone in the kitchen."

"Barni, stay with Ilona for a while," Grandmother requested. "I have to talk to her mother alone." A few minutes later she pushed Julika into the room to stay with us, so they could talk privately. I wondered what they had to talk about.

When I saw Julika looking sadly at me, I called her, "Julika come here please. I am sorry I was harsh with you moments ago. You can come into my bed now."

I had hardly finished the words before she was beside me. She was so pretty with her light curly hair and blue eyes. She was joyful and smart, but a chatterer.

"Ilona, I don't believe the storks bring the babies, and you know why?"

"I don't know. Why?" I answered. But, Barni's eyes got bigger and bigger.

"I'll tell you why. Because the babies are bigger than the stork and they would break the stork's beak. And that is why the babies must come from somewhere else." Barni and I smiled at each other. Grandmother came in and informed us that Mother changed her mind about our private talk.

"But why?" I asked.

"I straightened her out," Grandmother said.

"What was Mrs. Padar wanting to talk to us about?" Barni asked.

"Oh, something about the wedding."

I knew Grandmother was covering up her talk with Mother by the way she smiled at me. She walked out dragging Julika with her to give us some privacy. When she was gone Barni said, "Mother and I were shopping all day to find a black suit to fit me, but because of my height of 190 centimeters it was impossible. We had to buy material and I will have it tailored."

Just then Julika came back in to go to sleep in the bedroom we shared, and she asked Barni to tuck her in, which he did with delight. Then he came to me and said, "It is getting late; I have to leave." We kissed goodbye and he left.

"Ilona, why does Barni always kiss you on your lips, instead on the cheek like we do?" Julika asked.

"I will tell you when you get older. For now, go to sleep." I went to the kitchen to talk to Mother about her insinuation that I was pregnant. But I had to postpone our talk as my dear father came home from work very upset.

I asked calmly, "What's wrong *Apuka?*"

"Two of my co-workers, Laci and Sanyi, were fired without being given a reason, and the rest of the workers want to protest. There will be trouble at the mine," he predicted.

"That's Communism for you," Mother said and began to express her feelings about the system.

"Ilona, let's go to bed. You had a stressful day; you don't need to hear this."

"Yes, *Nagymama,* you are right," I agreed as I followed her into the bedroom.

When we were in our own bed, Grandmother said, "The only way we can help Laci and Sanyi is to include them in our prayer." So, we did. Later, I thought about Mother's suspicion about me being pregnant. I thought if only we could communicate, and she would listen to me, she would know the truth, and know me better. We were so far apart as mother and daughter that we were more like strangers. With the constant fighting between us, we were more like assailants.

CHAPTER 22

The following day, I had to put my disagreement with Mother about my wedding dress behind me, because we were going to buy my furniture. Mother would use my saved up salary to pay for the items. It didn't take too long, since under Communism we had a shortage of everything, and the word *choice* held no meaning. We purchased an off-white kitchen set with a dark green trim: a china cabinet, table with four chairs, and a laundry chest with arms and back to sit on. The bedroom suite had two upright cabinets, one with shelves, and the other with hangers for dresses; two night tables; and a full-length mirror with attached cabinets on each side that matched the night tables. Quickly we agreed on the selection due to the lack of any.

"When would you like this furniture delivered Mrs. Padar?" asked the clerk.

"Within two weeks. We will let you know the day," Mother replied. "Ilona, when you have lunch with Barni today, find out when the renovations will be finished so we can notify the furniture store."

"Yes Mother," I replied.

"We will wait for you and Barni for supper." As we parted she went to the station to take the train home.

I was so excited to meet Barni for lunch and tell him about our new furniture, but frightened to meet his co-workers for the first time. Walking the long walk to the office, suddenly Barni appeared at the door calling for me, and we walked in together. After the introductions we went for lunch. I was greatly disappointed that a woman named Magda, from the office, came with us.

In the restaurant, she quickly plunked herself next to Barni in the four-seat cubicle we were ushered to. I had no choice but to sit across from them. Magda and Barni carried on a conversation about work, just like I wasn't there. I tried to get eye contact with him to get his attention, but he was in another world - Magda's!

Granted, Barni was a handsome twenty-two years old with dark hair, big blue eyes, and a soft peachy complexion. Magda was about forty-five with bleached-blond hair. She wore bright red rouge to cover her freckled face, and a matching red nail polish on her chipped nails. Her tart appearance and her slang language really annoyed me. Several times I wanted to tell Barni about our new furniture, but Magda rudely cut me off. Analyzing my predicament, I realized that Barni was amused by her. Finally, my lunch from hell was over.

I still had my lingerie shopping to do, while waiting for Barni to finish work. After that we would go home together for supper as Mother was waiting for us. Just before we departed, Barni gave me a quick kiss on my forehead and said, "Ilona, I'm sorry that I can't take you home. I have to work late tonight, but I will see you tomorrow night."

They said goodbye and left. I was flabbergasted. I stood motionless in the middle of the sidewalk, watching as Magda slipped her arm in Barni's and they vanished around the corner. Suddenly I lost all interest in my lingerie shopping.

Taking the next train home, I tried to figure out this intimacy between Barni and Magda. It looked like more than co-workers to me, but Magda was old enough to be his mother, and we were getting married shortly. I couldn't believe what I had just seen. It appeared that just before our wedding Barni was having a love affair. My heart was torn between the humiliation and Barni's version of love for me. Would he do that to me? The thought would torment me for the rest of my life.

Racing home, I found only Grandmother was in the house. I wanted to pour my heart out, but I thought to myself, maybe I'm just jealous and immature.

"*Szervusz Nagymama!*" I greeted her.

"Come sit down dear. I will pour you a cup of tea and you can tell me all about your shopping." I described my furniture in detail. "I am so pleased that you are happy. You are happy, dear, aren't you?"

Pausing for a moment, thinking about Barni and Magda, I answered, "Yes *Nagymama,* I am happy."

"Show me the lingerie that you bought."

"*Nagymama,* I didn't feel up to lingerie shopping," I replied softly.

"How was your lunch with Barni?" she asked.

"It was fine *Nagymama,*" I answered as I walked out of the kitchen.

"Ilona, dear, come back here. You cannot hide your feelings from me. I know something is wrong. Please tell me."

"Nothing, nothing is wrong *Nagymama,*" and I closed the door behind me.

When my parents came home they wanted to discuss the guest list for the wedding, but still distraught about my lunch from hell, I had no desire to discuss my wedding. When Mother got carried away with the numbers, Father reminded her that we had to keep the guest list to a minimum because of the food shortage. They narrowed the list to about thirty guests. Father said that

Barni's parents would provide the music and liquor. We would supply the food and our house for the reception, plus the transportation for the wedding party, which included horses and carriages to *Szentkut's* church. Later Manci, Julika, and I discussed decorating the church. Everyone was so excited for me, but no one knew how I felt except my dear Grandmother.

The next evening, Barni arrived with shocking news: "The Communist government will give a good amount of money for young couples who are not getting married in church, just at City Hall. Isn't that wonderful?" he gleamed.

He seemed more interested in the money than the security of our marriage. We were shocked by this Communist bribery, and Grandmother said, "That's Communism for you. They will do anything to steer people away from God, especially the young generation. But that will be a sizable task for them, since most of us are Catholics, and very spiritual."

"But the money would help a young couple starting a new life," Barni said quietly.

"Not on your life Barni. It's a church wedding or no wedding. I'm not going to deceive God for money." At last my family agreed with me.

"Barni, do you agree with a church wedding?" Father asked.

"It is fine with me, Mr. Padar. I just thought we could have used the money."

"Barni, faith in God is more precious than money," Grandmother asserted firmly.

I was so proud of my grandmother; she was so kind and wise. She always knew how to say the right words at the right time. I wished Mother would inherit her vision. While Father and Barni discussed transferring our furniture to their house, Mother asked me about my lingerie.

"Mother I didn't buy any."

"But why not? I gave you money for it."

I hesitated for a moment, trying to think of a lie to cover up my heart-breaking lunch with Barni and Magda. Grandmother stared at me for a second, waiting for my answer. She quickly rescued me from a lie, by offering, "Ilona, next time when you go to your new place, please measure your windows and I will crochet some curtains for you."

"Oh, *Nagymama*, that is a lot of work for you."

"Just measure the windows dear, and I will do it for you with pleasure." By this time Mother gave up questioning me and got into a discussion with Father

138

and Barni. While they were talking, I kept looking at Barni with great disgust. I could hardly wait for him to leave, so we could be alone outside and I could question him about his relationship with Magda. Finally he said goodnight to my parents and I walked outside with him.

"Ilona, I am sorry that I didn't bring you home last night, but I had to work late."

"How late Barni? And who else was working with you?"

"Just Magda and I, " he answered nervously.

"Barni, what are your feelings for Magda? At lunch you gave her your undivided attention and you completely ignored me."

"Ilona, I have to be nice to her, since she is leaving the company and teaching me her job."

"So nice Barni that you had to brush your hand on her behind as we walked out of the restaurant. You can't deny it, Barni; I saw it."

Obviously defensive, he replied, "You are just imagining things."

"Barni, please don't insult me. She is old enough to be your mother. I wonder if her husband knows about her extra benefits at work."

"Just forget about Magda. She is divorced and leaving the company next week. And I love you!"

He wanted to kiss me, but I resisted. "Barni paying so much interest to a divorced woman, double your age, is not an honest way to show love to your fiancée." Without hesitation I turned and walked back into the house, and left him outside.

My heart was aching. I was glad Grandmother was asleep when I went in. I blew out the petroleum lamp and quietly went to bed, thinking about Barni's deceit and our marriage. To ease my broken heart I prayed for help: *"Dear Lord, help me not to rebel when the burdens of life weigh down upon me. I have to remember as Nagymama taught me that the great Burden-bearer walks beside me and understands it all. In His name I pray, Amen."*

Eventually, I cried myself to sleep.

CHAPTER 23

During Barni's next visit, when we were home alone, he declared, "Ilona you don't have to worry about Magda any more. She left the company yesterday, for good."

"Barni I wasn't worried about Magda, but I am worried about you. There are plenty of Magdas around. And how will you deal with the next one? Is it worth it to give up a lifetime of trust for a momentary pleasure? Is this the way to start a marriage?"

It looked like I hit a delicate nerve. He sprung up from his chair, seized his coffee mug, and walked to the window. He silently stared out for a long time...

"Barni, I insist on an explanation." Either he would admit his infidelity or he would lie about it. Either way, it was agonizing for me to deal with just before our wedding.

Still staring out the window, he whispered, "Yes, Ilona...it was wrong, not to bring you home."

He came to embrace me, but I turned away. I was hurt too deeply. We were alone, so I asked him to leave before someone came home. With tears rolling down my face, my heart pounding, I ran into the bedroom and locked the door. He tried to come in. From behind the locked door, he said, "Ilona, I am leaving as you wish, but I'll be back tomorrow. Don't forget I love you very much."

Mother came home. I heard her question, "Barni, where is Ilona?"

"She is in the bedroom."

"What's wrong with her?" Mother asked curiously.

"I hurt her feelings!" he said.

"Don't worry Barni; she'll get over it."

"Mrs. Padar, please don't badger her," Barni pleaded with Mother. "I have to go now. See you tomorrow."

Mother immediately pounded on the door. "Ilona open this door instantly. I want to talk to you. Why are you acting like a fool locking Barni out?"

I unlocked the door and Mother barged in.

"What's wrong with you? I want to know right now," Mother demanded. I told her the whole story about Barni and Magda. I thought for a moment that she understood my pain, but in a split second she was furious with me. "Ilona, you are just imagining things. I don't believe a word that you are saying about

Barni and Magda." She paused again and with a strong conviction, she harshly said, "He is marrying you, isn't he? That is good enough for me!"

"But Mother, this is not about you. This is about Barni's honesty and faithfulness toward our marriage and life together."

"Ilona, you're making a big thing about it. Just ignore it!" and she nonchalantly left the room.

I was infuriated with Mother's attitude toward my situation with Barni. Sobbing with rage, I felt like the forces of good and evil were having a tug-of-war in my mind, tearing me apart. Deeply distraught with closed eyes, suddenly the crossroad cross became so real in front of me, I reached out to touch it. Then Grandmother walked in and asked, "Ilona, what are you reaching for in front of you. There is nothing there!" As I opened my eyes I realized it was only a vision, but its vividness troubled me. Then Grandmother rushed to me and cuddled me in her arms saying, "Your mother told me about your accusation of Barni's affair."

"Grandmother, it is not an accusation. It is true."

"I believe every word of it darling. You have the right to be hurt and angry with him. This is a cruel thing to do, just before your wedding. I just wonder how much you can take."

"*Nagymama,* I have to go to the cross. It is drawing me there. I just have to go!" And I rushed out of the house.

Once at the cross I was on my knees praying and pleading for guidance. Is this life of mine worth living? The future holds nothing for me. I closed my tearful eyes and suddenly a Bible verse struck my mind: *"I have set before you life and death... So choose life."* Reciting this verse in my mind, I dozed off . . .

Later, the cool October evening breeze gently awakened me. I felt calm and peaceful within. On my way home I kept reciting the last part of the Bible verse over and over: *So choose life.* Grandmother was happy for my peaceful return. For Mother, my return made no difference.

Next morning, I went to Kisterenye for the fitting of my wedding dress. After that I stood in line for sugar and flour for the wedding cake. In our destitute Communist country, waiting in line brought out the inhumanity in us. There was pushing and shoving in line, because if you were at the back of the line or came late, you would just have to do without sugar or flour, regardless of how badly you needed it. Complaining was forbidden. Fortunately, after two hours in line I got some flour and sugar.

On my long walk home, I thought about how to treat Barni the next time I saw him. I had to let him know that I was not a fool, and that I was still deeply hurt about his actions. While approaching the house, Julika came from the well with a pail of water and informed me that Barni was in the house waiting for me with a surprise. I had hardly put my parcels down, when he handed me two red, long-stemmed roses with white baby's breath, saying, "Ilona let's walk to the meadow. I want to talk to you."

"I will have coffee and tea ready for you two," Mother said.

Barni clasped his strong hand over mine and dragged me out of the house. In the meadow he clutched me in his arms and whispered, "Ilona dear, I am sorry that I hurt you. I promise it will never happen again. Please forgive me."

"Barni, I can't. The anguish you caused me is unforgivable. Put yourself in my position; could you forgive that easily?" Abruptly he said, "Let's go home." And we reached home in silence.

At home, while having refreshments, Barni sadly let us know that the renovations wouldn't be ready before the wedding, because the windows were back-ordered. But they had purchased the liquor and hired the Gypsy band. Also his mother and grandmother would come early on the wedding day to help with the cooking. My father had hired two landau and three carriages. Mother said since we would have to empty our house for the reception, Aunty Margit next door had offered her house as a dressing room and sleeping quarters for long distance relatives. At that statement, Barni looked at me curiously. I was afraid he would ask where we would sleep. Even just his look and the thought of sleeping together made me blush; Mother had always forbidden any discussion about sex. After reviewing our wedding plans, Barni had to leave. Outside he seized me and held me tight saying, "Only a few more days and I can keep you with me all night."

"Barni let go of me. You are suffocating me."

"Sorry, but I was thinking of our honeymoon night. I'm so excited. How about you?"

I ignored his question. I doubted if he realized how terrified I was. He kissed me and he left. I walked into the house to an instant silence. My parents and grandmother just stared at me. Curiously I asked, "What's wrong?"

Finally Grandmother said, "Let me handle this Mari. Let me handle it."

She handed me a cup of tea and said, "Ilona come with me. We have something to discuss." And she closed the door behind us. "Ilona, since your place in Kisterenye won't be ready until after the wedding, we will organize the attic for you and Barni to sleep there." While saying this to me, she was looking down at her shoes. I almost said we could wait to sleep together until our place was finished, but quickly changed my mind remembering the advice in the book on *Sex and Marriage,* and I agreed with Grandmother. Then she said, "I will help you clear the stuff from the floor, take the cobwebs from the ceiling and put the mattress down. Do you have any questions dear?" I had lots, but I was too bashful to ask and just ignored her question.

"Are you still reading your book?"

"Yes, *Nagymama.*"

We said our prayer at the table and we went to our bed. I was still wide-awake thinking about my first night sleeping with Barni. All of a sudden, the recollection of Mrs. Szabo and her daughter's rape, the savage look in the Russian soldier's eyes when he tried to rip me out of my mother's arms, and Barni's forceful behavior in the garden terrified me. But I firmly believed I had to do whatever it took to get away from my mother's control. I wanted to be free to live my life. Free to make my own choices.

CHAPTER 24

On my wedding day, in 1952, I pledged to a lifetime commitment. I was free from my mother's control, but had to face Barni's. Hoping, with our marriage he would change, I prayed and recited, my favorite Bible verse: *Let not your heart be troubled, neither let it be afraid.* With this recitation I gained encouragement and strength to face my wedding day.

In the morning, I met some of my relations from different cities, which I had not seen for a long time. Soon, I had to leave them to get ready for my civil marriage in Matraverebely City Hall. I dressed at Aunty Margit's house in my elegant navy suit, off-white blouse, and shoes. Barni looked handsome in his light gray suit, waiting for me in the carriage with Father, who had to sign the marriage certificate. Our driver sat higher up in the driver's seat, waiting to lead his two black horses. The civil marriage was short, but I had to visit with friends, who had taken the time to come and wish us all the best for our big day. Shortly afterwards, we were home.

Grandmother caringly wanted me to eat something, but this time I wasn't hungry. She always looked after me with such loving care.

First, Barni changed and then he went to our house to welcome guests. Later my future mother-in-law came and brought me her famous cottage cheese pastry that I loved so much. Godmother helped me to dress, and secured my headpiece and veil, which I positioned on my head. She stepped back and said, "Oh, Ilona you look beautiful, in your white dress, with the white veil on your head." Then, she asked inquisitively, "Ilona, do you know what the white gown and the white veil mean on a bride?"

"Yes, *Keresztmama,* purity and innocence as Grandmother has taught me."

She gave me a sincere hug and wished me all the best for my future. Grandmother came in and said, "Please Julia I would like to talk to Ilona alone."

"Of course Aunty Rozi," and she left the room.

Grandmother pulled up a chair facing me and clasped my hands with hers in the praying position. She asked God's blessing for my marriage, then she advised me, "Ilona dear, you can't go into this marriage angry at Barni for his disloyalty. You have to forgive him in your heart, before you go to church."

"*Nagymama,* I have a hard time. It hurts so much. No one can feel my pain, not even you."

"Barni loves you, in his own peculiar way," she said.

"But, *Nagymama*, that is what frightens me: his *peculiar* ways!"

"I hope you can work that out with him, when you two are married, because your mother won't be there to interfere."

"*Nagymama*, I try to forgive him, but my jealous, rebellious teenage mind wants revenge."

"Ilona, we are waiting for you in the carriage," Manci called.

"I am coming." Grandmother helped me carry my veil to the carriage, where my wedding party was waiting.

Walking down the aisle in my familiar church, I felt rather unfamiliar. Instead of sitting in the corner of it, I was in the center of it. Even the church was different, or my situation made it so. Glancing at Grandmother, she gave me that assuring look and her affirmative smile that I had remembered since childhood. I picked up my head, focused my eyes on the cross above the altar, and I was transformed into tranquility. The pipe organ played my favorite hymn, and with a smile I reached my waiting groom at the altar. He touched my hand and whispered, "You look beautiful."

Father Feher conducted a divine ceremony and the main point he delivered was *the pillar of a marriage is honesty, loyalty, and respect for each other.* He was very convincing with his soft, clear voice, especially when he gave us his blessing.

While riding home with Barni, he said, "Now it is legal, Ilona. You are mine," and he pulled me closer. He alarmed me with his possessive assertions.

As we arrived, the Gypsy band played the violin solo of the famous Hungarian love song, *Csak Egy Kislany van a Vilagon* (There is Only One Girl in the World). Our guests cheered for us as we strolled to the head table. The celebration dinner was a success, with Hungarian chicken paprikas and other trimmings made under the supervision of our grandmothers. After dinner we started dancing to our favorite song, the *Blue Danube Waltz*. Barni commented, "Ilona, I remember not long ago dancing awkwardly to the same waltz with you, as a bashful fourteen-year-old in dancing school. And now you are my wife. You see, I always get what I want." His statement stung me, but the exquisite sound of the violin mellowed the hurt.

At midnight, I changed from my wedding dress to a red and white polka dot dress, and danced the traditional Hungarian *Menyaszony Tanc* (Bride's dance), that is dancing for money. Everyone asks the bride for a short dance, and puts some money in the collection basket. After about half an hour of dancing the fast *csardas* (because everyone knows how to dance the *csardas*), with all ages and genders, I was ready to sit down. This midnight dance is the highlight of a Hungarian wedding. After this dance most of the guests leave.

Our two families were enjoying each other's company, singing and laughing together. After finishing a *csardas* with my new father-in-law, Barni took me for a slow tango and commented, "You look so lovely in your red and white polka dot dress." Quickly he held me tight and claimed, "And now you are my wife." He stopped dancing and kissed me, whispering that we should leave shortly. Our guests were cheering him on for more kissing; I had to fight my way out of his arms.

Laci our neighbor called, "Ilona, you look beautiful when you blush. Your face matches the color of your dress." Barni led me to our table, and poured me a full glass of wine and toasted to our happiness, which everyone joined in on. Then he wanted me to drink the whole glass of wine, which is customary at cheering time. Still a teenager, I wasn't used to drinking alcohol and I refused to drink the whole glass. Shortly after, he said it again, "Already two a.m., we should leave."

"Soon, Barni, soon. I have to talk to Grandmother before we leave." I went to search for Grandmother and we had a private moment together. She gently hugged me saying, "Everything will be fine dear, everything will be fine. While you were dancing, your father had a talk with Barni." Then, without any eye contact, she quickly walked away when I needed her the most. I was frightened to face the initial part of my marriage. I had to go outside, to be alone for a moment, reassuring myself that everything would be fine. "Barni is my husband now; he won't hurt me," I tried to convince myself. I'm glad that I had read the book on sex and marriage, even though the intimacy was still to be discovered.

It was very sad that under Communism we had to give up our dreams for an elegant hotel suite for our honeymoon. Yet, most of us had to give it up for survival. I was startled to find Barni suddenly behind me. He grabbed me by my hand, led me up to the attic - our "honeymoon suite" - and locked the door behind us. In the candle-lit, small, attic room, he poured us a glass of wine, to toast our new beginning. We gazed into each other's eyes, mesmerized by the flickering candlelight, exchanging passionate kisses, while the violin softly echoed from downstairs on our honeymoon night.

CHAPTER 25

Awoken by some unusual racket, I had to think for a second where I was. I was up in the attic, lying on the mattress covered only by a sheet, and held by Barni's heavy arm, while he was sleeping. I realized the disturbance came from downstairs as the furniture was moved back in place after our wedding day. I had mixed feelings: free from my mother, but straight into Barni's web. I tried to free myself from his arm without waking him, when he yelled, "Ilona, where are you going?" grasping me tighter.

"Barni, Grandmother is calling me," I answered, and quickly fought my way out of his arms. I dressed in a hurry and sneaked downstairs, straight into the tool shed, hoping no one would see me. I felt bashful about sleeping with Barni, maybe because of my upbringing about sex, or maybe because I hadn't married the right man. I don't know exactly why, I just had this unusual, hurt, shameful feeling. Alone in the tool shed, behind closed doors, sitting on the big boulder - the same one I had struggled to move so I could steal a piece of ham as a young child - and I realized I'm a woman now. There came a gentle knock on the door, "Ilona this is *Nagymama*. May I come in?" she pleaded with her gentle voice.

"Yes, yes," and I jumped to the door to welcome her. "How did you know I needed to talk to you?"

"I saw you sneaking to the shed and wondered why."

"*Nagymama*, I need a bucket of water, and don't ask me why."

"All right dear. I'll bring it for you right now." Shortly Grandmother returned with a bucket of warm water saying, "Here you are dear. I brought you soap and a washcloth too. When you are finished just come in the house and I will empty the bucket for you."

"No! You can't!"

"Why not, dear? Your husband is waiting for you inside, to have breakfast with you."

"*Nagymama*, I have to wash this." I had tried to hide the soiled sheet behind me, while Grandmother hesitated to leave.

"Ilona, just put it in to the bucket and I will wash it for you."

"No, no, no you can't. I won't let you. Just go and tell Barni I will be there shortly," and I pushed her out the door.

When I came into the kitchen Barni asked, "Ilona, I looked out a few minutes ago and you were coming from behind the shed. What were you doing out there?"

"Just talking to Ilcsa," I answered.

By later in the day, with the help of our friends, the house was put back in order. Since we had no refrigerator, our helpers had to take home some of the left over food, which they cherished in our starving country.

The next day, Barni and I went to Kisterenye to help with the renovation of our house. When the windows were installed my mother-in-law helped me finish painting the bedroom. I could hardly wait for *Apu* and Barni to install our stove. When we lit the fire, even without any furniture, the warmth made the house cozier. Later *Anyu* and I finished painting the kitchen.

Barni's family welcomed me, especially his mother. She and I had connected since our first visit. *Anyu* asked, "Ilona do you mind if we will call you Ica. It is shorter and a nick name for Ilona."

"Of course not *Anyu*. On the contrary I like it." I called Barni's parents as he called them: Mother *Anyu*, Father *Apu*, and Barni called my parents as I called them: Mother *Anyuka*, Father *Apuka*.

We ate dinner with my in-laws, and *Anyu* said, "Ica, since your furniture is arriving early in the morning, why don't you two sleep downstairs in your home. I have an extra mattress for you."

Before I could answer, Barni exclaimed, "Excellent idea, *Anyu*. You just saved us from the long trip back to Kanyas."

It was a strange feeling for me, being alone in our new home with Barni. In fact, I felt uneasy in my new surroundings. We had electricity in the house for light. We also had a light in the yard, which I appreciated while going to the outhouse in the dark in my new setting.

The next day, we were overwhelmed as our furniture arrived. Barni and his family approved, and we arranged it tastefully. Barni's youngest brother, Istvan, said, "*Angyi*, (Aunty), I like this furniture the best," while he sprawled cozily on the settle, (the laundry chest) beside the warm stove. It was the first time I had been called Aunty. It felt good. I felt so mature.

I assured him, "Istvan, from now on that is your place."

He said, "Thank you, *Angyi*." And so our sincere friendship began.

The next thing we brought over was my personal belongings, dishes, and linen from Kanyas. It was a pleasure to set up our home with the new furniture and the beautiful carpets my dear *nagymama* had woven for me. I was finally settled in my new surroundings, but I already missed my beloved grandmother. Nevertheless, I was happy to be away from my mother's domination.

Now that I was married, instantly I wanted a baby of my own to love. But my mother-in-law said for a baby, I had to have patience. She was a very understanding, pleasant lady. We became good friends, especially after her mother passed away. She asked me to help her with the cooking and we would eat supper together. I was willing to help, because she still had to cook for the seven of them. She really appreciated my help since just bringing water to the house was a chore, carrying buckets from the fourth neighbor down the road.

One day, after picking peas in the garden and shelling them on the veranda, she told me about her life raising seven children and burying two at a very young age. She had lived a hard life. However difficult a life she had, she remained a calm, intelligent, ethical person. But she was bold enough to stand up to the belligerent attitude of my father-in-law. Also, she always protected me from Barni's manipulations, by saying to him, "Barni, Ica is your wife, and partner, not your slave, and I want you to respect her!"

I really believe that she was a blessing in my life. And I firmly believe that my God was always with me, sending me "mentors" like my dear grandmother, and now my mother-in-law.

I was happy with my newfound love for *Anyu*, and relieved to be away from my mother, but I was sad in my marriage. So often I thought and dreamed about Janos. I'm sure my life would have been more contented with him and my honeymoon would have been more pleasurable. I'm sure that was why I wished so desperately to get pregnant, so I could have a little boy of my own to love. As Grandmother always said, "We were created to love and be loved," and I was yearning for both. Yes, a little boy would be wonderful, since we had five females in our six-member family. My dear mother-in-law assured me that it would happen; I just had to be patient.

A couple of months later, Barni got an office job with better pay at Kanyas' mine office. It was closer, but he still had to take the train at Nagybatony to come home to Kisterenye. When he worked overtime, he would come home late. This situation bothered me deeply after the episode with Magda.

One day, *Anyu* stayed up with me waiting for him, while we embroidered and crocheted. I was watching the clock, getting angrier by the minute. She tried to distract me by telling me stories, but deep in our hearts we knew it was not working. We listened as the midnight train went by, predicting he would be home in twenty minutes, but no Barni. Finally at one in the morning he staggered in greatly intoxicated. I was furious.

"Barni, how come you are late and tipsy? Where were you? And with whom?" I was waiting for *Anyu* to say something, but she let me handle it.

"Don't worry about it Ilona," he muttered. "I am tired and I don't want to be grilled." He went to bed with his clothes on.

I broke down and wept. *Anyu* tried to cheer me up, but it was useless. She told me that she had to cope with hard times at the beginning of her marriage. I asked, "And then what happened?"

"Ica, I got fed up with it. I could not tolerate it any more. I was under stress. I was with one baby after another. I got assertive and firm and slowly the situation improved." She didn't tell me what to do, but I got the message.

Anyu left and I went into the bedroom to talk to Barni, but he was in a deep sleep. Angry and hurt, my hope in my marriage started to fade. I curled up on the single bunk bed in the kitchen and thought about *Anyu's* advice on how to confront Barni in the morning. For a newlywed I felt lonely, sad, unloved, and hurt. I kept asking the questions, "Why was life so cruel to me? Why was I continually tormented?" I asked my Creator, "Would I ever be happy deep in my heart?" Eventually, I sobbed myself to sleep in the early hours of the morning.

"Ica, Ica wake up. I'm late. I want some breakfast before I go to work."

While preparing the food, I questioned Barni, "What happened with you last night?"

"Oh, we went to the bar for a quick drink, and I missed the train."

"Who was with you?" I asked.

"The five of us co-workers," he replied.

"Barni, the three of you guys are married; the two girls are single. Do you think it is right to go drinking with single girls in the bar, until the early hour of the morning?"

"Nothing wrong with it. You are just jealous."

"Maybe Barni, but I am not a fool either. Do you remember the episode with Magda and what you promised? You said you would never hurt me that way again." There was silence. Remorsefully he came to hug me, but I was too hurt to let him near me. I was glad that he left before my tears flooded my eyes and ran rivers down my face. I thought, "I have to be strong like *Anyu*."

The following weekend my sister-in-law got married. It was a small civil wedding, with just the immediate family. The following day she moved in to her mother-in-law's big house.

Now there was just *Anyu* alone with six people to do the laundry and cook for. I could have had an easier life just to cook for the two of us, but I loved her dearly and was willing to help her. In the meantime, I learned a lot from her and we became more than just in-laws; we became more like mother and daughter. This was a completely different life for me, especially on the weekend. While we were cooking, it was a pleasure hearing the boys screaming and cheering as they played soccer in the backyard. The boys had great respect for their mother and me.

When we were alone, I continually questioned my mother-in-law about pregnancy. How does it feel to be pregnant? How long was she married before she got pregnant? She just smiled at me and said, "Don't focus on it so much dear, and it will happen."

"*Anyu*, what does it feel like to bear a child? Please explain it to me."

"Ica, I won't, because it is a different experience for each woman. Just wait patiently dear. It will happen sooner than you think." We had to close our conversation since some of the boys had come in.

After supper, while we were doing the dishes, *Apu* and the boys chopped wood, filled up the big wooden barrel outside with water, and picked some potatoes and berries for the next day. In the meantime, *Anyu* told me that she had a good heart-to-heart talk with Barni, about coming home late and intoxicated.

"Ica, I don't know how long my good influence will last. Barni is now twenty-three and at that age they don't want their mother telling them what to do. They want to live their own life regardless. It was easier with his older brother. Barni is more difficult, so much like his father when he was younger."

When the dishes were finished, *Anyu* gave some money to Barni and told him, "Barni take your wife to the movies tonight. I heard they are playing a love story." She winked at me with a smile, and I winked back with a big grin.

CHAPTER 26

The movie was a very affectionate love story, which showed that true love has no boundaries. And oh, how I hoped and dreamed for that in my life. Awakened by the alarm clock, my dream vanished.

After Barni left for work *Anyu* called, "Ica, don't forget today is Friday and you have to go for bread."

"Yes, *Anyu,* I will be up shortly."

I despised Mondays, Wednesdays, and Fridays for I had to stand for hours in a long line for bread. But, it was in the line-up that I could catch up on local and other news. At home, my mother-in-law forbade the family to discuss politics. She was very much afraid of any accusation against her six boys and my father-in-law, who had a good job at the railway's mail and baggage department. In the forties and fifties that was an important job, because most of the transportation was via train.

As we were standing in line, the usual, nasal-toned grievances started. "Isn't this disgusting. We have to stand in line, almost begging for food, while we supply Russia by the trainloads," said a gray-haired man wearing a torn, green jacket. "Thanks to the Stalinist Rakosi, who holds the top posts in both the party and the state, and who imposed collectivized farming and an agenda of heavy industry, we now live in economic misery," added a young man who had four children. "I have a hard time feeding my children; I despise this Communist system," he continued while shaking his cracked fist with rage. By this time, the crowd had become louder and more involved. Suddenly, the town's mayor showed up from nowhere. Instantly there was dead silence. He stood in line with us, but not for bread since he had that delivered. He just wanted to show his Communist authority, silencing the crowd with his accusing, searching eyes. Fortunately, the store opened and we charged in.

It had been an intense morning, and it was almost noon by the time I got home with two loaves of bread. *Anyu* was finished shredding the cabbage for the noodles that we still had to make. Making our own noodles for eight people was a tiresome and time-consuming task, but necessary since it was difficult to satisfy our youthful hunger without protein, such as meat.

I described to *Anyu* the political conversation from the bread line, wondering what her response would be. But, she said not a word. She didn't

152

express her opinion for or against Communism. I was still waiting. "*Anyu* you have nothing to say?"

"Yes dear. Let's focus on making the noodles, because my hungry boys will be home shortly." I realized she didn't want to voice her opinion, which might jeopardize the future of her boys.

After dinner, *Apu* was raging about what he saw at our borders on his shift work: box cars lined up with our barley, wheat, corn, and coal being shipped to Russia. Barni replied, "Those Communist bastards."

I started blurting out the store incident, when *Anyu* gave me that *keep quiet* look. The older boys wanted to get involved, but *Anyu* put an instant stop to it saying, "We can't do anything about it, so learn to tolerate it silently." She sent the boys to get water and chop some wood. When they had departed my father-in-law got the lecture of his life.

Barni changed the subject by saying, "Ilona, your mother asked if we could help them next weekend to harvest their barley. Your father, Uncle Pali, and I will scythe; *Anyuka*, Manci, and you can bundle the forage. My guess is it will take about two days."

"We would have to stay in Kanyas for the weekend." This time I wasn't excited about the harvest like when I was a child. It was hard work under the hot, summer sun, continually doubled over to pick and tie up the forage. Later, we would have to take the forage to another town for threshing. For the threshing the government retained 50% of our seeds, which infuriated us even more.

The next day, *Anyu* asked me to help her hill the potatoes early in the day to beat the heat. Around noon, *Apu* came home from work and called us for lunch. Coming from the garden, *Anyu* gathered a few eggs from the chicken coop and I picked up an armful of wood for cooking supper. *Apu* was busy in the kitchen making sandwiches for us from a big garlic sausage, which looked and smelled mouth-watering.

"Jani where did you get that big sausage? Meat is almost impossible to get," *Anyu* asked my father-in-law curiously.

"Never mind that Margit, just come and eat before the boys come home and make the whole thing disappear." Then he handed each of us a sandwich.

"I haven't eaten cold cuts for a long time. How about you Ica?"

"*Anyu*, never mind eating some, I haven't even seen any cold cuts for a long while."

"This sausage has an unusual taste," I said. *Anyu* nodded in agreement.

We looked at *Apu* for some explanation, but he just smiled and said, "Don't complain. Just eat what you get." Just when I swallowed the last morsel of that unusual tasting sausage, my father-in-law looked at us with a snickering smile, (at that moment he reminded me of my godfather) and cried out, "What you just ate was horsemeat!" And he roared with laughter, enjoying the distorted expressions on our faces.

The vision that sprung to my mind was the putrid odor of the half-decomposed horse, eaten by rodents and birds that we found as children during the war. I felt nauseated. The horsemeat upset my stomach and rose in my throat, choking me. I had to run outside and vomit. Still feeling nauseated, I went downstairs and lay down.

Later, *Anyu* came with a pot of chamomile tea to settle my stomach and asked me not to say anything to the boys about the sausage, because that's what they would be having for supper with the cabbage noodles. Assuring her with a nod, I just stayed in bed. Barni awakened me whispering, "Mother told me you are not feeling well. You must have a touch of flu. Can I get you anything?"

"Yes Barni, a glass of soda water."

After supper with his family, he came home and later crawled in beside me.

The next morning, feeling fine, I made cornmeal for breakfast drizzled with my mother's honey. *Anyu* brought a sausage sandwich for Barni to take for lunch. He thanked his mother for the delicious sandwich, gave her a hug, and left for work.

Just the thought of the sandwich turned my stomach and I had to vomit again. Now I was sure that I had food poisoning from the horse sausage. I decided to see the doctor without alarming the family. I told *Anyu* that I was going for some groceries and asked her if she needed anything from the store. Lucky for me there was only one person waiting in Dr. Nadasdi's office.

As I was ushered in he said, "Hello, Ilona. It's so nice to see you. I will never forget that I gave up on you when you were a baby. You were so malnourished and weak; it was amazing that you survived. The higher power showed to me that even us doctors could be wrong. I heard that you got married and moved here to Kisterenye."

"And now, how can I help you?" he asked.

I told him all about my problem with the horse sausage and that I was worried about food poisoning. Following my examination and questioning, he had a smile on his face as he reached for my hand, and said, "Ilona you can be sure that you have no food poisoning," and he patted my hand.

"Then what's wrong with me?"

"Ilona, you are going to have a baby. You will be a mother!"

I was so excited by the news that I got carried away and gave him a big hug. After our discussion about my pregnancy, we shook hands, and I joyfully flew out of his office. On my way home, I made a detour to the park and found a quiet place under the old pine tree. And I prayed gratefully for my baby boy, who I wanted so desperately. What a wonderful feeling it was to become a mother. Sitting there in silence I knew my baby would be a little boy, and the name Attila flashed into my mind, while the gentle breeze wafted the fragrance of the jasmine bush softly in my face. I felt completely tranquil and at peace with my Creator. I wished life could be like that all the time. But unfortunately it was not. Suddenly back came reality. I got up, brushed the pine needles off my skirt, and rushed home. I decided that night I would have dinner at home, alone with Barni, and tell him the delightful news.

I spent all afternoon cooking vegetable soup and cottage cheese noodles. I set the table, and put some candles and flowers on for a centerpiece. Just as I finished changing my clothes Barni walked in.

"Company is coming?" he asked.

"Yes, Barni," I replied.

"Who is coming?" he asked again.

I motioned him to sit down. "Your little boy Attila," and I put his hand on my abdomen.

He yelled, "I'm going to be a father!" He seized my hand and we ran upstairs to share the news with the rest of the family. Our announcement overjoyed everyone. Later we settled in bed. I gave Barni the book *Sex and Marriage* to read, and I immersed myself in the book Dr. Nadasdi gave me titled *Pregnancy and Childbirth*.

CHAPTER 27

I surrendered to my repulsive morning sickness, but I remembered the reward from God: the gift of my baby as a blessing. I could hardly wait to go home to Kanyas and share my blessing with my family, especially with my grandmother.

On my way to the well for water, I kept thinking about going to my beloved church in *Szentkut* with my baby, to worship God and pray for our well-being. When I reached the well I met Boriska, a blond, stocky, blue-eyed, young mother with her two-year-old little girl, Martika, who was the very image of her mother. Since I was new in the neighborhood, she invited me to her house for coffee. I accepted her invitation with excitement, thinking I could ask her all about pregnancy and childbirth.

Rushing home, I quickly put the buckets of water down to catch my breath. I told my mother in-law about Boriska and her invitation for coffee. There was a very long silence . . . I couldn't wait any longer, so I asked, "*Anyu* did you hear me telling you about the neighbor woman."

"Yes, Ica," and she came and sat beside me and continued, "I know you need a friend your age. I don't tell you whom you can or cannot choose, but Boriska is one I would not recommend."

"But why, *Anyu*? She seems so nice."

"She is nice, but her in-laws and her husband are very devoted Communists. You will have to be on alert all the time with them about what you say, especially about Barni's early dismissal from the military. For that reason, I strictly discourage your friendship with her."

"*Anyu*, I understand your point, if they are so prone to Communism. I better stay away from her. I can find some other friends."

"Ica, there's another thing I wanted to talk to you about, dear. I will miss your help with my cooking, but now you are expecting. You have to concentrate on your health with your own cooking."

"You know, *Anyu*, that is what Dr. Nadasdi advised me to do, because I still have an iron deficiency. He thinks it is diet related. He gave me a diet sheet to follow, if I can with our meat, milk, and cheese shortage. I'm worried about it, especially when I don't feel well."

"Not to worry dear, just try to follow your diet, and you will have a healthy little boy, just as you wish."

I was excited to be going home to Kanyas to tell my family about my baby. I wanted to shout to the whole world about my happiness. After supper, I packed for the two days we planned to harvest in Kanyas. We were up at five a.m. to catch the six a.m. train. While Barni was doing his routine shaving, I was doing my routine vomiting. As awful as it was, I was glad it happened at home, instead of on the train.

On the train I counted the minutes until we would reach our destination. I raced into the house with Barni lagging behind. Fortunately everyone was in the kitchen having breakfast. Grandmother said, "Sit down you two." She dished out some cream of wheat for us, and asked, "Ilona are you sick dear? You look so pale?"

"I am not sick, *Nagymama*." Hesitating for a moment, somehow I felt somewhat self-conscious in front of my family, especially Julika, because pregnancy involved sex. Barni could not wait and yelled, "Ilona, if you won't tell them right now, I will."

Finally, with great excitement, I blurted out, "I am going to have a baby! A little boy, and his name will be Attila." My announcement filled the house with excitement. Hugs and kisses were exchanged. I was overjoyed. Grandmother got up from the table and limped into the other room. I wondered, "Why?"

Father stated, "The name 'Attila' sounds very proper for my grandson," as he smiled at me with teary eyes. Julika was ecstatic and offered her babysitting services for free.

Manci asked, "Please, can I be his godmother, Ilona?"

"Of course Manci! I was just waiting to ask you."

Grandmother came back with a box in her hands. When she opened it, I was speechless. "This is for Attila's christening," she said. She pulled out a gorgeous, white, crocheted blanket with blue, satin ribbon woven around the edges, and a beautiful light blue outfit with a little bonnet and booties to match.

"*Nagymama*, why did you pick blue yarn?"

"Because I am praying for a little boy. I know that is what you want."

"*Nagymama*, you are God sent to me. Truly, I believe that."

We embraced and wept, while she whispered in my ear, "I miss you so much."

Barni called that they were going to the field to harvest the oats. Grandmother suggested that I shouldn't be doing that strenuous bending over, all day, in the summer heat.

"*Nagymama*, I am only sick in the mornings for a short while. I am fine."

"Not according to Dr. Nadasdi." Grandmother insisted.

Mother shrugged her shoulder, and said, "Regardless, I still want you out on the field. You are only pregnant, not crippled."

"You know what Mother, you are right. Thank God I'm pregnant and not crippled. I'll be there Mother; I'll be there to help you." She looked at me with a stunned face. Regardless of how much resentment I held against her, my heart was overflowing with happiness and I couldn't say no.

We worked hard and perspired in the heat of the summer day. Before supper, I wanted to go to the creek to cool off, so Barni came with me, bringing towels and soap. While sitting on the rock dangling our feet in the cool, fast-moving water, I showed him the exact spot where I nearly drowned in the rapid-moving current, with Julika in my arms, many years ago.

"I am glad that you were saved for me, and for our baby," he replied.

After cooling off and washing, I felt better and refreshed. Upon our arrival, supper was served. We had noodles with rabbit paprikas, cucumber salad, and watermelon for dessert. We had only one rabbit to share amongst the seven of us. Mother dished out one piece for each of us, but I was surprised that I had two pieces on my plate. Shocked at Mother's change of heart I said, "Thank you *Anyuka*."

"What for?" she replied. When she glanced over and saw me pointing at my plate, she said, "Don't thank me. I didn't give you the second piece."

Scanning the plates, I noticed everyone had one, except Grandmother. "*Nagymama*, you have to eat yours," and I put the piece of meat back on her plate.

"No, dear, I can't eat it. My stomach just doesn't feel right." I knew for sure she was fibbing. She put the meat back gently on my plate and said, "You need it, being anemic and pregnant."

"If neither of you want it, I'll take it." And with that remark, Barni quickly forked the meat off my plate and into his mouth. For a second, I thought Grandmother would stab him with her fork. She held her breath, rolled her eyes, and puckered her lips. There was absolute silence. Everyone was staring at Barni, but he just laughed it off as a joke. Everyone was shocked; even Mother's face twitched as she stared at him. That sight shocked me even more.

After supper, Father and Barni were sharpening their scythes, while the rest of the family cleaned up the kitchen. I wanted to be alone. Soon I was on the bike pedaling to the crossroad. Arriving there, to my amazement there was a bunch of flowers at the foot of the cross. I wondered who was sharing my cross. I thought it may be just some travelers who needed peace and a resting place, or perhaps it was a seeking soul like me. Since very early childhood, I had come to the cross to pray for peace, comfort, and tranquility. While immersed in prayer, braiding a wild-flower wreath for my cross, suddenly I became aware of someone moaning and heavy breathing.

I jumped up and hid behind a bush. I waited silently. The moaning came closer. Finally, a ragged, old, hunched-back, gray-haired woman appeared at the top of the hill. Exhausted from climbing, she oozed to the ground. Worried about her condition, I ran to her and asked, "Can I help you?"

She was so startled by my appearance, I thought her heart would stop right then. As I slid my left arm under her head she whispered, "Who are you - who are you? I didn't steal anything, I didn't steal anything, I swear."

I supported her head gently and said, " I know you didn't steal. I am here to help you." She opened her murky, black eyes and looked deeply into mine, and somehow she was convinced that she was safe in my arms. She softly asked me again who I was. I told her very little about myself. I wanted to know more about her.

Eventually she told me, "I'm a Gypsy, and they call me 'Borzos' because of my curly hair. I live in Matraverebely with the Gypsy tribe, and I came here to the cross to pray for my son, who was just arrested, accused of stealing a horse. Which he didn't do. But no one listens to or believes a Gypsy."

"But Borzos how can you be so sure he didn't do it?"

"*Kisaszony* (young-lady), I know. I am his mother. You will know too, when you have a child of your own. *Kisaszony*, do you have any water? I am extremely thirsty."

"No water, but I have an apple." I cracked it in half to share it with her.

She was so grateful for the few bites of apple that she insisted on telling my fortune by reading my palms. She stared at my palms silently, and then looked deep into my eyes, repeating this several times. She gently dropped my hands, and said, "You are going to have a tragic life, *Kisaszony*, a tragic life. That is all I will tell you."

"What? What? Tell me more."

She got up and started to walk away, then turned back and thanked me for my help and kindness. She hesitated for a moment before saying, "*Kisaszony*, your husband will deceive and mistreat you, and your marriage will result in divorce. That is all I'm telling you. May God bless; you will need it in your troubled life. I will pray for you." Then she vanished down the hillside. I was left standing there completely astounded.

Rushing home, I found Grandmother in the garden. I told her about my encounter with the Gypsy woman. To my amazement, she was calm about Borzos' predictions.

"I don't believe in the predictions of a Gypsy, but if it happens I won't be surprised. Barni's attitude and behavior is unacceptable. Just like tonight when he grabbed the meat from your plate. Sometimes I wonder . . . maybe he should be committed."

"*Nagymama*, I realize that, but he will change when the baby is born."

"I hope so dear, I hope so," she said sadly. "Now, darling, come and eat. I steamed some vegetables for your baby," and we exchanged a sincere smile. "Now just forget about the Gypsy's prediction and go to bed."

In bed, I told Barni about the prediction, but he just laughed it off as usual. Before I fell asleep I prayed for the Gypsy woman and her son, hoping that justice would prevail. She had said that she would pray for me, and I needed to return the favor.

CHAPTER 28

Monday morning, Barni went to work and I went back home to Kisterenye. My mother-in-law waited for me anxiously with gifts: six eggs, a piece of cheesecake, and some margarine she had saved. In exchange, I gave her some of the honey I brought from Kanyas. We chatted for a while, and then she rushed home as *Apu* was calling her.

On the bottom of the basket Grandmother had packed for me, I found an envelope. Curious, I tore it open. There was a ten *forint* (dollar) bill, and a note.

> *Darling,*
>   *I realize this is not much, but it is all I have. Buy some extra food for yourself. With love, Nagymama.*
>   *P.S. To avoid any argument with your mother, keep this between us.*

As my pregnancy advanced, my morning sickness got better. Shortly afterwards, the most amazing disturbance happened to me. I was having my afternoon nap, when suddenly I was awakened by a gentle activity inside of me. Still too sleepy to understand what was happening, I suddenly realized that my baby was telling me, "Mommy, I am here and alive." His movement felt so miraculous I was in complete blessedness, and I wept happy tears. There was a knock on the door.

"Ica this is *Anyu* again. Are you all right? With your window open I heard you sobbing."

"Yes, *Anyu*." I quickly ran to open the door, giving her a surprising hug. We shared my excitement about the baby's movement, while we had some tea. She also shared some of her pregnancy experiences with me, like good friends do.

"Ica the other reason I came is that I heard tomorrow there will be some oranges in the store, but you will have to go very early to stand in line to get some."

"I will go *Anyu*, regardless of the time. As you know first come, first served, and most likely they will have only a limited amount. I need the vitamins for my little boy." In my nineteen years I had never eaten an orange, a banana, or any tropical fruit.

Soon after *Anyu* left, I started supper: potato soup and noodles with fried eggs that *Anyu* had given me. I could hardly wait for Barni to get home, so I could share my excitement with him about the baby's activity. After school, Barni's youngest brother, Istvan, came regularly to see me. He was only ten, but such a delight to be with. He questioned me about the baby and how soon it would be born. He was looking forward to becoming an uncle. After he left, I set the table and anxiously waited for Barni. Hours went by with no sign of him. I became angry with him, thinking, "Why is he late this time? It isn't the end of the month or payday. How can he do this over, and over, and not feel guilty about it?"

Finally, after eleven I heard the gate close. Barni came in, with a quick hello, and said, "Ica, don't wait up for me any more. You need your rest."

As he passed by me, the blend of liquor and perfume nauseated me. A wave of pain, anger, and jealousy consumed my whole being. I sighed. "Please Lord don't let him destroy me. I must be strong for the benefit of the baby."

After he finished eating, I burst out, "Barni go and wash off that odor from you. I can't stand it any more. It makes me sick." Our eyes met, and his face blushed.

In the morning I told him about the baby's movement, but he wasn't excited. For him it wasn't as big a delight as it was for me. I was still angry and said, "Barni, you are violating our marriage vows with your unfaithfulness. Do you know that is grounds for divorce?"

"What are you talking about? You have no proof!" and he slammed the door behind him. He was silently torturing me. I thought the Gypsy Borzos was right about her prediction. And the military was also right for dismissing him. He was crafty, selfish, rude, and abusive to me. Would it be possible that he would change like *Anyu* and I hoped for?

Exhausted, but quickly dressing, I rushed to the store for oranges. To my amazement there were already about twenty people standing in line. After an intense one-hour wait, they let the older people and pregnant women in. I was excited, since I had never seen an orange. At the counter, I was handed two oranges for a high price. On my way home I stopped and smelled them several times. I carried them like precious jewels. On the way home I met *Anyu* rushing for her portions.

At home, I washed the precious fruit, like fragile eggs, and put them on the table. I was contemplating how to ration the oranges, when *Anyu* walked in and sadly told me that she and so many others got only one of the golden fruit, since they had run short. When Barni came home he wiped his eyes, picked up one of the oranges, examined it carefully and asked, "Is it real?" He handled them for a while, licked his lips and declared, "Let's eat them." He started to peel one, when *Anyu* quickly slapped his hand and snatched the orange away from him.

"Oh no, you don't. You will get a section from it. The rest is Ica's, for the baby." Barni made an angry face at his mother, but *Anyu* ignored it and handed the oranges to me. When she left I split one orange and gave half to Barni. I told him that the other one was for tomorrow. I took it into the bedroom and hid it in the drawers under the tea towels. When I came back I put some water on for boiling the orange peels for tea.

After supper *Anyu* and I went to a baby shower, which we thoroughly enjoyed. Jolanka, the young mother-to-be, was about my age. She was already in her ninth month, anxiously waiting for the little girl she was hoping for. When I came home, Barni was asleep. I gently slid in beside him so as not to awaken him.

The next morning, after Barni left for work, I decided to have some of my second orange. I went to get it, but it wasn't there. I thought, "Oh, maybe I put it in the second drawer," but it wasn't there. I looked in the third drawer and it was not there either. Now I was really puzzled. Maybe I put it somewhere else. I searched the whole house, but no orange. All of a sudden, the unbelievable thought flashed through my mind: Barni had eaten the orange! I had to sit down. I was completely shattered. I thought if he could do that - stealing the orange from us and eating it - then I lost all hope in him and our marriage. His dishonest behavior wiped out even the little feeling I had for him. I realized that he had no heart or feeling except for himself. While I was sure that he stole the orange, I would have to wait until he came home to confront him.

I did some washing and ironing, while listening to the radio broadcast about how wonderful our Communist Hungary was doing. "Yes," I said to myself, "it is doing so well that I had to get to the store at six a.m., stand in line for hours for two oranges, and pay a very high price. Even then, some people didn't get any." Later, I cooked dry bean soup for supper. *Anyu* brought some horsemeat sausage for Barni. I knew he would be home shortly. Still upset with him, I didn't want to believe that he could be so mean and selfish as to steal and eat the orange, but what other explanation was there? As soon as he walked in I told him, "Barni sit down. I want to ask you a question, and I want nothing but the truth."

"What about?" he asked defensively

"Barni, did you take the orange from the drawer?"

"What makes you think I did?"

"Because only you and I go into our bedroom, and I don't want to accuse innocent people in your family."

"Maybe it grew some feet and walked away," he answered sarcastically and laughed it off, just like he had when he devoured the meat from my plate at the Kanyas dinner table. I was convinced that he had taken the orange. I was furious and deeply hurt. Suddenly I had sharp pains in my chest and had to lie down. I went into the bedroom and closed the door behind me. He shouted after me.

"Where is my supper?"

With the pain in my chest and shortness of breath, I was frightened and in thought I turned to my Friend at the crossroad.

"Dear Lord how much more do I have to take? How can I cope with life with this selfish man? Please Lord; change him, before his son is born. My life is so complicated; I need your guidance at every turn of my life. Lead me and strengthen my faith in you, so that I can go on. Thank you. Amen."

The next morning, shortly after Barni left for work, *Anyu* came to see me and noticed my sadness.

"Ica, I can see something is wrong! I want to help you, but you have to tell me what is bothering you so deeply? Yesterday you were so elated, and now you look so distressed." I kept quiet, but she insisted, "Please tell me. Did Barni do something to you?" I sobbed out my story about the disappearance of the orange. She came and sat beside me, gently stroked my back saying, "I sympathize with you, dear. Please don't cry. I promise I will talk to him about his selfish behavior. But now you have to think about your baby and not let this incident destroy your happiness, regardless of how much it hurts. And you know what? Tonight I will take you to the movies to get you out of this depression."

"Thank you, *Anyu.* I would like that, since Barni has to work late again." At half past seven *Anyu* called and we were on our way to the movies. In the courtyard, people were lined up, already waiting to get in. Scanning the crowd, exchanging hand waves and smiles with some of my schoolmates, I suddenly grabbed *Anyu's* arms tightly and whispered, "*Anyu* I'm going to pass out!"

She led me to the nearby bench and asked me, "What is happening with you?"

I pointed behind me and muttered, "Look that way." I felt numb, seeing my husband and his friend going into the movies with their two single co-workers. *Anyu* instantly left me and marched straight to them to talk to Barni. I was hoping he would run to my aid, but *Anyu* returned alone.

The door opened and slowly the crowd moved into the theatre.

Furiously *Anyu* said, "Let's go home!" But my legs were still numb and I could not stand up. With my last glance I could see Barni and company going into the movies, ignoring our existence. *Anyu* was furious, pouring out unbelievable cuss words for Barni and the girls.

"Ica, dear, let's go home," and she reached for my arms, helping me up. Arm in arm we slowly and silently walked home. *Anyu* wanted to stay with me, but I strongly refused saying, "*Anyu,* I just want to be alone."

"I respect your wishes, dear, but don't forget I'm upstairs - just a call away." She left and I locked the door. When I am hurt and in pain, I just want to be alone - alone with God. That is the only way I find spiritual tranquillity and the assurance to go on. Finally, I settled on the bunk bed in the kitchen and shut off the light. I was still in shock, unable to control my trembling body, terrified of losing the baby. Lashing out that there must be more to life than this, "Please Lord, help me with my disintegrating marriage. Barni is hacking up my heart with his cruel actions. I can't take it any more!"

Suddenly there was a message . . . "Leave Barni. Go home to Kanyas and go to *Szentkut's* church." I felt it was a spiritual call to me.

Much later, slowly the key turned in the lock. I quickly turned facing the wall and pretended to sleep. Barni flicked the light on and off, and he tiptoed to the bedroom in the dark. I was glad he didn't disturb me; I didn't want to fight with him. My heart was still aching so deeply that I could hear its beat, as the scene flashed through my mind again: my husband taking another woman to the movies, right before my eyes.

CHAPTER 29

Silent breakfast. We didn't even look at each other. Barni had hardly closed the door behind him, when I burst into tears. I sobbed while packing to leave him and go home to Kanyas. My dear mother-in-law came in with breakfast on a tray for me.

"Dear *Anyu,* you are a wonderful mother-in-law, trying so hard to help me."

"Yes Ica, I try earnestly, but I am unable to change Barni's immoral attitude. Last night, I waited for him to come home; I wanted to talk to him. When I heard the gate close, I ran to the door and tried to call him into my kitchen to talk, but he curtly refused. Dear Ica, my heart is aching for you, but I don't know what to do! I beg you to stay with him. Have patience; he will change."

"*Anyu,* right now I am going home to Kanyas. I am not feeling well and fearful of losing my baby. He is the only one I live for."

When I was all packed, *Anyu* wanted to walk with me to the train station, but I firmly refused. I was planning to walk the seven km to Kanyas. I needed time to be alone. I needed time to sort out my shattered life. With a long warm hug, we said goodbye.

"Ica, I will miss you. Come back soon." And she walked away as she whispered, " I love you!" Hearing the words, "I love you" from her for the first time, I choked up and quickly rushed away.

On my way home I reached Godmother's house. I wanted to go in and have a short visit, but dreaded to see Godfather. But I tolerated him for the love of my dear Godmother. Fortunately only Godmother and Aunt Anna were home. I wanted to empty my grieving heart, but I couldn't utter the painful words.

They were delighted to see me. Aunty Anna's scanning eyes noticed my condition and said, "Ilona, are you pregnant?"

"Yes Aunty, and I feel in my heart that I carry a little boy and his name will be Attila."

"How does Barni feel about the baby?" Godmother asked.

"He is not as excited as I am." To avoid more questions I was quickly at the door and said, "I have to go. Kanyas is a long way yet."

"Ilona, how come you are walking instead of taking the train?"

" Aunty, I like to walk," I answered quickly and said goodbye.

On my long journey I enjoyed my solitude, just listening to my thoughts and spiritual musings. When I arrived home unexpectedly, my family was puzzled and Grandmother demanded an instant explanation. Since only my parents and grandmother were at home, I told them the heart-breaking movie incident. "Right now I have to leave Barni, before I do some evil thing in my confused mind. I am traumatized, and I am worried about losing my baby."

Grandmother got furious, shaking her finger at Mother. "I told you Mari this marriage would never work, but you didn't listen." And she cursed Barni with dreadful words, but Mother defended him.

Out of fury I said, "Mother I wish that Father would cheat on you, maybe then, maybe then, you would understand!" Mother wanted to utter something, but Father answered with anger.

"Hold on, Mari, hold on. Ilona's mother-in-law was with her and wanted to stop Barni from going into the movie with this girl and company, but he didn't listen even to his mother."

This time Mother stayed quiet, and Father cried out, "No one talk to Barni about this except me. Ilona will stay home until Barni makes a solemn pledge that he will stop his disgraceful behavior. Enough is enough! Now I have to go to work, and I sincerely hope I run into Barni at the mine."

Instantly, Grandmother took me under her wing, serving lunch. After our meal she called me into the bedroom, for privacy, to give me her advice. "Darling we have to be silent about your problem with Barni. Friends or neighbors cannot help you, and some may rejoice in it. Now listen very carefully dear. Tomorrow morning you go to *Szentkut* for the late Mass. After that you go to Father Feher's office and ask him for consultation. He can guide you, the right way, the Godly way. And then, you will be able to go on with life. Now, lie down and have a rest. You need it."

The next day, following my spiritual intuition and Grandmother's advice, I went to church. It was a weekday and not too many people attended. Father conducted the Mass. Listening to his devotional worship filled me with peace. After Mass just sitting there in silence, it felt like being in another world.

Suddenly, a gentle touch on my shoulder, followed by a soft whisper, "Hello Ilona, it is so nice to see you." He slowly sat down beside me. "I was wondering how you are doing."

"Father, that is why I am here. I need your help. I am expecting and I left my husband. I have a serious problem with my marriage. Barni is unfaithful and I am deeply hurt by it. I'm becoming an angry, hateful, malicious person, and I can't live like this. I desperately need your guidance."

With a soft tone he answered, "My child, smoldering rage and unresolved hatred is destructive for you and for your unborn child."

"Father, how can I rid myself of this destructive feeling, before it destroys me?"

"Begin with forgiveness Ilona."

"Forgive? I am hurt, humiliated, and crushed. I can't forgive." I lashed out with anger.

"Yes, you can, Ilona. Forgiveness is the only way for healing. I realize that you have been hurt by Barni's actions, but don't dwell on hate and anger. I will counsel you and teach you through the Bible to learn forgiveness. Ilona, next time you come, bring Barni with you; together we could solve this problem."

After our conversation, Father walked me out and we said our goodbyes with a tender hug. On my way home, I prayed that Barni would come to counselling, but I doubted it. He was not a believer. Weeks passed and I didn't hear anything at all from Barni. Father at *Szentkut's* church counselled me daily after the morning mass. I tried to find an answer to the problem in the Bible as we studied chapters and verses, while reciting the special part of the Lord's Prayer: "... *forgive us our trespasses as we forgive those who trespass against us; . . .*"

During counselling Father would reinforce, "My child, I realize you are hurt deeply by your husband, but you have to forgive. There is no other way, my child, but to forgive." Finally, I started to grasp what he was saying.

Prior to my counselling, I did not believe that I could ever forgive Barni. But the Father of *Szentkut's* church taught me the way: how to forgive. It is not easy, but it is truly possible.

Only Grandmother knew about my counselling, and I discussed every session with her. She commented, "Ilona one thing I know for sure, your faith in God has empowered you enormously."

"Yes, *Nagymama*, immensely. I am sure now I can go on, even if I have to raise my baby alone."

Manci heard that I was home, so she came home for the evening from her nanny job and surprised me with some baby gifts. They included a gorgeous, turquoise, thermal outfit; six flannel diapers; a rattle; and a pacifier for the baby. I was very thankful for her generosity, to which she responded, "I'm his godmother, aren't I?"

Julika was puzzled every time we talked about the baby, and always focused her eyes on my stomach. One day, Grandmother called me into the bedroom to discuss something privately. Julika rushed behind and sandwiched herself between us. Quizzing me about the baby and his birth, she asked, "Ilona, how will you know when the baby wants to come out?"

I loved her. She was so sweet and innocent. Later my father came in and informed me that he had had serious, daily talks with Barni at the mine for the past weeks; he would come to take me home tomorrow.

CHAPTER 30

Barni walked in the house; Grandmother walked out. Barni came to me and arrogantly said, "Let's go home, Ilona." I sat in the chair motionless, until Mother came to me.

"Ilona, I'll help you to pack." I was startled even deeper by her statement; then I realized I wasn't welcome any more. I had no choice but go back to Kisterenye with Barni, without any apology for his actions.

On the train he had every opportunity to apologize, but he acted like nothing even happened. This tormented me even more. Instead he announced, "I have good news for us. I got one of the ten duplexes the mine had built in Kanyas. I'm so excited. How about you?"

"I am excited Barni, but my aching heart holds me down."

He ignored what I said and continued, "The duplex is a small unit with one bedroom, a living room, kitchen, bathroom, and a small storage room. But what is most important is the electricity and indoor plumbing. Even if we have to warm up the hot water tank by wood, it will be easier, especially with the baby on the way. It is costly for my wages, but I won't have to travel to work by train." He glanced at me when he made the last statement.

"Barni the fault is not in the circumstances, it is in you."

He turned his head and stared out the train window for a long time. I closed my eyes thinking, "Life is not fair, but God is so good to me. Moving back to Kanyas, I'll be close to Grandmother, the crossroad and my beloved *Szentkut*. Thank you Lord!"

Later on, we were discussing moving and arranging the furniture, when suddenly Barni said, "Ilona, we have to buy a crib for the baby. We will put it close to the fireplace to keep our little guy warm. The house is ready, so we can move in right now." In that moment it felt like a reflection of a true marriage. But it wasn't mine.

At home in Kisterenye *Anyu* sadly helped me to pack, but she was happy for our new home. In Kanyas, Grandmother helped me to unpack, and she was the happiest I had ever seen her. We were now only a ten-minute walk away from each other. I met my next-door neighbors over the railing of our joint veranda. They were a very nice family with two girls, ages nine and twelve. Seeing my condition they offered me help to get settled.

Time passed quickly, while settling into our new home. Mother came and tried to arrange the house and control my life, but her authority did not have the same weight in my home as it did in hers. Ilcsa and friends came with gifts, to wish me happiness in my new home. While we were chatting over tea, they said how envious they were that I was married to such a handsome man, had a baby on the way, and a nice new home. But, they didn't know about my troubled life with Barni. Shortly after finishing our tea, the girls left.

While alone, I was thinking and worried about the high rent. With the baby on the way, how were we were going to manage? But under Communism most people just barely got by, so we were not alone. With that thought, I brushed my fear away.

The government built these houses in an orchard that they had confiscated from previous owners. The tenants divided the fruit trees, which helped us with our food supply. Grandmother and I were busy dehydrating and canning fruit for winter. My dear *nagymama* was there every day to help me, but only during the day. She deeply despised my husband, and as soon as Barni came home, she quickly said goodbye and left.

My mother on the other hand adored him, so much so that one night at eleven she knocked on our bedroom window, calling with a whisper, "Ilona, open the window." Thinking it must be an emergency, I quickly opened the window and she handed me something rolled up in a piece of newspaper.

"Mother, what is this?" I asked.

"Six cigarettes for Barni, just in case he runs out," she whispered.

"Where did you get them Mother?"

"I stole them, one at a time, from your father's package."

"Mother, I know cigarettes are very expensive and hard to get, and that is not fair to Father."

Suddenly, Barni turned over and I quickly shut the window. I didn't want to give him the cigarettes, because he would sit up in bed and light one immediately, polluting the air in the bedroom. I continuously begged him not to smoke in the house, but Barni always did what Barni wanted. I gave him the cigarettes the next morning, just before he left for work.

With time, I got heavier and more and more tired, but looked forward to having my baby. I suffered through the Christmas holidays, with a terrible flu virus that greatly agitated my doctor. He did not want to give me a high dose of antibiotic, but at the same time he wanted to eliminate the virus as quickly as possible. From Christmas on I spent almost two months as an invalid, trying to be very cautious about the baby's health.

With the good winter rest, I had recovered by spring. I had to. It was time for my baby to see the world. My doctor urged me to check into the hospital, which was about a two-hour train ride away. Arriving at Paszto's hospital, Barni waited until they admitted me. Soon after he left, I slowly settled in with three other mothers. Since I had never been in a hospital, bearing my first child frightened me. These ladies were very encouraging, since it wasn't their first experience with childbirth.

I was ecstatic and scared at the same time. I was captivated by the way these mothers breast-fed their babies. When, for some reason, one of them lost their lifeline to their mother, they would cry out in anger until their mouth was filled again with their mother's breast. The demand for survival was strong, even at that young age. Survival is one of life's mysteries.

March 18, 1954, I felt utterly elated, as the excruciating labor pain delivered its fruit, and my beautiful little boy was born. Attila looked so adorable with his perfect little, angelic face, like a little fuzzy peach. He had big, blue eyes and tiny curls of light hair. Even the maternity nurses complimented him, saying he was the most handsome little boy they had ever seen. Of course that didn't hurt his mother's pride. I hardly could wait to show him off to my family and friends, especially to my grandmother.

I waited impatiently for my first breastfeeding at five p.m. We did fine with the guidance of the maternity nurse. While nursing, Barni walked in and he was astounded to see me breastfeeding our baby. He was speechless. Then he said, "Ilona, you two look absolutely beautiful. Mother's first breastfeeding. You just need a frame around you two, for a perfect portrait." His blue eyes got misty as he admired his son, while holding his little hand. After the feeding he wanted desperately to hold him, which he did quite awkwardly, while he kissed him tenderly.

When they took the baby away, Barni was just staring at me. Finally, he said it again, "Ilona, you look so beautiful and radiant. Actually, you are glowing."

"Barni that is what the ladies here are telling me. It comes with the birth of the first baby, the sign of metamorphosing to motherhood."

"Ilona whatever you call it, you look beautiful." Glancing at his watch, he quickly kissed me and ran to catch his train home.

After visiting hours, I heard one of the babies crying. Not yet recognizing my baby's cry, I wanted to rush out to check. But, the nurse told me that it wasn't Attila. Satisfied, I settled in my bed, closed my eyes, and pretended to sleep. I was wide awake, praying, and trying to figure out the mystical miracle of birth. Just the brain connections alone are phenomenal. Such a mystery. I thanked God for my healthy baby. Mine, mine to love, with all my heart. Slowly my medication took effect and I peacefully fell asleep.

After a week's stay in the hospital, we were allowed to go home.

CHAPTER 31

Arriving home from the hospital, I could smell the mouth-watering aroma of Grandmother's savory goulash soup. To my amazement the whole family was waiting for us. While everyone hovered over my baby, I noticed my father sat in the background waiting politely. I stepped out of the circle, walked to him, and said, "*Apuka*, here is your grandson." And I gently placed the baby in his arms.

He reached for him and said proudly, "Come to Granddad my precious child. We will have special times together, I promise you that." One of my father's tears dropped on baby's tender little face, while they gazed at each other. We watched silently while Granddad kissed him gently. As we watched that moment, we were spiritually touched.

Grandmother sat beside my father impatiently. Finally, Father handed him over to her. She called out, "Come here my little darling. I am your great-grandmother, and we will pray for you right now." She traced the sign of the cross on baby's forehead, tenderly kissed him, and she led us into the *Lord's Prayer.*

By the time our introductions were over, Attila was restless. It was feeding time. At that moment, Julika perched herself right in front of me and started asking questions, "Ilona, how come Attila knows how to suck the milk from your breast? And how did he get into your stomach?"

"Julika, go and ask Grandmother. She can explain it to you better than I can."

After supper I was exhausted, and we went into the bedroom to have a nap. When I returned to the kitchen, it stunk like a smokehouse. I was furious. I tried reasoning with Barni again about his smoking in the house. He promised from then on he would smoke only in the bathroom, which had a big window that could be opened for fresh air.

A week later, while visiting my in-laws, everyone adored Attila. However in the family of nine, with seven males and only two females, I am sure a little girl would have thrilled them even more. Barni's older brother's wife also had a boy, now one year old. *Anyu* softly but demandingly declared that we needed more females in this family, while pointing to each of us with her eyes. To my amazement, no one smoked in the house. Later, I found out that my dear mother-in-law had ordered the smokers not to smoke in the house, while the baby was there. She was so thoughtful, such a wonderful person and a great mother-in-law. As we were saying goodbye with a hug, *Anyu* put something in my pocket and whispered, "Buy something for the baby as a gift from me."

We enjoyed our visit with Barni's family, but we had to get home as I was getting very tired. Breastfeeding required a lot of energy, and besides, I had to prepare for Attila's christening.

Sunday after Mass was the christening celebration, for which Manci was delighted to be Attila's godmother. In the ceremony she proudly said her vows: if anything would happen to me, she would help to look after Attila.

Time went by, and my precious child grew and he started to look at things curiously, giving me funny smiles. One day while nursing him, I noticed a small, dilated, blood vessel on his angelic little face. A couple of days later I noticed the vein was spreading. I panicked and rushed him to our doctor, who arranged an appointment at a special clinic in Budapest. We had a long four-hour train ride to the clinic.

Upon our arrival, we registered with the nurse and had to wait for the doctor. At our turn we were called in. The doctor looked at my son and asked, "What is the problem with this beautiful little child?" I showed him the blood vessel on Attila's right cheek. He darkened the room by shutting off the light, and used a special flashlight to examine the baby's face. Minutes later, he turned the light back on, and with his chilling personality declared, "I am not sure what exactly caused this small capillary to break, but if we don't treat it immediately it could spread on the baby's face. To stop the spreading, he requires radiation treatment."

The thought of radiation treatment caused me to panic, and I asked, "Doctor, is there an alternative way to treat this problem? He is so tiny, only four months old!"

He insisted, "No, Ilona there isn't! Please come back in two hours and I will do the procedure."

I went out into the clinic's garden, heeding the call for my soul's desire for solitude. I sat under a tree, with my precious baby in my arms, praying for guidance. I was terrified thinking about what would happen if the blood vessel spread, but worried about what harm the radiation treatment could do to my tiny infant. During my prayer, I got a definite message to have the procedure done. I was sure the Lord was guiding me. As I carried him downstairs, deep into the basement, I tripped on the dimly lit stairway, falling on my left arm.

Luckily I didn't hurt my baby, but he became so frightened he started to cry. I didn't realize I was holding him so tight I was suffocating him.

Though guided by prayer, I was extremely frightened by the procedure to be done. Attila and I were given protective gowns to wear during the radiation treatment. Waiting for the doctor, I held my little darling tenderly. I looked into his eyes and he seemed to sense my anxiety. And I heard the pleading in his cry. The doctor came in and measured the size of the vein on his little face with a special instrument, and said, "Ilona, sit absolutely still and hold the baby motionless."

By this time I was shaking in the semi-darkened room, while my baby screamed as I held him down. The doctor asked the nurse to strap me down over the shoulder so that I couldn't move. That made me panic. That instant, the doctor's cool face warmed up. With his hand on my shoulder and looking straight into my eyes, he said, "Ilona, don't be afraid, but listen to me carefully. The baby is in your hands. You have to hold him absolutely still, otherwise the radiation beam will hit on the wrong place." He stroked my shoulders several times, before he took an object like a funnel and placed it exactly over the measured place on the baby's face. He darkened the room more, switched on the radiation for a second or so, and it was over. I was determined to get loose from the tightly binding strap, to calm my screaming, frightened child. I was frightened also. I just wanted to escape, so I rushed upstairs to get out of the building.

Upstairs, at a table, there were other mothers dressing their babies. I stood next to a young mother who asked, "What is the matter with your baby?" I showed her Attila's face and she asked if I had to come back for more treatment. When I said yes, she shivered with a shrug, and begged me not to have more radiation on Attila's face.

I asked, "Why not?"

She lifted up her little daughter's blouse and I could see an open sore about the size of a thumbnail on her tiny stomach. She explained, "After several radiation treatments the skin opened up, and now it won't heal, regardless of what the doctors do." We stood there in silence. Two young mothers agonizing over their babies. She touched my arm and, with tears in her eyes, pleaded with me not to come back for more treatments.

On the way home I prayed for the young mother's baby, and asked, "What would I do if my son's face wouldn't heal?" Deeply troubled, I looked down at my son's previously flawless little face, marked with a dime-sized pink circle. At home, we discussed Attila's care with my family, and decided to end the radiation treatment and have faith.

That night Attila was very restless. I tried to nurse him, but he refused to eat or sleep, regardless of how long I rocked him. Alone with my baby in the depth of the night, I lashed out in despair, "Why did this have to happen to my child? Why is life so cruel to me? Why do I only have flashes of happiness in my life Lord? Why?"

CHAPTER 32

I was still greatly worried about the radiation treatment on my baby's face, especially since he had developed a severe diarrhea. Our local doctor said the problem could be caused by the radiation or something else. Now, I was troubled by the radiation more than ever. I asked, "Doctor, please tell me, will this radiation mark ever vanish from my son's face?"

"Ilona, radiation is very dangerous. It is very harmful for living tissues." He must have noticed my distress as he reached for my hand and clutched it saying, "I can see as a young mother how devastated you are, but my answer to your question is 'no'. That radiation circle on your baby's face is permanent. Ilona, I wish I could help you, but I can't." And he stretched out his right hand while saying goodbye.

On our walk home from the train, I stopped at the crossroad cross to pray, and to show off my son to my childhood friend, Jesus Christ, while breastfeeding him at the foot of the old, rugged cross. After our spiritual rest we continued our walk home.

At home, around five in the afternoon, I found a note from Barni: *Ilona I had to go out. I will explain things when I come home.*

Crumpling his note with anger, I thought out loud, "Yes Barni, you're lying again. I don't know where you are, what you are doing, or with whom. If you keep it up, you will lose your son, just as you lost even the fraction of love I had for you at the movies in Kisterenye." I had had enough trouble for one day. After bathing and feeding Attila, he fell asleep in my arms. When I gently put him down, he gave me a funny grin that warmed my heart.

I was just about dozing off when Barni came home. Thinking I wasn't up to more lies or arguments, I pretended to be asleep. He came into the bedroom and gently shook my shoulder to wake me, "Ilona! Wake up. I want to talk to you." Slowly I opened my eyes, sat up, and listened to him.

"Three friends and I bid for this five acre parcel of land from the government. We will cut the hay; it's a fifty-fifty share. We will cut it manually and make some extra money for us."

I was delighted for his effort and felt awful about my mental accusations. To eliminate my guilt I gave him a hug. "Barni, that is very nice of you. The extra money will be handy for Christmas."

After his last cigarette in the bathroom, he kissed the baby and came to bed. We discussed my day with Attila at the doctor. His answer was, "Ilona, leave it up to the doctor."

"Barni, I trust my faith will guide me." He didn't believe in Communism, and he didn't believe in the Creator like I did.

Around 10 a.m. the next morning I answered a knock on the door. To my shocking surprise it was the Communist leader from the mine. In my amazement, I blurted out, "What are you doing here?"

"Ilona, let me in. I came to see your new baby." I realized this intrusion would infuriate Barni, but I had no choice as he forced himself in. I walked with him into the bedroom where Attila was sleeping. He commented that he definitely inherited Barni's looks, but he hoped not his scheming, obnoxious attitude. I didn't like his remark, but I had to be silent since he was the Communist leader at the mine where Barni was employed. Since the government owned everything including the mine, and the duplex we were renting, I knew I had to be cautious. Quickly, I offered him some coffee, but he refused saying he was in a hurry.

However, instead of leaving, he stayed and badgered me with more questions, "Ilona, how do you like the house?"

"I love it. Barni was lucky to get it, over so many applicants."

"I arranged that Ilona," he said with authority.

I was totally shocked. "But why did you do that? You don't even like Barni."

"Ilona, I like my friends close, but my enemies even closer." It confirmed he was keeping close tabs on Barni. He must have sensed my puzzlement about his statement. He got up and hastily said goodbye.

I sat there completely perplexed about his visit.

Later Barni was home and rushed me with supper, as he had to go haying again. While we ate, I asked him, "Barni, who is haying with you?"

"Laci, Pista, and Jeno. Why are you asking?"

"Just curious," I said. I was afraid to tell him about my visitor, but I had to or he would find out from someone else.

"I had an unusual visitor today."

"Who was it?"

"Your Communist leader from the mine."

"What the hell was he doing here?" he shouted at me.

179

"He came to see our baby," I uttered softly, trying to calm him down.

"The hell he did. He came to get some information from you about me. What did you tell him? What did you tell him?"

"Why would he do that Barni?"

"They are afraid that someone will blow up the mine."

"Barni, who would do such a thing?" I asked curiously.

"Jeno would. He works in the mine which he hates, and he utterly despises Communism; but Ilona don't you dare tell that to anyone. I know you can keep secrets."

"Barni, I hope you will talk him out of it. Jeno's hatred of Communism is not reason enough to justify a malicious act of violence." He just laughed and rushed out to meet the others for haying. I was worried; maybe the haying was just a cover up.

His attitude scared me to death. I had to tell someone. If this notion were followed, too many innocent people would be killed. I had to tell my father. Instantly I rushed home.

Upon my arrival, Mother reached for Attila from me with a different kind of attitude like, "Ilona, please can I hold him?" It looked like Mother started to realize to whom Attila belonged. I hesitated for a moment, and then handed him over to Mother. Quickly I found Father in the tool shed and told him about my surprise visitor and Barni's reaction. Father was startled to hear about the terrifying plot.

"Ilona, dear, you are so upset, please come sit down. I really don't know how to deal with Barni's mentality. I am so afraid that his actions put you and the baby in danger! The Communists are ruthless. They can imprison you and the baby until Barni confesses to crimes he didn't even commit. Leave this problem with me. I have to talk to him, I have to."

Just then Grandmother shuffled in asking, "To whom will you talk Jozsi?"

"I will tell you later *Mama*!" and Father rushed out. Then Grandmother quickly closed the door and sat on the toolbox, pulling me beside her. She whispered, "Ilona, why was that Communist snoop at your house in the morning?"

"Who told you that *Nagymama*?"

"On my way to you, I saw him go into your house, so I turned back home."

"Oh, *Nagymama*, he came to see the baby. Isn't that nice of him?"

"Ilona, I don't believe that nonsense for a moment. A harsh Communist leader like him would not leave his work, just to see your baby. No, dear, there is more to it. I can feel it. I'm sure he is tracking Barni," Grandmother predicted.

I told her about the leader calling Barni his enemy.

"Dear, I'm not surprised. Not too many people like Barni, including me. I hope one day they will arrest him and take him away for good."

"Grandmother, you don't really mean that!"

"Yes I do!"

I rose to my feet and urged Grandmother into the house, where Julika was holding Attila, while Mother was combing his curly hair.

On our way home, I visited with some of the neighbors briefly. Arriving home, I noticed a beautiful bunch of wild roses on the table, and I called out for Barni. He was home, taking a bath. While I nursed Attila in bed, Barni came in just as we were finished.

He lay beside us and played with his son for a while saying, "I just can not believe how fast he is growing. The way he crawls, it will be not too long before he can walk."

I put Attila in his crib to sleep. Neither of us mentioned our Communist visitor. We talked about raising some rabbits for meat. After Barni slumbered away, I was worried to death about the price Attila and I would have to pay at the hands of the Communists, for Barni's actions.

CHAPTER 33

Early Friday afternoon, I left Attila with Grandmother while I went to the dentist in Salgotarjan. Boarding the train in Nagybatony, to my pleasant surprise, I noticed Dinyos Mariska and her twin sons, Pali and Jani, on the train. I hadn't seen them since they moved away years ago.

Watching them from a distance it seemed to me that Mariska had aged a lot, and I could see why. Pali had grown to be a 180 cm tall, handsome, young man, but sadly Jani, due to a crippling accident, was only about 100 cm tall. Jani's face had changed into a young man's, but his height stayed as a young child's. Unfortunately the train was packed and I was standing a short distance away from them. They didn't notice me. Seeing them, I reflected upon Jani's life.

A disastrous human error had caused his misfortune. His godfather, while tossing him up in the air as a baby, failed to catch him. Jani fell to the ground and the injury stunted his growth and left him with a hunchback. Even though the kids in school ridiculed him by being called *the hunch back of Notre Dame,* he never got angry. On the contrary, he was always ready to help us children with our homework, as he was a top student.

Finally our eyes met. Mariska waved me over and Pali offered me his seat. Between watery eyes and hugs both of us inquired at the same time, "How are you doing?"

"I am very well Mariska," I answered. "How about you?"

"I am coping Ilona, just coping." Pali gave me a hug, while Jani waited for his turn.

With a happy grin he looked up at me and said, "Bend down to me, you beautiful creature. I want to give you a hug." I stooped down to his height and he gave me a tender, but firm embrace. "You remember, Ilona, when we were kids, you promised me you would marry me."

"Yes, Jani, we were always playing husband and wife, weren't we?"

"Yes, Ilona, those were the good old days," he said softly. At the next station an old couple came in looking for seats and Jani politely gave up his for them. While the boys were standing a little distance away, Mariska poured out her sad heart.

"Ilona, we are going to pick up a wedding suit for Pali. He is getting married in two weeks. He is so ecstatic about his wedding, but Jani's heart is shattered. He is terrified that after the wedding, his twin brother will leave

182

home. Ilona, I am afraid he will have a nervous breakdown or will commit suicide. With his disability, he has become so dependent on Pali. His *giant brother*, that's what he calls him."

"Mariska, he will not commit suicide. Just pray and trust God. He is the supreme master on healing broken hearts. Trust me, I've been there."

"Ilona, how devoted you are. You still have that strong faith. I watched you many times going to the crossroad cross as a young child."

"You know, Mariska, in all my troubles it's that faith that keeps me going."

"Ilona, tell me about you and the rest of your family."

"I am married and have a baby boy; his name is Attila. And the rest of the family are doing fine."

Just then the loud speaker announced that we were arriving in Salgotarjan. After wishing happiness for Pali and good luck for Mariska, I hugged Jani and he whispered in my ear, "Can I come and see you sometimes?"

I answered with a whisper, "Anytime, dear, anytime." Then we sadly parted.

I was distressed about Jani and felt the pain in the dentist's chair more intensely. My entire journey home was focused on Jani and Mariska. It must be devastating for a mother to see one of her sons elated to get married, while the other was suicidal.

Reaching the house, I spotted Grandmother in the garden. I got upset and asked harshly, "*Nagymama*, how could you leave Attila alone in the house? Even if he is asleep, he could fall off your bed?"

"Now, dear, don't get upset with me. I fought with Barni bitterly not to take Attila home, but he insisted."

"*Nagymama*, I don't trust Barni alone with the baby. He plays too rough with him!"

I ran home breathlessly. On my way up the steps I heard Attila whining. As I burst into the kitchen, my heart skipped a beat at the sight of Attila's frightened little face, all alone sitting on the top of the kitchen table, while Barni was visiting with our neighbor at the back door. I screamed, "Barni what on earth are you doing, leaving the baby alone on the table?"

"He was on the floor a minute ago, how did he get up there?"

"By the chair next to the table, Barni. By the chair, can you see that?" I scolded him with anger.

"Barni he could break his head open or break his neck if he falls on the cement floor." He just shrugged his shoulder and said, "He won't fall."

"Barni you are brainless! Babies are terrified of falling. This is not the way to take care of a year-old baby."

I took Attila to the bedroom and started to nurse him to quiet him down. Later, I explained to Barni the tragic accident that had crippled Mariska's son, Jani.

I was deeply worried to leave Barni alone with the baby. From then on I had to make sure that it wouldn't happen again. He worried me to death, especially when he slipped into his peculiar state of mind, and made up his own rules about reality. Just like agreeing with Jeno to blow up the mine. From then on I had to be there when he was around the baby. I didn't trust him.

One miserable, fall night, awakened by Attila's moaning, I quickly picked him up and noticed that he was burning up with fever. I sighed, "Please Lord, not the flu virus." I tried to nurse him, but he refused, just sobbing and rubbing his ears. I knew something was desperately wrong.

Early in the morning I took him to our doctor. After a very short examination, we were rushed to emergency in the Salgotarjan hospital. The doctors quickly discovered that Attila had contracted a very serious, rare, ear infection called *mastoiditis*. He needed immediate surgery. I was shocked. Due to the extreme pain, he was crying constantly. I was frightened; everything was happening so fast. Blood was needed for the operation, so the nurse rushed me to the lab for a test.

Just as I returned to my distressed child in the pre-operating room, the nurse ran after me with shocking news. "Ilona, your blood is not suitable for your son. Call your husband right now." I was stunned for a second: my blood is not suitable for my son? I carried him for nine months. But no time for this question now. I reached Barni and while the surgical team prepared for the dangerous, delicate operation, he arrived. His blood was a match to Attila's.

The doctor must have realized my confusion as he tried to explain to me what was going on. "If the infection and pus have moved into the adjacent mastoid bone, just behind the baby's ear, there is excruciating pain. The only course of treatment we have for this condition is to cut into the eardrum for drainage. If that doesn't help, we surgically have to remove the mastoid part of the skull, leaving his head disfigured. If we don't do that, fatal *meningitis* is the result."

I wish he hadn't explained all that to me. Now, I felt completely distraught. I was not only feeling my son's pain and suffering, I feared for his life. I wished I could take all his pain away. Holding my baby close to my heart, I was allowed to carry him only to the door of the operating room. As the door opened, I smelled the disinfectant; it smelled like death. I was horrified. The room looked like something from outer space: with big round bright ceiling lights; people dressed in surgical clothing, with masks covering their noses and mouths and their shiny bug eyes staring silently at me. One of the aliens came to take my baby away from me. I hung on to him tightly; I didn't want to let go of him. I feared his death. As he was taken from me by force, the pressured door slammed shut in front of me. I cried out in anguish, "Please Lord don't take him away from me. He is my life; he is the only thing I live for!" And I passed out.

I came to with a sharp pain in my arm, as a nurse had injected me with a sedative. I was drowsy, in and out of consciousness. After the agonizing two hours of the operation, I was finally allowed to see him.

His little head was bandaged; just his tiny face was showing. I knew he was alive, as the blanket gently rose and fell with his heartbeat. The doctor explained, since the bone wasn't infected yet, only cuts were made behind both of his ears, for drainage. The specialist said he would be fine, but he had to stay in the hospital on intravenous and antibiotics to prevent the spread of further infection. He advised me to nurse him as much as I could to help with his recovery.

I went to the hospital every day for two weeks to feed him. Between intervals of feeding Attila, most of my time was spent in the chapel. My savior, my crossroad Friend, proved his love for me time and time again.

CHAPTER 34

Finally we were released from the hospital. On our way home we stopped in at Mother's. She ran to us and possessively took the baby from me. "Come to Grandmother, my little darling." She cuddled him tenderly, gently stroked his little head, and kissed him softly. My mother's humanity shocked me; it made me wonder, where was all her kindness, compassion and love called humanity when I was growing up? Reasoning it was in the past, I let it be. My heart had some satisfaction to see Mother happy.

Grandmother made me some lunch, after which I had a nap while Mother and Grandmother looked after Attila. To my amazement they did it in perfect harmony. God works in mysterious ways. He gave us a child to bring some peace between the three of us. Whenever I went somewhere Grandmother had Attila. Mother adored him and begged Grandmother to let her hold him. That gave Grandmother and I a power over Mother.

Later, I hurried home to make supper. When Barni came home, he quickly ran into the bedroom to see Attila. He was shocked to see his tiny head all bandaged, with just his fragile little face showing. He remarked, "He is sleeping so peacefully, just like he knows he is home safe."

At the supper table, Barni announced that tomorrow, Saturday, afternoon he would be going to the soccer game with his friend Pista. It was a very important game: Kisterenye versus Hatvan for the provincial championship. He was staring at me, waiting for my reaction.

"Barni suit yourself, but don't go drinking and forget the time and come home late. I have had enough stress with Attila's dangerous surgery. I don't need your carousing."

In the afternoon, after Barni had left for the soccer game, my dear grandmother brought over bean soup and cornmeal squares for supper. I was pleased, because recently I had felt too exhausted to cook. Grandmother watched while I gave baby a bath. She waited patiently for me to finish, so she could hold him. In the meantime I set the table, since it was time for Barni to come home and Grandmother to leave.

Now alone, I read my new book, *Parenting*, while waiting for Barni to come home. Even as I tried to bury myself in my reading, my mind was wondering about him. Maybe the soccer game was just a cover to take the office girl to the movies again. Why is he doing this? I don't deny him intimacy. With Barni that would be impossible!

Midnight and there was still no sign of Barni. I got more and more infuriated. I felt jealous, humiliated, hurt, and taken for a fool again. This time I wouldn't forgive so fast and easy. I couldn't sleep; with rage, I paced the bedroom floor.

Suddenly there was an auto tire screech. Instantly I shut off the light and listened. Then, the slam of a car door; I peeked through the window and saw a car take off. I was startled, too afraid to move...Who could that be? Not too many people around here had cars, only the big shot Communists. Abruptly there was a knock on the door. I listened silently...then another knock and a whisper.

"Ilona, this is me, Barni. Open the door."

I ran to the door. As the door opened he staggered in! I got so angry I didn't even look at him. I just walked into the bedroom. Before the door closed behind me, he collapsed. When I tried to help him, I saw his badly beaten face. I panicked, asking, "Barni, what on earth happened to you?"

"I got into a fight! Just help me to the chesterfield." Then I noticed blood trickling down behind his ears. "Help me to take off my jacket, and give me a cold towel and a couple of aspirin." Helping with his jacket, I discovered more blood and bruises on his body. He had been beaten badly.

"Barni, who beat you up?"

"A couple of guys."

"Why?"

"I don't know."

"Where did they beat you?"

"Outside the bar, in Nagybatony."

"Who brought you home?"

"I walked home."

"You are lying. I saw a car pulling out of our driveway."

"I don't know what you talking about. I walked home," he protested in anger.

"Barni, tell me the truth."

He yelled at me, "I don't want to talk about it any more, and I forbid you to tell this to anyone, not even our families."

"Barni, you need a doctor."

Grinding his teeth from pain, he licked the blood from his bleeding lips, and looked at me with his swollen, blood-shot eyes and yelled, "Ilona, when I say no one, I mean no one, especially not a doctor." With rage he hit the end table and broke the lamp. The sudden, loud noise frightened Attila and he started to cry. I quickly put the soother in his mouth to quiet him, and he went back to sleep.

Next morning, Barni asked me to go to the office to let them know that he was sick. From the office, they sent me to the Communist leader's office, since he was the chief of personnel. By this time, I was suspecting that he might have had something to do with Barni's beating. I was dreading seeing him, but I had to or Barni would lose his job and also the duplex we rented from the mine. When I walked in, he wasn't surprised at all. He just motioned me to sit down.

"Thank you Comrade, but I have to run. My baby is sick and I have to hurry home. I just came to tell you that Barni has the flu and won't be at work for a while."

"Are you sure Ilona? Is he sick because of the flu or could it be something else?" He stared straight into my eyes. I almost panicked and blurted out the truth about Barni. The temptation to tell the truth and free myself was in my mind…but for some reason I couldn't.

"He should see a doctor and I want his report!" he demanded.

To change the subject I asked, "Comrade, something has been puzzling me ever since we moved into the mine's duplex. Previously, you stated that you helped us get the house to rent from the mine because you like your friends to be close to you, but your enemy even closer. I realize we are not friends, but we are not your enemy either."

"Not you, Ilona, just that instigating husband of yours. He made it clear in the military that he despised Communism! Well that includes me, because I am a devoted follower of the glorious Communism. Ilona, since his deranged behavior at the military, we've kept a very close eye on him and will continue to do so. If he is instigating people against Communism, we are here to show him what Communism can do with its power." His words of warning frightened me; I had to leave in a hurry before I said something that I would greatly regret.

On my way home I realized again the enormous tribulations Barni could bring down upon us. Ruthless Communism could make you pay: with your life, or in Siberia laboring a lifetime. Arriving home, I heard Attila whimper. I rushed into the living room where Barni was holding him and talking to him, saying, "Daddy loves you and I will teach you to be a fighter."

I was listening through the half-opened door. He didn't notice me. Love and hate were churning in my heart. I felt compassion for him, for being beaten up like that. At the same time I thought: he is so selfish, putting his family in danger, and hurting me mercilessly. I walked in and took the baby away from him, thinking perhaps Attila was frightened by his father's injured face. I thought to myself, "I have to find a way to escape, before Barni destroys us."

After a long silence Barni asked, "Ilona what did that Communist bastard have to say?"

"Barni you have been branded by them, ever since the military. They are watching you. That was what he said. Barni, do you realize you can vanish without a trace?"

"I'm careful. I can't be killed, because we will kill them and Communism as well."

"Barni, who are we?" I asked

"Forget that, Ilona, just forget it. Their time is coming soon."

"Barni, that is your choice, but don't take us with you. We are not up for sacrifice for your vendetta. Why can't you see that you can't win? Savage Stalin supports them with Russia's powers. You have to find a way out of this hostility, for the sake of our lives. Please give it up, or I will have to do something in desperation. You give me no choice."

"Ilona, I will never go along with them as long as I live, even if you and the baby have to suffer. Do you understand that?" he shouted, as if he were deranged.

I was utterly shocked. He frightened me. I panicked, quickly grabbed the baby, and rushed to my parent's house. I desperately needed help. I was glad Grandmother was alone, so I could tell her the whole episode with Barni and the mine leader.

"Ilona, you are shaking. Give me the baby and go make some tea, while I am thinking what to do."

While serving the tea, Grandmother instructed me to sit down and listen very carefully to her plan.

"Ilona, dear, you have to get away from Barni. I will look after Attila and you go to Budapest, stay with Mrs. Nemet, and find a job. Barni will have to realize that you are serious and won't tolerate his irrational actions any more. Also, if you leave Barni, the Communists will see that you don't agree with him, and you don't support his anti-Communist rage. Hopefully, this will bring Barni to his senses and protect you and the baby."

"But *Nagymama*! I can't leave Attila behind. Please don't ask me to do that. He is my life."

"Darling you have to, if you want to live with your son! But not a word to Barni about this, or he would stop you. I will discuss this plan further with your parents."

The next day, in the tool shed, Father and I agreed on the plan for our safety. Back home while Barni was taking a bath, I quickly packed my suitcase, and put it outside the back door. While waiting for him to finish I was worried someone would notice my suitcase outside. He hardly was done when I informed him, "Barni I have to run to Mother's for more goat's milk for Attila."

"We still have some in the jar, in the pantry," he replied.

"That went sour," I lied. "I will be back in ten minutes," and dashed out in a hurry. Luckily, in the dark, no one saw me with my suitcase on the way to my parents. Later I informed Barni, "Early tomorrow I am going to Mother's to help them harvest the sugar beets. I'll be home by supper time." I felt sorry to leave my belligerent husband in his condition, but Grandmother and Father were right. I had to! The most heart-wrenching action was yet to come. I was dreading leaving my son behind the next morning, but I had absolute faith in my Creator and I trusted Grandmother's love for him.

The plan was the following night, instead of me going home, Father would go and explain the situation to Barni. We hoped he would realize what he was doing to us, and he would stop his revengefulness, before he destroyed our whole family.

I was utterly distressed about what I had to leave behind and what I had to face. The unknown scared me. Finding a job to make a living, while adapting to the big city of Budapest, frightened me. But with my unwavering faith I was sure I would make it.

CHAPTER 35

With a broken heart, I boarded the train to Budapest. Alone in my compartment I closed my eyes very tightly to stop my endlessly rolling tears. The fear of the unknown ahead of me took over my whole being, and I cried out for divine help, *"Dear Lord, teach me the secret of inner peace. Strengthen my faith in you, so that I may not be haunted by fear. Give me the assurance that you are always near. I need your help facing the big city alone."* I recited this prayer several times on my four-hour train ride and got control of my racing heart.

Finally, I arrived in Budapest, and shortly afterwards at Mrs. Nemet's. She was surprised, but elated to see me. She cheerfully welcomed me in and greeted me with a firm hug. While sipping on our tea, I revealed my troubled life with Barni.

"Dear Ilona, I certainly understand your fright about Barni's plotting against the cruel Stalinism." Mrs. Nemet was very compassionate and assured me that she would assist me in every way. "But to find work in Budapest is not an easy task," she said. "Not only because of the job shortage, but also because you are not a resident. You need some connection or a resume." I couldn't ask the mine office for a reference because I would need permission from the government to move to Budapest, which could take a month to a year, if I were allowed to move at all.

After our sweet and sour rabbit venison supper, I ran down to the corner store for a newspaper to search for a job. I picked up the *Szabad Nep* (Free People). The title must have originated in the mind of a deluded Communist. I quickly searched the paper and circled three possibilities: filing clerk, switchboard operator, and worker in the paper bag factory.

When I returned, I satisfied Mrs. Nemet's further curiosity about my troubled married life. She asked about my family and Grandmother's health, and she endlessly thanked me for the food I brought for her.

Early the next morning I started job hunting. The filing clerk and the receptionist jobs were impossible because of the many applicants, and I wasn't a resident of Budapest. After becoming completely lost a couple times, I finally found the Paper Packing Products Company. It was a dirty old building in the industrial area of Kis Pest (outskirt of Budapest), about an hour streetcar ride from Mrs. Nemet's. When I entered the office, there were four other people waiting for an interview. They were chatting about how difficult it was to find a job in Budapest, but I had a different outlook: there is a job out there for me and I will find it.

At last, I was called in. A mature lady, about fifty, pointed to the chair for me to sit. While she was reading my self-written resume, I noticed the gray roots under her red hair. Her face was covered with heavy makeup, similar to most city women. She fiddled with my paper for a long time, a typical Communist act that was premeditated to show power and intimidate people. It worked briefly, but mentally I repeated the golden words, "Peace, I choose peace," and I waited patiently. Finally, she introduced herself, "My name is Comrade Molnar." Showing her authority, she continued, "I hire and fire people in this company, Ilona." She didn't even ask me if she could call me by my first name (which is rude in Hungarian culture, but ignored by the Communists). " Do you believe in Communism?"

I answered, "Communism is our future and way of life. And Communism is a new horizon for us. If we open our mind to it, we can learn the way to a new life." I presumed she approved of my answer, because of her quick grin.

She continued, "This is a hard job. We make different sizes of paper bags on each machine. Each one of them has to be handled with speed, for minimum wages. I will fire you instantly, if your work is not satisfactory."

"I will do my best Comrade Molnar."

"You can start tomorrow morning at eight a.m., and I mean start, not just walk in."

"Yes, Comrade Molnar, I understand. I will be here," and quickly said goodbye.

I had mixed feelings: happy for the job, but fearful of the future working with Comrade Molnar. I hopped on the streetcar for home, realizing that my wake up time would be at six a.m., to be at work by eight a.m. Walking home from the streetcar, I picked up the newspaper and a pink carnation for Mrs. Nemet.

Bless her soul; she was waiting for me with supper. She was delighted with the carnation, and thanked God for my job. After a long bath, I felt exhausted and retired early.

My first day at work at the *csomagolo anyag arugyarba* (paper bag factory) was laborious. I had to keep up with the fast moving machine, by picking up and stacking the bundled paper bags. In the meantime I still had to carry buckets of thick, heavy, liquid glue to fill up the machine's tray. But with time, I managed well.

Soon I realized the lady on the next machine would be fired, as she was not able to handle the job. She looked so sad. I thought if I ran faster I could carry her share of the glue and fill up her machine as well. But, when our intimidating Comrade was around, she didn't allow that.

As the months passed, deep loneliness sat in my heart, longing for my son. I was worn out physically and mentally. Later... a promising letter from Barni arrived via Grandmother. But could I trust him? Is he really changed? Should I go home? Not yet.

With time I mastered the job and got a raise in pay. Later, I became friends with Comrade Molnar and discovered that she was human after all. She even dropped the Comrade title in the bistro, while we were sipping on our espresso coffee. She put on the red mask just for the working title and the good salary.

From Grandmother's letters I got detailed reports about how fast Attila was growing. And from those reports, I was desperate to cuddle him. In Budapest I lived a regimented life: work on weekdays, church on weekend mornings, and cruising Margit Island for solitude, so I could be alone and connect to my source. Since early childhood, that was the only way for me to regain my faith and strength.

One day, I got a letter from Grandmother, "Ilona please come home immediately. Attila is sick with a fever."

I ran into the office, where Comrade Molnar issued my pay immediately, and I was on the train for home. During the trip, I reflected on the time when I came to Budapest and how terrified I was. This time, I felt even worse: desperate to see my ill son. It felt like the train was only crawling. I was upset, I was anxious, and I was shaking while reciting my calming verse, *"O Lord teach me the secret of inner peace . . ."*

CHAPTER 36

I raced home from the railway station to see my beloved, sick baby. Storming into the house, like a savage, I ripped my child out of my grandmother's arms. Smothering him with my kisses, dampening him with my dripping tears, I pledged to God that I would never leave him again. Nothing on earth would separate us from now on.

"Ilona, dear, come to your senses. You are out of control."

"*Nagymama*, he is everything I live for."

Suddenly, he stopped whimpering and recognized me. He clung to my neck whispering, "*Mama, mama.*" Quickly, I sprung to my feet, clasped him tighter in my arms and headed to the doctor. After our long walk, we reached the crowded doctor's office, where we had to wait patiently for our turn.

Following a thorough examination the doctor said, "Ilona, there is nothing wrong with your child physically."

"Doctor, I trust my Grandmother's judgment. She said Attila had a fever; he was extremely quiet and refused to eat. He's always been a very active and hungry child."

"Ilona, you said earlier that you were away from him for a long time. What I can detect is he is broken-hearted; his little heart was yearning for you. Deep longing for his mother is not unusual. That could be what made him sick. He was lonesome for you, but now that you are home, he will be fine. Trust me. Some children are tightly bound to their mothers, and your son is one of them."

That information eased my mind and I loved him even more. On our way home, I became exhausted while carrying my heavy toddler. We rested on the roadside for a while, and to my amazement, he was happy and crawled all over me. And he kissed me for the first time! We were exhilarated, rolling joyfully in the grass by the roadside.

Later at home, Barni admitted that he missed me and wanted to come for me, but my parents had not given him Mrs. Nemet's address. He was happy that we were back home. As time passed, it seemed that maybe Barni had changed. He hadn't caused any grief lately, but as Grandmother said, "With Barni, you never could be sure." I was hoping that in my absence, he had had time to think about our marriage. Now, two months had passed since I came back home and he still hadn't talked about the mine explosion or the revolution.

I thought a miracle had happened and he really had changed. I felt like giving him a hug, while in bed sleeping beside me.

In the middle of the night, I was awakened with a pain in my right breast. To my touch, I discovered a painful lump. By the morning it was intolerable. Grandmother urged me to see the doctor. Due to the excruciating pain I rushed to seek advice. After a check-up the doctor sent me to the Salgotarjan hospital to see the specialist. In the office, the plump young nurse introduced me to Dr. Szigeti. He greeted me with a strong handshake and a soft voice. After a thorough examination and blood test, I asked, "Doctor, why all these intense examinations? I only have a pain in my breast."

He hesitated and with his soft voice said, "Ilona, you have an infected milk gland in your breast and you need surgery. I will contact the other surgeon and will let you know the time of the operation. (Communism had one honest act: good Medicare.)

I was frightened. Later, the specialist and the surgeon came to see me in my room. They looked puzzled and without hesitation the specialist spoke, "Ilona, we have a complication. Not only do you need surgery on your breast, but you are also pregnant."

"Pregnant!" I yelled with joy.

Ignoring my happiness, he continued, "Your pregnancy is in the very early stage and we should terminate it. After that, we can do the breast surgery. The pregnancy is causing your breast to go through changes, and we cannot guarantee a successful healing, and you could lose your breast."

I was stunned by this news. After getting my thoughts together, I asked, "Doctor would you please repeat what you just said? I want to be sure that I understand the decision I have to make." My mind was stuck on the word "terminate." That meant an abortion! To take my baby's life is a heart-rending decision. The doctor restated the diagnosis and affirmed that this was the only way to save my breast.

Later in the afternoon, the doctors, my husband, and I discussed the procedure again. I was in conflict with the doctors, but very frightened, so I agreed to their suggestion verbally, but not in my heart. I was scheduled for an abortion the next morning, and two days later for breast surgery. When the doctors left my room I asked Barni to leave as well. I wanted to be alone, to connect with my Creator for guidance.

Later the nurse came with a sedative, but I refused to take it. I wanted to make my decision with a clear mind. After she left, I got out of bed, shut off the light, and knelt beside my bed and recited the *Lord's Prayer*. Having experienced motherhood with a beautiful child like Attila, how can I permit a life to be terminated? I would rather lose my breast!

I went back to bed and lay there in numbness. With tear-flooded eyes, I stared out the window at the shining streetlight that resembled a brilliant star. Captivated by this mysterious beaming light, I had a quick awakening, a definite intuition repeatedly flashing in my mind: "You keep your baby." Amazingly I felt assured and slowly drifted into a peaceful sleep.

In the morning, the nurse wanted to prepare me for the abortion. Instead I walked into the operating room, and I confidently said to the surgeon, "Dr. Kazari, I have changed my mind. I am not going to have the abortion."

Totally surprised he asked, "Who, or what, changed your mind?"

I replied, "My prayers were answered. I have been assured that everything will be fine without the abortion."

He must have read the determined expression on my face and said, "Then so be it. It is your choice, but you will have to sign some papers. And we can do the breast surgery this afternoon." The following day I was released, but I had to see the local doctor for check-ups.

Due to my pregnancy I had a long and difficult time with the healing of my breast, but I made a remarkable recovery, for which I praised God.

CHAPTER 37

While coping with morning sickness again, it was difficult to look after my one-year-old son. By the trickle of tears on his face, I knew he disapproved of being confined to his playpen. When he was loose in the house he was determined to rearrange everything within his reach, including my pots and pans in the lower cabinet. I was blessed with my grandmother, who came to help me daily, not only with my son, but also with the canning and fruit dehydrating. We were blessed to be able to do this; in the winter we would trade the canning for other foods or heating fuels, like coal and wood. It was a shame, but under Communism you could barter even your soul.

With my lack of energy I was unable to prepare for Christmas, so we spent Christmas Eve with my parents and Christmas day with Barni's. This greatly helped me, as I didn't have to cook, yet we were able to eat well. This was important for the health of my soon to be born little girl. Even before my first pregnancy, I knew I would have two children: a boy and a girl and their names would be Attila and Beatrix.

December was very cold and we ran out of heating fuel. We begged for coal at the mine, but their harsh refusal was very hard for us to accept, since most of our coal was shipped to Russia.

Throughout Hungary, the economic situation continued to decline. In the last few years, there had been some attempt to make reforms in the political system. Matyas Rakosi, our Moscow-trained, former Prime Minister, succeeded in disrupting the reforms and forced Imre Nagy from power in 1955 for "right-Wing revisionism." Hungary joined the Soviet-led Warsaw Pact Treaty Organization. Rakosi attempted to restore Stalinist orthodoxy within the party, among students, and in other organizations; chaos persisted in the government. There was a prediction, which quickly spread countrywide, that we were near a revolution.

That news elated Barni. He raged, "Retaliation time!" His anger scared me, but this time I was too pregnant and too busy, looking after my active son, to really care. So I ignored him when he went out in the evenings for hours. He didn't tell me where he went, and I didn't ask.

With the small amount of coal we traded for on the black market, we survived the hard winter. Grandmother and I were busy knitting and crocheting little pink outfits for my Beatrix. Often I thought about how nice and peaceful it was with Grandmother, and I wished the same would be true with my mother. In my heart, I missed my mother, but she had not been there for me when I needed her. I wondered if we would ever be close like a mother and a daughter should be. Would I favor one of my children over the other? Such favoritism can affect a child forever, as I sadly knew from experience.

It was interesting to watch Attila start to get crafty. When I said "no" to something, he went to Grandmother, batted his big, blue eyes, put on a sad face and asked for it from her. Then Grandmother, won over by Attila's pleading face, would look over at me with a plea, and I just had to give in.

One evening Barni came home from work and handed me a package. I asked, "What is this?"

"Just open it, Ilona, just open it. "

As I opened the package, I could not believe my eyes. "Barni where did you get this much sausage (*kolbasz*)? It must have cost a fortune." Meanwhile my rolling stomach reminded me of *Apu's* horsemeat sandwich, and I gagged.

"Never mind where it came from, or how much it cost. Just prepare some for supper. And *Nagymama*, I would like you to stay and have supper with us."

He quickly helped Grandmother to take off her shawl. Usually she was on her way out when Barni came in. To my shocking amazement she replied, "Yes, Barni I will stay," and she began rolling up her sleeves to prepare some of the sausage for supper. I sat there astounded, asking myself what was going on. Had Grandmother's hatred suddenly vanished toward Barni? Not long ago she had wished him in hell.

"Ilona, I will make some hot potato salad (*rakot crumpli*) for supper with the sausage."

"That will be fine, Grandmother, and I will come and help you," I answered with amazement. While Barni went outside for wood with Attila, I quickly asked Grandmother to sample the sausage to determine if it was horsemeat or not. It wasn't. Then I questioned Grandmother about her staying.

"Ilona, dear, since Barni asked me, I decided to stay. He will never change his idiosyncrasies or attitude, so I decided to change for your sake. Another thing, dear, you can't fight fire with fire."

"Thank you, thank you, *Nagymama*. Your genuine love has lifted me."

Barni came in with an armful of wood, with Attila tagging behind him with a couple of twigs in his arm, trying to hold it just like his father. He insisted on putting the twigs in the stove by himself. I opened the hot stove door; he put the twigs in and wanted to play with the fire. This scared me, since he had no fear of fire. He was fascinated by burning candles, cigarette lighters, and matches.

After supper, we cleaned up and Grandmother left for home. I lay on the chesterfield for a short rest, holding my stomach, and treasuring the movement of my little girl. I heard the echo of the laughter as Barni and Attila played in the bathtub. I praised God for the moment of family happiness, which had seeped into my troubled life. Grandmother had really touched my heart when she forgave Barni.

"Mother, come and take your played out little mischief from the tub!" When I went in, I nearly slipped on the wet floor. There was water all over. I carefully carried Attila to the bedroom. He was hardly awake while I dressed him in his pajamas.

In bed, I asked Barni again where he got the sausage and the money to buy it. With a sharp reply, he said, "Ilona, never mind where it come from. Just enjoy it." I knew meat was very hard to get, even on the black market. To purchase that amount of meat on the black market you would have to have cash. We had no bank account, not too many people did under the Communist regime. We lived from pay-day to pay-day and every penny was accounted for. Since it was Saturday, Barni had paid the miners with cash. Oh no, had he embezzled some money from the mine office? If he had, the cruel Communists would crucify him. Barni was so unpredictable, sometimes making up his own rules and believing his own version of reality. But I was too exhausted to think about his actions any more.

For the past couple of days I had had irritating lower back pain and the constant urge to go to the bathroom, even though my bladder was empty. Later that night I felt a rapidly rising fever with nausea, and I noticed some blood in my urine. I woke Barni to call an ambulance - I was in labor. Since we had no phone, he ran to the mine office to call the ambulance.

We had no time to notify Grandmother to come and babysit Attila, so Barni stayed at home to get a hold of her, and he would come later. After a quick examination at Pasto's emergency, I was told that I had a kidney infection, which had complicated my labor pain. The doctors stopped the labor to treat the kidney infection, and then they monitored my pregnancy very closely. After about a week, the infection cleared, and the doctors tried to induce labor for days.

Finally on March 1, 1956, after long hours of excruciating labor pain, my Beatrix was born. But my happiness was short lived as I was told that she had a heart complication. She had s*eptal defects,* that is a failure for the holes in the partitions between the heart chambers to close properly. The doctors monitored her heart and hoped the heart chamber would close naturally. I was devastated, but the heart specialist tried to assure me that she was a strong baby and she would make it.

At my first breastfeeding I was worried about my previously operated upon right breast, but it seemed to be fine. While I was touching and examining Beatrix's little body, I found a bone sticking out of her neck, almost piercing through her skin. I called the nurse and she quickly took her away. Later she returned with further devastating news: Beatrix also had a broken collarbone. I was distraught again and desperately longing for my son, but children were restricted from visiting in the hospital. Finally, after about a month in the hospital we were allowed to go home, but we had to go back for regular check-ups for Beatrix. I felt too fatigued to take care of two small children, so Grandmother moved in with us temporarily. She was a blessing!

With my newborn, ailing, little girl, my very active toddler son, and my constantly plotting husband, I was physically and mentally exhausted. I definitely needed Grandmother's spirituality. After Barni and the children were asleep, Grandmother lit a candle in the living room, opened the Bible, and read Romans 5:3-5, and said, "Now, Ilona dear, please recite this scripture until you know it by heart. And darling your wavering faith will be like solid rock. Trust God's words, dear, and you will be fine with your immense love for your children. Goodnight dear. I will attend to the children's cries."

"Thank you, *Nagymama.* You are truly a Guardian Angel."

CHAPTER 38

Julika came regularly to take Attila to the park. Grandmother had dressed him while I nursed Beatrix. Even though I went through a lengthy, painful, healing with my breast surgery, I felt blessed that I could nurse again. As Julika walked out with Attila, I realized that at fifteen she had grown up to be a very pretty young lady, who enjoyed mothering Attila openly, but secretly with my mother, which she insisted on. Of course I didn't let on that I knew it. Let Mother channel her accumulated love to Attila, which passed me by. It looks like she truly missed having a son of her own.

Grandmother and I labored to wash diapers by hand for two infants. While outside hanging the diapers on the line, the mailman gave me a few letters. One was addressed to Barni. Curiously I held it up to the light, but I couldn't read it. Then unintentionally, the envelope just opened. The very short note read: *Barni, meet me Saturday at the Matraverebely soccer game. It is urgent.*

There was no signature. What was he up to now? Should I burn this note, or give it to him? Before going into the house, I folded the envelope and slipped it in my pocket.

That night, in bed, I decided to give Barni the note and questioned him about it. As he read it, a quick rage flashed on his face, and he jumped up and threw the note into the fireplace. Silently he stood by the window staring out into the night.

"Barni, you are scaring me. Please tell me what that note is all about. And the more you say 'it's nothing for you to worry about,' the more it's killing me."

With an instant anger he said, "With the revolution, the bastards will be wiped out for good."

"What revolution Barni?" Grandmother yelled from the other room. We didn't realize that she could hear us.

"No revolution, Grandmother. Barni is talking nonsense," I answered quickly to calm her.

Then Barni whispered, "Ilona, the revolution is coming. You will see, and I will collaborate with them." His last statement was whispered very softly, but with a stronger conviction.

"Barni, I have so much to cope with: my fragile health, two infants to care for, and your constant conspiracy against Communism. But the most painful to endure is your cheating."

"That is not true!" He tried to deny it with a snicker on his face.

"Oh yes, Barni, it is true! Someone walked into the office the other night, when you had to work overtime. You were cuddling one of the office girls, who was sitting in your lap. And you know very well who saw you, because you apologized to him. Each infidelity feels like you are twisting a knife deeper and deeper into my already crushed heart." He quickly turned away as I continued. "And now you are plotting with the revolutionaries. You are jeopardizing our lives again."

"I don't care; the Communists have to be wiped out."

At that instant, I was ready to scream at him with rage and frightened about my evil thoughts for him. But quickly I came to my senses. I could not slay anyone, regardless of my anger. There is no other way but to hand our lives over to the Lord. And let Barni self-destruct.

With time, and the doctor's help, Beatrix got better. She looked beautiful with her ocean-green eyes, blonde, curly hair, and round, little face. However, Attila was resentful of her. He would come to me and try to push her out of my arms, saying with a sad face, "I don't like baby." Then he hit her in anger. Seeing his action I had to watch him closely, until he finally accepted her.

As we got stronger, Grandmother went home to Mother's, and I tried to manage on my own. By this time the food shortage had gotten even worse. We had to stand in line for hours for almost everything. One day, approaching home, I saw two men come out of our house.

I rushed up to them and asked, "What on earth were you doing in my house?"

"We just inspected the electrical wiring."

"There is nothing wrong with it," I replied. " And how did you get in?"

"Just in case you forgot, this house belongs to the mine and we have the key to it," one replied sarcastically.

I was completely flabbergasted. My thoughts raced. Why didn't they come when we were at home, or let us know when they were going to come? Even if they have a key from the mine office, invading our privacy is not acceptable. Barni will have to report this incident at the mine office. As I put my wallet in the cabinet behind the towels, I noticed that the whole cabinet was disturbed. I was greatly puzzled and wondered, "Who were those two men? Could they be from the AVO, the Communist secret police again?"

Still distraught when Barni came home, I described the event and urged him to go back to the mine office and report the incident. He wasn't as shocked, but furious and started to search the house.

"Barni what are you doing?"

He put his finger on his lips and wrote on a piece of paper, "I'm searching for a *bug*, a hidden microphone, so they can hear our conversations." With that statement he completely freaked me out. He saw how upset I was, he waved me over to the table where he was writing. "Ilona from now on, not a word about the government, Communism, or the mine, not if we want to live. We can't be sure if the house is bugged or not."

With that statement, a feeling of faintness took over my body and I grasped the chair to sit down, utterly beside myself with fear. I was terrorized and a prisoner in my own home. My first thought was of reporting Barni. The sooner he was arrested the better. Oh Lord, forgive me for my thoughts, but it is impossible to live with him any more. Short of breath and shaking, I attended to my children's cries.

Barni carefully searched the whole house for any listening devices, shaking his head and mumbling. "They were definitely searching for something, by the way they upset the whole house."

"Barni, what can we do about it? What were they really looking for?"

"Guns, Ilona, guns; the revolution is near," he whispered.

"Barni, I am moving home to Mother's. I can't live like this."

"No, Ilona you are not. If you leave me, they would become even more suspicious about me. You and the children will stay right here with me. And, we have to keep silent about this, not a word to anyone!" he whispered rolling his fiery, red eyes as he continued mumbling. "Retaliation time. We going to wipe out the . . ."

In my trapped situation, I swore to ignore Barni's activities and behavior. I had to! It was the only way to retain my sanity, and to focus on my health, and on my children's welfare. With prayer and the faith my dear grandmother had rooted in me an enormous strength possessed and guided me.

With fall, the tradition of making sauerkraut at Mother's approached as well. I cleaned the old leaves from the cabbage and cut them in half to be shredded, while Manci and Julika mothered my babies. Father shred the cabbage, just before Mother hammered it down with a special tool in the big crock. Grandmother sprinkled on just the right amount of peppercorns, bay leaves, and salt. Suddenly Father asked, "Ilona, where is Barni?"

I ignored his question. Shortly after, he rushed in and took over the shredding from Father.

"By the way, where were you all afternoon Barni?" Father asked.

"I had to pay the night maintenance miners this morning, and I had some paper work to do in the office," he replied.

Since Mother liked to talk about politics she asked, "Barni, what do you think about the approaching revolution?"

Instantly our eyes met and rage infused my body. "Not another word about politics! One more word of politics, I am taking the children and going home. And I mean it." Shaking with rage, thinking about the two invaders, I slammed the cabbage and the knife on the table accidentally cutting my finger, and yelled, "Ouch, " Dead silence . . .

Father gazed at me curiously. Finally he said gently, "Ilona is right. This is Sunday and a family day, not a time for politics."

"Amen for that Jozsi!" Grandmother answered promptly, while bandaging my finger.

Somehow Barni seemed nervous and shortly after supper he rushed us home. Just before we went to bed he handed me a sealed bulky envelope and whispered, "Put this in your purse and guard it with your life. Take it with you wherever you go. Keep it for me until I ask you for it."

Quickly I flipped the envelope open, and to my amazement there was a large amount of money in the envelope.

"Barni where did you get this much cash?" I should have known better than to ask.

"Don't worry about it. Just hide it, and keep it a secret."

I couldn't sleep that night wondering what Barni had done to get all that money. I was thinking to give the money back to Barni to return it to wherever he got it from. It was terrifying to be a part of his embezzlement scheme: to be jailed? Oh, no, not on his life; I couldn't live without my children.

In the morning, I approached him and said, "Barni, here is the money. I won't keep it for you. Wherever you got it from, give it back." He didn't say a word, just put it in the inside pocket of his jacket and left for work. I wondered if the two phony electricians had been looking for that money.

As the months went by, Barni and I were almost like strangers in our own home. He went to work and stayed out until all hours of the night. I ignored his activities with great difficulty and just focused on my health and on my babies. I despised going to the store and standing in line, while hearing the bitter disputes between friends and neighbors about the nearness of a revolution. The topic couldn't be avoided as it spread quickly across the country.

1956 October 23, the forces to reform reached the turning point. Security forces fired on Budapest students marching to aid Poland's confrontation with the Soviet Union. The following battle suddenly turned into an immense, well predicted, sought-after revolution. That was what Barni was waiting for.

Imre Nagy, named by the Central committee as Prime Minister on October 25, negotiated with the U.S.S.R. to withdraw its troops from Hungary. Nagy announced Hungary's neutrality and withdrawal from the Warsaw Pact. He appealed to the United Nations and the Western powers for protection of its neutrality. Engrossed with the Suez Crisis, the UN and the West failed to respond, and on November 3 the Soviet Union started a vast military attack on Hungary. In our small community the streets were empty; everyone was in their house listening to the radio, hoping to over-throw the Communist government, and to free ourselves from their bondage.

Being alone with the children I was afraid, especially at night. I wouldn't dare to tell anyone that Barni wasn't home. I was terrified to be interrogated again by the AVO or lose my children, because of his involvement. This silent terror consumed my whole being.

Nagy and his associates took refuge in the Yugoslav Embassy. Janos Kadar, who had previously defected from the cabinet to the Soviet Union, returned to Budapest, and on November 4 announced the formation of a new government. With Soviet support, he tyrannized the country with severe retaliation. Thousands of people were incarcerated or murdered. Later we heard that Nagy and other former officials had been executed.

After days of absence, Barni came home. He quickly got washed, changed his grimy clothes, and got into his pajamas, placing his soiled clothes in a garbage bag and taking it outside. He returned empty handed, crawled into bed exhausted, and he called me, "Ilona, I have the flu, and I've been in bed for five days (while he was away from home) regardless of who is asking for me." Then he ordered me out of the room and asked me to close the door.

I was terrified and slumped on the chesterfield with my babies in my arms. Fearing to lose my children, because of his retaliation, I panicked. Should I report him? I could go to the Comrade leader. He would stop Barni, or silence him forever. Suddenly, reality hit me. I couldn't do that; he was the father of my children, and they would never understand my motives. It was out of my control to end this continuous torment.

The bloody fight on the streets of Budapest continued. The multitude joined in, with thirteen- and fourteen-year-old children fighting the mighty Russian tanks with Molotov cocktails. Tanks ran over humans, compressing them to a smear of blood and flesh, to be trampled on like rubbish. There were dead bodies all over: some were garrotted on trees or lampposts, some had bullet holes, and some had cut throats with their genitals stuffed in their mouths. Streetcar lines and pavement stones had been piled into barricades around Kilian barrack and Parliament Square. Many historical buildings were reduced to rubble. There was not a single Red star to be seen, or a Soviet monument still standing. Budapest was in ruins.

As the Russians came back with ten-fold-strength, they reclaimed Hungary from its famous *Five Days of Freedom*. Hearing these detailed tragic actions first hand from a survivor of the revolution, I felt like I was there. But, thank God that I wasn't.

CHAPTER 39

We didn't suffer to as great an extent as Budapest or the bigger cities had. We lived in a small community, so there were no Russian tanks or soldiers. However, we were broken hearted for the many who had paid with their lives for our very short-lived freedom.

Now, the future of the country and the lives of the revolutionaries were in more danger than ever. The Communists gained more authority, to freely kill anyone, and answered to no one. They were judge and jury. We restrained our hatred behind a wall of silence: hatred that caused revolutions, hatred that corrupts even the most honest people.

The country was in total chaos. Work didn't resume at the mine. Barni kept talking about escaping. He tried to convince me that it would be for our own good. I told him, with two small babies, he was out of his mind. We heard that thousands of people had fled the country, even in December, when the border was more secure.

In the afternoon, while the children were sleeping, we decorated our small Christmas tree. In the meantime, Barni kept pleading with me to escape, telling me how much better off we would be in a free country.

I tried to explain, "Barni, this is the middle of winter, and I am not strong enough to walk kilometers in the dark of night, on isolated country fields, in freezing snow, carrying a ten-month-old baby."

"But Ilona, we should do it for the children's sake! We have to do it!"

"Barni, I don't want to talk about escaping any more. Just the thought of it scares me to death. Please, let's just enjoy Christmas Eve," and I started to sing *Silent Night.*

When the children awoke, we showed them the Christmas tree, but as babies they didn't know the real meaning of Christmas. However, the sparkles and the flickering candles on the tree fascinated them. Attila was anxious to touch them. He was captivated by fire, having no fear of it.

Since we had no money to buy any toys, Grandmother's creations of a rag doll for Beatrix and a home-made football and rag horse for Attila were treasures. Barni got a shirt that he needed badly, and I got a warm nightgown. We played with the children for a while, and then Barni glanced at his watch and said, "Ilona, I have to go out for a short time."

"Where are you going, Barni? This is Christmas Eve?"

207

"I will tell you later."

"Barni, this is our big problem. You are not honest with me."

"I have to go. See you later." Swiftly he was out the door.

It was cruel and frustrating to be left alone on Christmas Eve. With a troubled heart and misty eyes I watched the children play. Attila was still jealous whenever Beatrix crawled onto my lap; he still tried to push her out.

Later, while feeding the children some pudding, Barni came home. He looked very troubled. Silently he helped me to put the children to bed and waited for me, sitting beside our little Christmas tree deep in thought. As I approached he reached for my hand and pulled me down beside him, and said, "Ilona, let us pray."

I was utterly shocked to hear this from Barni. I believed in miracles, but not that one! However, acting naturally I started the *Lord's Prayer*. To my shock I discovered he didn't know the prayer, he just mumbled it following my lead. This is all right, a first step in the right direction. Thank you Lord! Can I have hope, or does he just want to convince me to escape? We had hardly finished with our prayer when he pleaded again with me.

"Ilona please don't get upset, just hear me out. We have to escape from Hungary. We have to; it is not a choice. We must leave or I could be in Siberia for the rest of my life."

"Barni you are scaring me again. Why do we have to escape?"

"Now with the revolution lost, the Communists will be after me."

"What did you do that is so frightening?" He didn't answer my question and just continued.

"As you know, the mine is shut down until after the Christmas holidays. Last night I snuck into the office and someone stalked me and whispered as I was quietly locking the door, 'Barni I will report you!' then his tall shadow vanished at the corner of the building."

"Who was it Barni?"

"I don't know, but now I am scared. You see, Ilona, we have to go. We have only two days to escape."

"Barni, is this true, or are you just lying to convince me to escape?"

"I hate living under the Communist dictatorship. We have to escape for the children's sake."

"Barni, it looks like you are willing to sacrifice the children's lives to save your own." But he didn't hear me and just went on again.

"Ilona, we will have a good life in Canada."

"Canada!" I yelled. "How can we have a good life without anything and not knowing the language? We would have absolutely nothing, except two small children."

"Ilona, everything will be fine. You will see. I know you have absolute faith, and that is what I am leaning on. We have no choice."

"Barni, how about the children? They will not survive the long journey. It is the middle of winter; it's freezing and snowing out there! Attila is only two and a half; Beatrix is only ten months old, and both are still in diapers. Barni, think about this seriously. You are sacrificing your children's lives to save your own."

"Ilona, I trust in your faith. I am certain that your faith will bring us through safely."

"Barni, you go. And if you make it, then when you have the money, send for us."

"Ilona, you can't stay! They will torture you, take your children away from you. You know how ruthless the AVO can be."

"Barni, you are using the children to scare me to death."

"You see, Ilona, you have no choice either."

I felt petrified of the thought that they might take my children away and hated Barni for putting me in this situation. I swore to God that if the children would perish, Barni would also.

"Here is the plan, Ilona. Tomorrow, early on Christmas morning, we go to your parents to wish them holiday greetings and stay for a very short time. We'll tell them that we are going to Kisterenye to stay with my parents for a couple of days. We'll give your keys to Grandmother to stay in our house until we come home. When they find out that we escaped, your parents can take our belongings. Otherwise, our dishonest government will, as they did with so many people's belongings, who escaped before us. We will meet Laci, with whom I rendezvoused at soccer games, his wife, Marta, and their three children, aged fifteen, ten, and eight, in Nagybatony. We'll take the train to Kapuvar and from there we will cross the border to Austria."

"How far do we have to walk in this severe winter Barni? How far will we have to walk?" I was confused by this life-threatening decision. It was happening too fast.

Ignoring my question, he continued, "We must go tomorrow morning, because they are already closing the borders." I wanted to see my parents secretly, to say goodbye, but I couldn't reveal to anyone our escape plan. If the Communists found out, we would be shot before we stepped out the door.

I waited for Barni to fall asleep, then went to the living room and lit a candle. In my prayer I asked God what I should do: "This is a major decision to make, and I can't make it alone. We can journey to freedom only with your help Lord," and I just sat there, in silence. My eyes started to gaze over every piece of furniture, then the pictures, doilies and figurines. I said goodbye to each piece with rolling tears, choking throat, and painful heart. I realized I couldn't bring any of my precious things with me, except Beatrix in my arms and the love and memories in my heart for my family and country. Early in the morning, Barni awakened me on the couch, where I had fallen asleep with the candle still burning, which had filled the house with its spiritual fragrance. We fed and dressed the children in complete silence, as we both realized the giant geographical leap we had to take from Hungary to Canada. With two babies, we were taking an extremely dangerous risk to escape. I felt numb; what we were about to do was beyond my comprehension.

When we were ready to leave, I had to go into each room one last time, to say goodbye to our precious belongings and our little Christmas tree. Gazing around the rooms, I wanted to take everything. In the final moment in our bedroom, I glanced at Beatrix's crib and Attila's bed. Suddenly my eyes focused on the glistening small cross, which I had never see glisten before, while it was hanging on the wall above our bed. I rushed over, and picked it off the wall and put it in my pocket. Now, I felt some what assured that my Lord Jesus Christ was with me.

"Ilona, let's go!"

In the kitchen, Barni and the children were waiting for me. When Barni locked the door, the click sound of the key turning in the lock became engraved in my heart forever. Even after fifty years, sometimes for a moment I have misty eyes when I hear that metal click as I lock the door. Everything we ever owned stayed behind.

At my parent's house, Father wanted to undress Attila to play with him, but Barni stopped him and said that we had to hurry to catch the train. Christmas greetings and hugs for everyone, but I could not look into their eyes. My heart was pounding from the worry that I would break down. When I came to

Grandmother, I could control my mind not to reveal our actions, but my heart was uncontrollable and the tears rolled.

Grandmother said, "Ilona dear, don't be so emotional. You are going only for a couple of days." While still holding Grandmother, my heart whispered, "*Nagymama*, this is goodbye forever. I will never see you again." Suddenly Grandmother's words came to me. When I was in a dilemma, she used to say, "Ilona you can't hide your feelings from me." She knew me better than I did myself. Holding her just a little longer, our eyes met and she whispered, "I will pray for you." With that intense look in her eyes, I knew that she was aware of what we were doing.

Barni called again, "Ilona, hurry or else we will miss the train." I will never forget that picture as my family was at the window waving goodbye. I was torn apart, with throbbing pain in my whole being. I hesitated... I wanted to go back. Then, quickly I rushed after Barni as he carried my crying son in his arms and walked down the road.

We walked half an hour to the station in the snow and slush, with only our babies in our arms and a bag with some food and diapers. On our walk to the station, Attila was chatting and pleading with his father to put him down. He wanted to play in the snow. Beatrix quietly clung to my neck; she must have felt my anxiety.

In Nagybatony station we met the other family briefly. Barni and Laci stepped outside to talk privately; then, we quickly separated so as not to arouse suspicion that we were traveling together. At the station I bought two more soothers to add to the six I had in my pocket full of sugar. My plan was to wet the soothers in my mouth and dip them in the sugar to silence the children's cries, especially at the border crossing.

As we were waiting for the train, two uniformed AVO men rushed into the waiting room and scanned the people with their suspicious looks. Barni whispered, "If they ask us where we are going, just say to Kapuvar to visit our friend Sos Miklos." Fortunately, they didn't approach us.

The train was packed and the crowd was very quiet. A deep sadness and confusion reflected on everyone's face. Finally, I got a seat, changed diapers, and started to feed the children some cookies and dried fruit, which I had to chew for Beatrix while she whimpered impatiently. I was worried about Attila. He cried for some more, but we had so little. Later, on the long train ride, we dozed for short intervals.

CHAPTER 40

We were brutally awakened with, "Inspection! Inspection! I want to see everyone's red I.D. book," shouted by the AVO policeman, standing right in front of me. Beatrix was frightened by his yell, and she started to cry. "Give me your book! Where are you going with these small babies in the middle of the winter? You are desperate to get there aren't you?" With that suspicious remark, he peered into my eyes and kicked my feet.

While I searched in my bag for the book, I tried to calm my frightened child. As he checked my document, I could see from the corner of my eye Barni grinding his teeth and tensing his jaw muscles. For a moment I thought he was going to hit the AVO man, but suddenly he smiled and answered, "We are going to visit our friends for the Christmas holidays."

"I ask you once more: where are you going?" he growled and moved closer to Barni. He looked wicked, ready to kill Barni, while punching his right fist into his left palm and kicking Barni's feet with power.

Barni answered calmly, "To Kapuvar." The Inspector started to hand the book back, but defiantly dropped it on the floor in front of Barni. For a second, I thought that would be the end of us, but Barni picked up the document and said, "Thank you, Comrade."

He looked surprised at Barni's answer, then he turned to provoke the next person. Beatrix was still frightened, but she calmed down with a sugared pacifier. When the AVO police left our compartment, Laci and Barni went to the back of the coach for a smoke, secretly discussing our course of action. I had time to calm my restless children. Our tension increased even further as we got closer to Kapuvar.

After our arrival, we quickly sneaked down a narrow, dark alley, where we met Sos Miklos, a dark-haired, middle-aged man, with a nervous shake, and fearful look in his eyes. He hurried us on his wagon. We traveled about an hour on a narrow, dirt road, chilled to the bones in December's cold. We were dropped off in a dimly lit barn, where we waited quietly until Laci and his family arrived.

Then, quickly we had to climb up on a hay wagon, lie down and be covered by some blankets and about a meter of hay. Before we pulled out, the driver warned us, "Silence from now on, not even a sigh." He gently whipped the horses to go. Attila was confused and tried to crawl out. Beatrix also got frightened and let out a cry. "Keep that baby quiet or I will turn back," whispered the driver, with a guttural voice. I quickly reached in my pocket with my right hand for another sugared soother, while holding her down with my left hand. Suddenly a call, "Stop!" The harsh call and the dim shine of the flashlight permeated through the hay.

"Where are you going Comrade Kovacs?"

Realizing he lied about his name, I wondered if he was afraid to smuggle us.

"Just to the next farm," he answered calmly. "They ran out of hay and I'm helping out by bringing this load for them."

"We are close to the border, and you know there is a curfew. Be back before ten or I will arrest you."

"I will be back," murmured the driver as he whipped the horses to get away quickly from the outer zone border guard. By the sound of their conversation, the guard knew our driver. Due to the hay dust, I sneezed. Our driver whispered foul words and Barni kicked me warning not to sneeze again. Shortly afterwards we stopped.

"Come out all of you! From now on you are on your own." As we crawled out, he instructed further. "The border is about one kilometer, and you have to make that on foot. Close to the border there will be watchtowers and Russian guards, who will send up flares. They shoot at anything that moves, so stay as close to the ground as possible, and when the flares rise, freeze instantly. They can only see clearly what moves."

Barni and Laci handed something over to him, and then he asked, "It is all there?"

"Yes," Barni and Laci whispered at the same time.

"God be with you all," and he turned back toward the distant light, where a far-off dog's bark echoed.

Standing there, silently, we could see on the horizon the flickering lights of Austria.

I thought, "In front of us lies our tomorrows; behind us our yesterdays; in between the two is the border zone, the death-trap which we have to cross."

We journeyed forward on the frozen snow. There were some hills, hardly visible in the dim nightlight. It started to snow again, this time an icy drizzle, with a gusty wind blowing. Its painful sting was freezing my face. I quickly pulled Beatrix's toque down to cover her face, as she cried out from the pain of the freezing wind. I glanced at Attila; he was sleeping with his face close to his father's neck. Our footsteps crunched on the frozen ground as we trudged to our destination: the border zone. We seemed to endlessly mount one hill after another. I felt weaker and weaker. Suddenly a flare went up a short distance away. We dropped to the ground and lay motionless on the frozen snow.

I whispered, "Barni, I'm terrified. It feels like I have no strength left. I don't know if I can go another step."

Beside me, Marta answered and patted my shoulder, "Yes, Ilona, you can make it. You have to, for your children's sake. You have to take them to freedom."

Instantly, another flare lighted the sky. I heard the rushing beat of my own heart, while laying flat on the ground trying to cover Beatrix's face with mine. When we thought it was safe, we tried to run, but with Beatrix in my arms it was difficult. More flares, and a yell, "*Stoy!*" We were captured. With machine guns in our faces, the guards talked to us in Russian; some of it we understood. We were told to wait right there. Frightened, we looked into the cold barrel of their machine guns.

Shortly, an army truck arrived and they took us to the border station, where we joined many other escapees. They kept us overnight and debated between a firing squad or a trip to Siberia's labor camp. Hearing this I was furious at Barni for dragging me into this gruesome situation with the children. Barni and Laci were secretly passing notes to each other, via Laci's oldest son. The crowd was silent. We wouldn't dare to talk.

Since we were too crowded in one room, the guards ordered all the men outside to an open fire, where they were closely guarded. I was huddled in the corner with my children on the floor. Laci's oldest son came in to see his mother and surprisingly gave me a hug, to camouflage the note he dropped beside me. It said,

> *Ilona on our way to Siberia, when the train slows down at the Budapest station, we will jump the train on the side opposite the station. We will rush to the southbound train station to catch a train to the Yugoslavian border where we will cross over. We have to! It's either Siberia or a chance at the Yugoslavian border to "freedom." As soon as you've read my note, put it in your mouth to wet it, so it won't be readable and then tear it up.*

I felt numb. I couldn't think of anything, except to pray, and to cuddle my tired, hungry, restless children.

Early the next morning, we were forced into an open army truck, like cattle, and shipped back to Kapuvar train station. There the guards allowed us to go to the washroom, which was guarded outside. Barni, on his way, bought some apples from a peddler to feed our starving children.

On the train, four soldiers were constantly walking from coach to coach to keep an eye on the escapees. I had never seen a coach full of people in dead silence. The only sounds were my children's whimpers from hunger and diaper discomfort, between sugared soothers. They were the only babies among us. As I thought about what our future life might be, I looked outside to hide my tears. The drizzling rain had frozen on the train window and formed a lace-like curtain. It reminded me of the one my dear grandmother had crocheted for my windows back home. Tears flooded down my cheeks. I was completely petrified of the thought of reaching Budapest and jumping off the moving train with my baby in my arms.

Barni stared at me with his vacant eyes, as I was wiping my tears. He whispered, "Ilona, think of your crossroad Friend; he is with us," and he squeezed my hand. But I quickly withdrew it. I hated him for the pain and suffering he put us through to save his life.

Since it was the end of December, it was dark early, and the darkness frightened me even more. By our calculations we would reach Budapest around six p.m. I had two hours to decide whether to die in Hungary jumping off the moving train, or be shipped to Siberia for the rest of my life.

Just before six, Barni came back from his smoking trip with Laci. He leaned over, pretending to talk to Beatrix. He whispered, "When I get up with Attila in my arms, you quickly follow me out, and when I signal, jump off the train."

I whispered back, "I can't. I am shaking already."

"Yes, you can. Just think of your crossroad Friend where you find peace." He put his finger on his lips to silence me, then he quickly turned away from me as the Russian guards walked in.

As we got close to Budapest, the people got restless and started to move around. The guards were running in and out of the coach, checking different people's IDs, terrorizing us by yelling, "Sit down, sit down all of you!" and then running to the next coach, trying to control the restless people. Approaching

Budapest station, even in the dim light, I saw the rubble, the evil of destruction. The train tracked slower as we were in Budapest. I was trembling. Beatrix sensed my anxiety. Barni kept eye contact with me. The train got slower and slower. Barni quickly rose and touched my shoulder with a strong grip; he pushed me in front of him. Outside we reached the small platform, and with the train still moving, Barni whispered, "Ilona, jump." I was frightened beyond human comprehension.

"Ilona, jump!"

"I'm scared! I can't move."

And, with a strong force, he pushed me off the moving train. I rolled several times on the gravel, clasping my moaning baby tightly in my arms and quickly covering her mouth with my hand, as she started to cry. Lying on the ground, I could only see, between the still moving wheels, boots of the lined up AVO police waiting for the train to stop and take us off.

Instantly, Barni helped me up and tried to rush us away from the station. To reach the south train station, to the Yugoslavian border, we had to get by the patrolling AVO police. It was difficult to walk between the rubble in the dark. My leg throbbed, while I held the baby with my painful shoulder. Wet with perspiration, on the verge of passing out, we suddenly heard Russian words spoken!

Two patrolling soldiers with machine guns stopped about twenty feet from us. We were breathless, crouching behind a barricade. Beatrix moaned. Lying on my side, with my injured arm I couldn't reach into my pocket for a soother. She moaned again. I panicked. Quickly I locked my mouth on hers, and she started to suck on my tongue. I held her this way, while the patrolling soldiers listened and slowly passed us. Walking and ducking between the ruins, we had a rest behind a burned out Russian tank. Attila wanted to come to me, but we couldn't switch children; he was too heavy for me to carry. I gave them each a sugared soother, and shortly we reached the station. Laci and his family were inside, nervously waiting for us. We communicated only with eye contact. Barni and Laci went outside to review our next move. We found out that we had one hour to wait. I needed that time to recover from my exhaustion.

The station was full, but a dark-haired, chubby man waved me over to take his seat. I slumped on the bench and put Beatrix down to rest my arms. She cried out, favoring her right leg. I picked her up and checked her little leg; it was bruised from our fall. I massaged it gently and she quieted down. Attila got jealous and tried to push his sister out of my lap. I was exhausted, but desperate to cuddle my babies.

Barni came back with some buns and juice, and we fed our starving children. Feeding the children aroused my own hunger, but I had to satisfy myself with the yeasty fragrance of the dried up bun and the last drops from the juice bottle before I threw it away. The man next to me saw our struggle with the children and gave his seat to Barni. He wanted to take the children from me, so I could nap, but Attila clung to me tighter than Beatrix. While I gently kissed his face, cuddled him close, and stroked his back, he finally fell asleep. I leaned my head on the back of the bench, as I scanned the people around us.

Everyone was withdrawn, just gazing into the emptiness, with their distant looks. I was afraid to close my eyes because of my thinking. Are we going to make it, or will some of us perish? I was worried about my failing strength. What would happen to my children, if I died? I felt so tired and weak. With closed eyes I pleaded, "Dear Lord! I need help. I need strength. I have to live." Then I felt Barni wipe away my rolling tears, and he whispered, "I love you. Go to sleep now."

Shortly, I was awakened. Two AVO men walked in and demanded our red ID book for inspection again. I panicked. Beatrix was sleeping beside me on the bench. Barni was outside, and I didn't know our next plan. I started to walk outside with the children, when one of the AVO men yelled at me, "Where are you going?"

Without hesitation, I answered, "Taking the children to the bathroom."

"OK, just be back, or else I will come and get you."

Outside I alerted the boys. They went in, and shortly afterwards I followed them. Barni reached for Beatrix and whispered, "We are going to Szeged to see our friend Kocsis Jozsef." I nodded.

While one of them checked my papers, Beatrix giggled at him and he smiled back at her. I thought the ruthless AVO man was human for a second. After a while, we boarded the train to the Yugoslavian border, and we began the push and shove to get a seat on the train. We shared the compartment with four other people: two young men, and an older lady with her husband.

We were all dispirited, except for my two lively children, who had no awareness of the danger yet to come. The children were happy just to move around at our feet, and the two young men played with Attila. The children were contented to play until the lady across from us opened a bag and started to eat. The children's eyes lit up and focused on the bag of food. I had one bun left, which I quickly shared between them. Their eyes were still focused on the lady, while she tried to enjoy her pastry. Finally, she could no longer tolerate the children's hungry eyes, and she handed me the bag with two pieces of my favorite pastry. Bashfully, I accepted the food for my children's sake. Suddenly, that deed reminded me of the time I gave my food to Anna and her children on a train not so long ago. Grandmother's right when she says that universal law: what goes around comes around.

After the children finished the pastry, they fell asleep. Everyone looked sad. We kept our inner thoughts to ourselves. Most of us had closed our eyes, to shut out reality and buried our thoughts in the continued sound of the clickedy-click of the train wheels.

I was awakened by the shriek of the wheels as the train pulled into Szeged station. The old lady gave me a goodbye hug and whispered in my ear, "God bless you, my child, on your long journey. You will need his help." She must have figured out that we were escaping. I hoped she would not report us.

At the station Barni and Laci disappeared. Shortly, Barni came to me and led me behind the building, where we met a young man with a motorcycle that had a sidecar. Barni rushed me to sit in it with the baby, and nervously whispered, "We will meet you later." Attila cried out for me, but quickly I gave him a sugared soother as we left.

We left the city, speeding in the darkness on a snowy, slippery road. I covered Beatrix's face with my scarf, as mine was throbbing from the sting of the cold wind caused by the speeding motorcycle. When my side of the wheel hit a deep pothole, I nearly flew out of my seat with the baby. The driver didn't even slow down. He said we had to speed for time. After our rough ride we were dropped off in a small, dimly lit barn.

The driver firmly instructed me, "Stay here and keep silent. Don't you dare go in the house, no matter what. Now, I will go back and get the rest of you." He went out and locked me in. I was terrified: alone with my baby, in the middle of nowhere, with danger only steps away from me in the house. I wondered who was in the house that the driver was so afraid of. I waited there silently.

Startled when the cow let out a loud "Moo," I felt my heart skip a beat, started choking and coughed for air. Suddenly, a dog wanted to come in, growling and scratching at the door from outside. Sitting on a bale of hay in the dim light, I held my breath. I thought with the scratching and bark of the dog, surely the mysterious terror would reach me from the house. My frightened baby also sensed the danger. She didn't cry; she just clung to my neck and pressed her little face to mine. Then, I noticed the countable ribs on the skinny, old, gray horse, as he was staring at me with his golf-ball eyes, looking like a corpse in the gloomy light. I had to go to the bathroom badly, but I didn't dare to move. Then, a deep voice yelled, "Satan . . . Satan, come for supper," and the dog ran away with a rapid bark. I was numb from fright.

Suddenly the inspirational Bible verse came to my mind again: *Let not your heart be troubled, neither let it be afraid.* I recited this verse rapidly, not letting any other thought enter my mind, to overcome my uncontrollable fear.

Finally, we were together in the barn. The driver, Laci, and Barni moved away from us. Barni handed him the gray envelope with the money, which he should have returned. The driver lifted out one item from Laci's bag that glistened like a piece of jewelry. He quickly put it in his pocket and said, "I will be back shortly."

Quickly he returned with some bread hidden in his bucket. He must have been afraid of someone in the house. The nine of us devoured the small loaf like vultures. Grandmother was right: when we are starved we become greedy and lose our dignity. We were impatient while the driver milked the cow, but when he dished out the milk our patience was tested even more, as he had only one tin cup which we had to share. Even though we were in this situation together, greed occurred amongst us. Marta boldly pushed her children in front of me, ignoring the whimpers of my babies. The driver noticed that, and he handed me the half-liter measuring cup of milk. Quickly I tried to fill the children's bottles, while they were already reaching for them. Afterwards, he gave me four tea towels to use as diapers. Then he said, "Hurry up! Let's go! Not a sound from now on." We quickly snuck away from the suspicious house and got on his wagon. "I will lead you close to the border, and when I turn back you are on your own. When you reach the gorge, cross it. Once you come up on the other side you will be in Yugoslavia. God bless you all. Dead silence, from now on."

The word "dead" made me shiver. After a while the wagon stopped and we got off. Then he turned back and vanished into the dark frigid night. Silently, we trudged on our fearful journey through the freezing night. We tried to walk softly, to keep down the loud crunch of our footsteps on the frosted snow. A harsh, frigid wind forced us closer together. After our long walk, my arms went numb from carrying my heavy toddler. With the deterioration of my energy, slowly, I stayed further and further behind the others. Quietly a "Hush!" sound from Laci, telling us that they were at the edge of the gorge. Suddenly they vanished into it. I tried to rush after them, but with my increasing fear my energy quickly decreased. I strove to crawl up the other side of the gorge, when suddenly my right, injured foot sunk into a snowdrift up to my groin. I tried to put Beatrix down to pull my foot out, but she started whimpering. I quickly picked her up.

Barni whispered, "We are near the top. Hurry up."

"Barni, I am stuck! I can't pull my foot out of the snowdrift. You just go."

"I can't leave you. Just try for the children's sake."

I put Beatrix down again. She got frightened, she whimpered, she spit out the sugared soother, and cried out. I was terrified.

Barni whispered louder, "Ilona, think of your crossroad Friend on the cross, who always helps you."

Glancing down at Beatrix's frightened, little face, I picked her up again. I was exhausted, but panicked to stay behind. Confused and gasping for air... Just as I lifted up my head, to cry out for divine help, I noticed a strange sight and whispered, "Barni, I see a glistening cross up there."

He muttered, "That is the frosted hydro pole . . . Oh no, no. Ilona that is your crossroad cross. Hurry up here to see it better."

"Yes, yes, I am coming, I am coming." Without awareness, I forced myself to the top.

Instantly, a searchlight reflected in our faces and there was a shout, "*Stoy!*" We were captured again. And I passed out.

CHAPTER 41

As I regained consciousness, I heard Barni saying, "Ilona wake up, wake up, we are free." Then I heard Attila, "Mommy, Mommy, wake up, we flee, we flee." As I lay on the snow-covered ground, I opened my eyes. Barni and the children were hovering over me. I had such a joyous feeling, as if I had been reborn. I began hugging my children; I was so happy to be alive.

We had been captured, but this time by the Yugoslavian border guards. They were more sympathetic than the Russians, but they knew we had escaped from the Stalinist Communism. Yugoslavia's President Josep Broz, codename Tito, was a Communist leader, but not under Stalin's dictatorship.

From the border we were transported to Beograd. In a short time the border guards captured about one hundred fifty escapees, and they later transported us in open army trucks, somewhere. We were tightly guarded, and that puzzled us. There were twenty-five of us in each truck, and we were restrained by four guards with machine guns. We were frightened again, wondering, "If we were free, why the strict security?"

We traveled on a dusty, winding, dirt road, up and up into a secluded forest. We had no idea where we were. In the middle of the night, we arrived somewhere and we were ordered into a gloomy, unusually structured building, with no windows. All one hundred fifty of us were put in a big room with no beds, just about two feet of straw for us to sleep on like cattle.

The washroom was even more freakish, with a long, cement sink mounted on the wall. It looked like a watering trough for animals. I was scared of being alone in this dimly lit, strange washroom, where there were six holes for toilets in the rough cement floor. The whole place was creepy. There were only a few small, dim lights and no windows on the whole building. I rushed back the long, dark hall to the room where we were gathered. As I tried to explain to Barni about the washroom, the guards called us with gestures and dished out some food.

At the announcement of food, we behaved like animals. The food was one slice of bread, some Brussels sprouts and potato stew, in an aluminum container with a handle, which looked like an army pot. Puzzled more by the minute, I wondered why they had all the same pots. The supper was awful, but it eased our hunger and filled our stomachs. After supper I lay down on the straw with my children and started to pray. I was so frightened by this cryptic place.

The next morning, we found out that our short-lived freedom was over. We had been transported to the Albanian and Greek border, completely isolated in a former concentration camp. The Hungarian government pleaded with Yugoslavia's President Tito to throw us back, but he couldn't because of the Geneva Convention. Under this agreement, Tito received money to keep us, until they sorted out emigration for us to different countries. We were under extremely tight security. Tito was afraid that Stalin's Communists would attack him from Hungary to take over Yugoslavia, which Stalin had wanted to do for many years. It was for this reason that we were secluded and closely guarded in this former concentration camp - isolated from the world.

The following day I took the children outside to play. Attila ran into an empty building to hide. The building was one room about 80 square meters, with a low ceiling like a matchbox. Built of concrete, with no windows, just two heavy steel doors at each end, it looked like a vault. After further study of the structure, I discovered four holes at the lower corners, each end about ten cm in diameter. Suddenly, I froze, with shivers rushing through my body, and tears running down my face, gasping for air, I realized I was standing in the middle of a real gas chamber, thinking of all those innocent human beings who had lost their lives here. I thought instantly about my childhood friend, Terri, when the German SS soldiers gathered the Jewish people and took them away. I leaned against the wall, slid down onto the cold cement floor of the gas chamber and wept. Gathering my children, I rushed back to the shelter and asked Barni about the building. "Yes, Ilona it is real; this is a former concentration camp, but we can't talk about it." In my heart, I pledged daily visits to the Chamber of Horror, to pray for all those innocent souls who were murdered so brutally. And we could also be the victims of it.

As time went by we began to hear rumors that Tito feared of an uprising in his own country, with all the angry Hungarians flooding into Yugoslavia. He was skeptical about the escapees: were they really escaping the Stalinist revolution, or were they coming to ignite one in his country. One day when I played with the children in the hallway, I overheard a group of men discussing that Tito was a ruthless statesman. He played political monopoly with Stalin and Hitler in World War II. According to some we were not safe in his country: on the contrary we were in more danger than ever. Maybe that was why he had transported us to this isolated location, in this former concentration camp, with a gas chamber - to eliminate us quickly if it was necessary.

By spring our health was deteriorating rapidly. People started to get sick and were taken away. That frightened me as I worried about my two toddlers. We gave most of our food to them to save their lives. We were kept in this isolated camp, tightly guarded by the Yugoslavian army. Since the room was too crowded for all of us, we were allowed to be out in the yard. In the spring the dandelions and chickweed were growing in the yard, and I taught the children how to eat grass and dandelion leaves. Feeding most of my food to the children, I was so malnourished that while picking leaves without consciousness I picked up a handful of earth and ate it. It tasted awful, but the minerals it contained satisfied my hunger.

We picked roots and leaves everyday. Luckily Grandmother Batta had taught me which leaves were good, like dandelion, chickweed, and pigweed. As I picked them, I chewed them up, and injected the juice from my mouth into the children's sucking bottles, and diluted it with water to nourish the children. It tasted potent, but they got used to it. I never thought I would have to do that for survival. I was just a child myself when Grandmother taught me the value of herbs. Day-by-day more people got sick and were taken away somewhere.

One afternoon, while Barni and the children were sleeping, I went to pick some more leaves and roots. On my way I stopped in the Chamber of Horror . to pray. Abruptly two guards were right behind me. They grabbed me by my arms and dragged me outside, aiming their guns at me and pointing in the direction of our building, while talking harshly in Yugoslavian. Frightened, I ran back to our building and dropped down on the straw beside Barni and the children. Barni woke up, glanced at me, and asked, "What's the matter with you? You look so frightened?"

"No, Barni. I'm just tired." I quickly turned away from him to hide my frightened face. I thought they could have raped me; there was no one around. The next time I went out with the children, we stayed close to the building for safety. I went into the gas chamber only when people were around.

I was worried about Barni's failing health. He didn't believe that he could survive the long wait on so little food. I had to assure him periodically that with faith we would survive.

About the end of May 1957 a miracle happened: the emigration delegates arrived. We had our pictures taken, were fingerprinted and documented, and ready for emigration. But we were so malnourished that we didn't even feel excited any more. Suddenly, Beatrix developed a high fever. I was terrified.

Without a doctor in camp I was afraid they would take her away from me, or I would have to go with her and we would be separated. Barni couldn't look after Attila. I was torn apart on whether or not to report her illness. To conceal her sickness and her constant crying, I told people that she was just teething. She hadn't eaten or drunk anything for the second day. I asked for some baby food in the kitchen, but was told they didn't have any. On my way back, I heard that two young men were regularly sneaking out to the village and smuggling food into the compound, in exchange for jewelry. Some people had some treasures, but for us we had only our children and our wedding bands. Looking down at my finger, I pulled off my wedding band without hesitation and I asked Barni for his. He slipped his off and handed it to me. I located the men and gave them the two gold rings to bring me some fruit.

Inside, rocking my whimpering baby in my arms, I waited anxiously for their return. Finally, one of them showed up at the door and waved me to go outside. I quickly gave the baby to Barni and rushed after him. Behind the building, the other man waited with a bag of fruit. He reached in the bag and handed me three oranges. Holding my hands out for some more, he said, "That is all you get."

"What are you talking about? Only three oranges, for the two gold rings? They have value, even on the black market."

"That's all we got for it."

"You are a liar. You are cheating your own people. I will report you,"

"To whom lady? To whom?"

Their cynical smiles infuriated me. I turned away with rage and helpless tears. When Barni saw the three oranges for our wedding bands, he was angry as well.

"Barni you can't report them to anyone; we need the oranges for Beatrix."

Quickly I hid the oranges in our bag. I secretly peeled one and put some pieces in Attila's mouth, so that others wouldn't see it in his hand. I chewed up one section and a small piece of peel into a liquid and hourly mouth-fed Beatrix. This time I discovered my God-given, immense control over my mind. At the point of starvation, I chewed the orange section to a liquid and didn't swallow it. That was the most difficult temptation I ever had to overcome in my life.

The day we were transported to Italy, we left four more people behind, which petrified me. What would I do if I had to part with my children? Staring out the window of the fast moving train, I saw only the dark sky and the smoky, gray clouds gliding through the top of the forest. Holding my baby in my arms, I pledged that if she would die, I wouldn't let anyone know - not even Barni. I would smuggle her body to Canada, no matter what. Checking her in the bundle of blankets, I found her motionless with her eyes closed, but she was still breathing. I kept feeding her mouth-to-mouth with the orange sections, hoping for miracles, since I only had two orange sections left.

Attila got restless again and wanted to come and sit in my lap. I handed Beatrix to Barni, while I cuddled Attila until he fell asleep. I also closed my eyes and agonized over the possibility of Beatrix's death. How would I hide her, if her body starts to decay and smell? To escape my pain temporarily, I kept reciting this Bible verse:

> *"Peace I leave you. My peace I give unto you, let not your heart be troubled, neither let it be afraid. I will never leave you or forsake you."*

Later I gave Attila back to Barni, so I could feed Beatrix the last piece of orange. Hesitantly, uncovering her little face, I was astonished by her big, blue-green eyes gazing at me intently, just like I was a stranger. I could not hold my happiness back, sobbing and repeating, "Thank you, thank you, thank you Lord that you are still with me."

As I glanced out the window, I noticed a radiant, blue sky, and people were yelling as the train crossed over the Yugoslavian border to Italy, "We are Free! We are really free!" Even though we were exhausted, the sight of Italy shed a light of hope for our survival. Later we reached Milan, where we were treated humanely.

We received care packages from the Pope, and for that we were so thankful. During a peaceful week in Italy, we gained enough strength to face our immense journey to Canada. First we were transported through the Swiss Alps to France's harbor city, Le-Havre, where we boarded an old warship destined for Quebec City, Canada.

CHAPTER 42

In Le-Havre France, we boarded an old, squeaking, run-down warship along with thirteen hundred other Hungarians destined for Canada. On the ship, the men occupied the fore and the aft cabins; the women and the children were in the middle of the ship. As we sailed out of Le-Havre I was scared, but anxious to see the *Land of Milk and Honey*, Canada, our future country.

My happiness didn't last long; the second day the ship sailed into a violent storm. I became seasick. I had this continuous feeling of vomiting and a horrible sense of swirling dizziness. The only smell and taste I sensed was raw fish. I had difficulty looking after two lively toddlers. Therefore, my husband took Attila with him, even though I was greatly worried about his safety. Now at age three, Attila was a curious child with no sense of fear. He had to be watched every minute. I pleaded with Barni not to let him out of his sight on the big ship.

One day, when I looked out of the porthole, the rough sea seemed to be two or three stories below us as our ship was being tossed about like a matchbox. This was terrifying for me since I had never been on a boat before. My strong faith for survival was fading again. I was fortunate to have another lady, Margit, and her twin daughters, aged eleven, sharing the cabin with us. When they tired of enjoying themselves on deck, watching the whales following our boat, they helped me to look after my energetic little girl. The savage sea didn't affect their health. Despite the help they provided me, a part of me was envious and angry about that. Why did I always have to pay a price?

One day, Barni ran into our cabin very upset and said that Attila was missing. Hearing this, I became hysterical. I crawled up on deck, and with the help of the other people on board, started to search for my lost son. While searching at the back of the ship, I saw a pod of whales following our vessel, and that devastated me even more. I thought Attila had fallen overboard and had been devoured by the whales. I was distraught. I questioned God: Why is this happening? How much heartache can I handle? Leaning over the rail, distraught and momentarily disoriented, I thought the only solution was for me to jump overboard and search for my son. Seconds afterwards, with a clear vision, somehow I realized I couldn't leave my baby daughter, who also needed me. The words rushed through my mind over and over, "You can't leave her; you can't leave her," and I staggered back to our cabin. Possessively I grabbed

226

Beatrix from Margit and cradled her in my arms. Torn apart and sobbing, I prayed for a miracle that Attila would be found. I tried to recite the rosary, but my evil thoughts of Barni's carelessness, drinking and gambling diverted me.

For dinner each table of four people got a bottle of wine. Because of my seasickness and the children, Barni had the bottle of wine to himself at each dinner. So Barni and some of the other men got together, drinking and playing cards. When Attila disappeared, Barni was engaged with the card game and not paying attention to our son. As I prayed to God for my son to be found, I swore that if he had fallen overboard because of Barni's carelessness that Barni didn't deserve to live either. I was fearful of the evil thoughts I fostered towards Barni.

After about two hours of agony, Barni walked into the cabin with Attila in his arms. Stunned, I felt as though I was somewhere else. Was I hallucinating? I cried out, "Where did you find him?"

Barni answered, "He was in a safe place - in the chapel by himself, playing on the floor between the benches."

I seized Attila from Barni and thanked God for his safety. Right then, I decided he would stay with me for the rest of our journey.

Seeing all this, Margit said, "Ilona, keep him here, and I will help you to look after him."

"Thank you Margit, and bless your heart." I felt relieved that he was with me. I firmly let Barni know what an irresponsible father he was risking our son's life. He had put me through such agony again. His selfish carelessness was unforgivable in my heart. For the remaining time of our journey, we exchanged very few words. Barni continued his card games, while I was busy looking after the children, mostly from a horizontal position to ease my seasickness. I was blessed to share the cabin with Margit and her children as they took over periodically.

July 1957, after eleven days of suffering, we arrived in Quebec City. Stepping off the boat, onto the land of Canada, we realized our true *Freedom* - our dream! Tears streamed down our faces, as the Canadian crowd cheered us from the shore. I wondered if they really felt our deep happiness? Quickly I realized they could not. They had no idea what we had been through in the six months of struggle and agony for freedom. As we were slowly getting off from the boat, I was overwhelmed gazing over the attractive, white buildings sitting on top the landscaped hill, sprinkled with trees, shrubs and flowers, under a clear sky and warm, radiant sun. It reminded me of being in Buda, during my early childhood, with my dear grandmother, whom I had left behind. As the gentle, summer breeze softly swirled the fragrance of the flowers and trees in my face, I tasted their sweetness instead of raw fish. I looked up to the majestic sky and thanked God for our journey to freedom. In this state of ecstasy, my motion sickness was replaced with a tingling feeling running through my body and veins: I felt real *Freedom* - the greatest gift. May we never forget...

CHAPTER 43

In Quebec City, Barni's cousin, Charles Kolonics, picked us up. His parents immigrated to Canada long before. With our secluded Communist regime the families had lost contact, but when Barni inquired about him, the immigration bureau contacted Mr. Kolonics, and we stayed with them for a short time. Charles found a job for Barni in a machine shop owned by a Hungarian, Jewish man. Soon we moved out because their two-bedroom apartment on Park Ave. was too small for the eight of us. We were thankful and appreciated even the short time we had with such wonderful people.

We moved into a studio apartment on St. Michael Blvd. in Montreal, with only a table, four chairs, a few dishes, cutlery, some blankets, and a double mattress on the floor for the four of us to sleep on. To start a new life in a foreign country, without any money, or the knowledge of the English language to earn some, looked very grim. But, we felt blessed that we were free.

One day I went for a walk with the children to explore Montreal's streets. Everything looked so different and lavish compared to the poor Communist country I had left behind. After a short walk, I realized what danger we were in if we got lost. Not knowing the language I wouldn't be able to tell the police or anyone else where we lived. Without the language I felt handicapped. Quickly we went back for a pencil and paper, and I wrote down every street we crossed, so we could find our way back home.

Later I found a job with a Jewish family, who emigrated from Hungary before WW II. I had to look after their two young children and teach them the Hungarian language. Since the parents still spoke some Hungarian I got along fine with them. I cared for the four children, my two and their two, did some housework, washing, and ironing. I also prepared supper before Mrs. Adler came home. Since our meals were included, I didn't get much salary, but we had good food to eat and were happy to be fed. Mrs. Adler was so wonderful at giving me clothes, dishes, and food to take home. She even slipped some extra money in my pocket periodically. She continually encouraged me to learn the language, so I could get a better job. I was blessed with the Jewish people; they were always willing to help me.

Later the Canadian government offered conversational English classes for new immigrants. I knew this was essential for a better life and eagerly signed up for the class.

That fall Attila started school. Almost immediately, the name-calling began about the mark on his face. The radiation had left a dime-sized, permanent mark on the lower part of his right cheek.

He complained to me, "Mom, I feel so humiliated when the children start laughing at me and calling me Spot Face."

"Attila you have the mark on your face, but some children have big ears or noses. Some even have crossed eyes. They tease you because you are new and you speak a broken English. Just ignore them, and they will stop." I think he was convinced, but I was worried because kids can be cruel, especially if they gang up on one.

To earn more money, I found a job in a sock factory. I got more money all right, but I was under tremendous pressure because it was piecework. Coming home on the long bus route, with my first big pay, I stroked my first, treasured salary that was tucked safely inside my canvas bag. I planned to buy some clothing for the children. Attila needed some for school. My happiness was short lived again. As soon as Barni counted the money, he put it in his pocket and said, "From now on, I will keep all the money."

For me, his action was like a red flag waved at a bullfight. It reminded me of the time when my godfather took my babysitting money away from me. I said, "No Barni. We will open a joint bank account and save some of our money."

He took out the exact amount for my bus fare to work and said he would put the rest in the bank. That bothered me, but I thought it would be fine in the bank. What I found out later infuriated me. I had to give him all my earnings and I had no signing authority at the bank; the account was only in his name. He only gave me money for groceries and bus fare to work. I didn't like the arrangement, but I could not fight Barni alone. There was no *Anyu* or Grandmother to side with me. Barni took over my life completely. I was free in this country, but not in my existence. My dream was to bring my grandmother out to live with us permanently. I needed support. We struggled in Montreal's cold weather for nine years.

After that we moved to Toronto, hoping there we could find a job much easier without being bilingual.

Shortly after our arrival Barni got a job at the Ford Motor Company in Oakville, Ontario. I applied for a filing clerk position at the Northern Insurance

Company in Toronto. Barni belittled me about the job saying, "With your broken English you are stupid to apply for that position."

"Barni, I know I speak broken English, but the filing will be numerical, that is why I applied, and I am sure of myself that I can do it. You should encourage me instead of running me down." But he ignored my words and continued.

"You will never get it. You are nothing, just an immigrant and you don't count." I asked him not to call me names and to lower his voice, as the people walking by the door of the apartment could hear it.

He replied, "You see how stupid you are. I'm speaking Hungarian, and they don't understand the language."

"But, Barni they can hear that you are loud and dictatorial."

He answered, "I don't care." His verbal abusiveness bothered me. He started calling me names more often, like stupid, idiot, and ignorant. I resented those names because I felt I was none of those. It looked clear to me that he was jealous. But two weeks later he was even more jealous when I got the filing clerk job. He found faults in almost everything. The shadow of his silent terror not only followed me from Hungary, but it was getting worse. I wondered if I would ever be free from it.

The new school in Toronto greatly intrigued Beatrix, but with Attila it was different. He was shy and modest. In the new school the name-calling started again. *The marked faced new boy.* Attila was upset. I knew he was suffering because of it. He needed my reassurance again. With him I had to sit down to talk face-to-face. With Beatrix I could carry on a conversation from the next room. It's so amazing: the same parents and yet the children were so distinctly different. With time, Attila found good friends, but there were always a few who picked on him because of the noticeable mark on his face.

After a year of hard work at the insurance company, I achieved my dream. I got my own desk with my name cardholder on it. I was promoted to a processing clerk, modifying policies according to the endorsements we received daily, from lawyers and insurance agents in the property department. To make some extra money, Barni and I worked on our holidays on the tobacco farms of Windsor, Ontario. After two weeks of hard labor, I was glad to go back to work in the office. The girls in the office admired my suntan; they thought I had been vacationing on some tropical island. Little did they know that I had to soak my hands in bleach for hours to get rid of the black tobacco tar from my hands and nails. Of course, I let them believe the tropical island fantasy.

As we finished on the tobacco farm I had a big argument with Barni about my money, because I refused to give him my two-week's of hard-earned cash. I told him that I would open a bank account and save the money to bring my beloved grandmother to Canada. At my announcement Barni's face turned pale, then blue and green from anger. The way he was grinding his teeth and pacing in front of me, I thought that he would kill me, but I stood my ground. Somehow I wasn't afraid of him any more. Now that I was alone, God gave me the strength to defend myself. I wasn't going to let him bully me any more.

Barni was miserable. He hated his job at the Ford Motor Company. He was constantly complaining and fighting with the foreman, and the company suspended him for a week. His attitude really bothered me. I hoped he would change in the free country, but he didn't. He acted the same way at the Ford Motor Company as he had in the military and at the mine in Hungary. He was angry, rebellious, no one could tell him what to do. He complained about the job and his foreman to our Hungarian friends, so they started to stay away. Three days after returning from his suspension, he was fired. Then my life became hell on earth. I hated to come home from work, but I had to because my children needed me. Since he had no work, he started drinking heavier and dwelled on his anger and hatred for the company, which he took out on me. I told him to go and find another job.

His answer was, "Not until my unemployment time runs out."

It reaffirmed my belief that Barni didn't like to work and his attitude would never change. I tried to tolerate him, but he worsened with his verbal abuse.

Of course I didn't write about this in my letters to Grandmother. I didn't want her to worry about me.

CHAPTER 44

After six years in Toronto, Barni was restless, and he forced us to move again. From Toronto we moved to Pitt Meadows, British Columbia. I hated to leave my good job with the insurance company in Toronto, but I got a transfer to the Vancouver office. In Pitt Meadows we put a down payment on a dilapidated old house on an acre of land, with the dream that later we would build a new house on it. The children were happy, since now we had room for a dog. We bought them a German shepherd puppy, and they named him Solec.

The neighborhood children welcomed them, but in school the name-calling started again. The mark was obvious and I was thinking of plastic surgery to fix it. Attila was a good student and he was involved in sports, especially lacrosse. He was a sociable teenager until a new boy, Gino, was transferred into his class. Gino was two years behind his class and very domineering in the schoolyard. He organized a small gang and they were bullying the weaker children. Attila resented being called *Attila, the marked man*. I knew he was upset, and I realized that the mystery of that mark followed him. The more I questioned him about what was happening in school, the less he revealed. He always said, "Mom, I can handle it."

One day he came home with a black eye and a torn shirt. Regardless of how much I questioned him, he wouldn't tell me what had happened. This troubled me. His grades fell and his enthusiasm for sports disappeared. I became extremely concerned, and I suspected serious bullying. Barni made the situation worse by encouraging Attila to carry a baseball bat and fight Gino. I disagreed with Barni's solution. I made an appointment with the principal, but he was unconcerned and said, "They are teenagers and they just like to fight. A black eye doesn't point to bullying."

I was very upset by his attitude and I informed him that I would go to higher authorities with this problem. I waited about a week to proceed, and then I heard the good news that Gino had been transferred to a special school.

Since Vancouver was too far to travel to work, I had to look for a job closer to home. Searching the paper, I found that Star Insurance Agency in Port Coquitlam was looking for a clerk. I applied for the job, and the next day I met my new boss, Mr. Nach. He was of Jewish descent, and like all the Jews I had met he was ready to help me. He lent me a typewriter for two weeks to practice my typing skills at home before I started to work. Mr. Nach could have hired a

Canadian with experience, but he gave me a chance, for which I greatly respected him.

By this time, Barni had run out of unemployment insurance again and had to find a job. He began working in an aluminum window factory. That work didn't suit him either. He planned to stay there only until he collected enough stamps to collect unemployment again. I asked him, "How will you stop working to collect unemployment? You have to be laid off, don't you?"

"It will happen, just watch me," he replied.

His attitude scared me. He was drinking heavily and hiding the bottles around the house. The more he drank, the more abusive he got with me. One day he wanted some sugar in his coffee, but the sugar canister was empty. He ordered me to fill it up immediately, since that was my job. I was straining noodles above the sink and said, "Do it yourself. I am busy." He filled up the canister with about a kilogram of sugar, and then he came to the sink where I was and poured all the sugar on my head. He said, "That's your job," with a smirk on his face; he roared with laughter. I stood there flabbergasted while the small grains of the sugar ran down from my hair, past my neck, and into my inner garments. Ignoring my anger, he poured himself another glass of wine and continued with his verbal abuse. I refused to talk to him.

I didn't know what to do about Barni's behavior, so I buried myself in my work. As he drank, his abusiveness got more and more frightening, especially when the children weren't home. Due to our constant quarrelling the children stayed more and more at their friends' homes, especially Attila. I felt so alone. I wrote a letter to Grandmother asking her to come and see me, but she was unable for health reasons. She wrote me that Father was desperate to come to see me and Mother insisted on accompanying him. I would be happy to see my father, but I was afraid I couldn't cope with Mother and Barni together. Wanting desperately to see Father, I went to the immigration office and started the paper work that would take about six months to process.

They arrived in May 1973 for three months. We were excited waiting for them at Vancouver Airport. Finally, I spotted them in the slow-moving crowd. Upon taking a closer look, I was shocked by how much they had aged. I realized it was almost twenty years since I had left home. They had aged and I had matured. I hoped that while they were here Barni would change. About a week after their arrival, I took my vacation and we went blueberry picking down the road from our house. Mother and Father wanted to earn some money to buy some gifts to take back to Hungary. Barni had managed to get laid off from the window factory - for what reason I never found out. Mother asked him to come berry picking with us, but he refused. He said he was sick. To our surprise, when we came home he was having a good time drinking and watching TV.

I rushed to have a shower to wash off the dust and sweat of the summer heat. Just as I was lathering up, my heart almost stopped. I realized I had lost my precious silver chain and cross that I had bought with my very first pay cheque in Canada.

I had it blessed at Mount Royal church in Montreal. I thought even if I went back to the berry farm I would never find it in that big field. I stood there frustrated, hearing Barni with his loud voice demanding supper in English. I also heard him pop another bottle open. Later I found out he had spilled some of the wine while taking it to Father. Mother warned him, "Barni, you shouldn't drink any more."

"Mind your own business woman!" he slurred in English with a guttural voice, which Mother didn't understand. Quickly I ran out to stop the argument. Mother was on her hands and knees cleaning up the wine spill. Barni pushed her roughly as he walked by her, saying, "Leave it! Ilona will clean it up." Absorbing all this from the bathroom door, I noticed Mother was staring at the two empty wine bottles beside the garbage can, when she was getting rid of the wine-soaked paper towels. She motioned me to see the bottles. I put my finger to my lips to hush her. Telling Barni not to drink when he is highly intoxicated was not a good idea. Despite my attempt to quiet her, she mumbled, "Barni is a disgrace," as she began to help me with supper. Later, she wanted to go for a walk with me. As soon as we left the yard she said, "Ilona, dear, we are here for only a short time, and I can see the trouble you have to cope with."

"Mother, this is my problem. I handle it as best as I can, but you can't talk to Barni when he is drinking. He can get violent."

"Looks to me like you cannot reason with him at any time."

I thought, "Thank God. Finally, Mother noticed. But, you should have noticed it before you forced me to marry him."

"You are working all the time. It should be the other way around. How can you stand it?" Mother questioned.

"*Anyuka* don't worry. Everything will be fine."

235

"Not as I can see it, dear. You need to do something about it." For the first time in my life I felt my mother's concern for me. Finally, we reached home. Father was asleep. Attila lived with a friend, and Beatrix had stayed over at Debbie's.

Mother and Barni started an argument about drinking. I had to stop it, as I was worried about Mother's heart condition. I took Mother away to wash her hair. Before I left the room she asked me to pray with her. Surely, God works in mysterious ways. I had never thought that Mother and I would understand each other, none-the-less pray together. Afterwards I tucked her in and kissed her goodnight. Father asked, "How about my kiss?" I gave him one and gently brushed his gray hair out of his face. I felt safe with them near.

While they were with us we took them to see and explore some of the natural beauty around our area. On one trip we took my parents to Victoria where they enjoyed the Island, especially Butchard Garden. They were fascinated with the variety of flowers they had never seen before. At home, Father would sit in the backyard for hours fascinated by Mount Baker's snow-capped peaks in the middle of the summer heat. One day we surprised them by taking them up to the snow-capped mountain. We had quite a bit of trouble crossing the border to the United States since they were from a Communist country, and they had passports only to Canada. They had never seen snow in the summer time. Mother had to pick up the snow and eat it to make it sure it was real. Father was amazed that in July he was standing on the icy snow and could feel the coolness through his shoes. Looking at him, I was worried about him because he was so pale. Father wasn't a good traveler and was often carsick. On the way home he ate Gravol pills like they were candy and stayed in bed for two days to recover from the trip.

One day, I looked out the window, and to my amazement Mother and my neighbor, Dolly, were carrying on a conversation - Mother in Hungarian and Dolly in English. They seemed to understand each other. Even with the language difference they formed a deep friendship.

The summer went by quickly, and just before they left, Barni, Father, and Attila went fishing one last time. Mother and I went shopping at the Lougheed Mall for gifts to take home to Hungary. When we arrived at the mall, Mother said, "Ilona let's go to the restaurant and have a cup of tea. I want to talk to you about something that has been bothering me." Worried about her heart condition I gently ushered her to a table and sat her down.

"*Anyuka*, are you all right? You look troubled?"

"I am fine, dear, I just have to get something off my heart. I need to ease my guilt. I now see the pain I caused you when I insisted that you marry Barni. After three months in your home, I realize what I forced upon you." She reached over with her shaking hands to clasp mine. Tears trickled down her face. She took a deep breath and whispered, "I am begging for your forgiveness, dear. Could you ever forgive what I did to your life?"

I quickly answered to ease her pain. "Yes, *Anyuka*, let's forgive each other." I thought, please Lord forgive me for my evil thoughts for her. Holding each other's hands over the table, she bowed her head and kissed my hand clutched in hers. I rushed to sit beside her. We embraced and our trickling tears became cascades.

A peace fell between us. I finally felt my mother's love, something I had wished for since childhood. I felt that God, my heavenly negotiator, was with us. I utterly believed it was arranged by Him for us to find each other. With great delight, I watched and smiled at her as she enjoyed her favorite Canadian food: about two centimeters of thick peanut butter smothered on her toast with a glass of chocolate milk.

"*Kis lanyom*, dear daughter, I have one more thing to tell you. Even if you and Barni speak English, I feel that you two are always arguing. Furthermore, Barni is full of hate, anger, and malice. Ilona, dear, promise me right here and now that you will divorce him before he destroys you."

"*Anyuka* just forget about Barni and our troubles. Let's just enjoy our new found love for each other for the remaining two days while you are here."

Our shopping was finished when we found the gold chain with a cross that Mother wanted so badly. On our drive home we felt united and sang my favorite Hungarian hymn, which is similar to *Amazing Grace*.

At home, Mother helped me prepare supper. After supper, I helped Mother to pack. She tried to figure out how she could take a lifetime supply of peanut butter with her, since it wasn't available in Communist Hungary. While polishing her shoes outside, I overheard Mother plead with Barni to treat me with more respect, help me more with the big, vegetable garden and the poultry, of about one hundred or so chickens, ducks, and geese, as I was working full-time. But there was no answer from Barni. Mother's plea had fallen on deaf ears.

I ran in and calmed her. "Don't worry Mother, everything will be fine."

On Sunday at five a.m. we took my parents to Vancouver Airport. The departure was stressful for Mother and I, since we had just found each other. Before departure Mother said, "Ilona, dear, this was meant to be; I had to come to visit you. If you had written me about your life with Barni, in my skeptical mind, I would never have believed the difficult life you have had to live with him. Swear to me before I leave that you will divorce him." I didn't answer. I just nodded. Then she slipped something in my pocket. She hugged and kissed the children and said goodbye to Barni. While I embraced my dear father, I finally told him openly how much I loved him. Mother traced the cross on my forehead and said, "God bless you my darling. I will pray for you." One more trembling hug and we departed . . .

On the way home I reached into my pocket for tissues and there was the small envelope, which Mother had slipped into my pocket at the airport. With shaking hands I opened the envelope and a gold chain with a cross fell out. This was the chain Mother had pretended to buy for herself. Her short note said,

> *My darling I bought this chain and cross for you to replace the silver one you lost on the blueberry fields. God will help you, darling. You will see. Grandmother and I will pray for you in Szentkut's church. I'm going home to Hungary, but I leave my heart with you, my darling. Love Anyuka.*

Life was very cruel. I had just found her and I had to lose her again. Not only did we find each other, but also Mother had found her way to Grandmother. She said they would pray together for me in *Szentkut's* church, which they had never done before. This was the reason why Mother had to take the long, tiresome journey to Canada with her heart condition, and perhaps the reason Grandmother couldn't come to Canada. I believe the universe operates on purpose. And our Creator arranged Mother's long journey to make peace between us, before she passed away.

CHAPTER 45

As my parents left it was impossible to control my broken heart. My life with Barni had reached its crisis. I tried to take my life with a massive dose of sleeping pills, but I was saved by the power of the Almighty. When I came to, they were pumping my stomach in the Maple Ridge hospital. Barni was reported to the police for his abusiveness and cruelty. My dearest friend and neighbor, Mrs. Brown, knew about my troubled life, but she never interfered.

After failing my suicide attempt, my life continued to be hell on earth. I was busy working full-time, and trying to guide my teenagers, which I think I failed at, because the children spent most of their time with friends away from home. I tried not to involve the children with my difficulties with their father. I didn't complain. I didn't want to destroy their relationship with their father; our conflict was between husband and wife. However, Attila was worried about his father's behavior and said, "Mom, divorce him. You deserve a better husband than he is."

I felt so alone and so afraid of Barni. But still I kept my problem to myself, except for the endless prayers to my God, for guidance and strength.

About a week before Christmas, I came home from work and noticed immediately that Barni was highly intoxicated and angry. He came to me at the door, grabbed my face with his hand, and squeezed my cheeks together. I felt the excruciating pain as my teeth cut into the inside flesh of my half-open mouth. As I tried to fight my way out of his hands, I tasted the bitter sweetness of my blood. Finally, he let go of my face and yelled, "Where is my supper? That is your duty as a wife." He continued cursing at me with foul words. I was glad the children weren't home to see and hear this. Since Attila defended me a few times, Barni did most of his abuse when we were alone. I was terrified that he would kill me. I wanted to escape from him, but he locked the door, and he put the key beside him on the table. I hoped someone would come by so I could escape. Shaking from fear, I started supper, as he had demanded. Moment by moment, he got more and more violent because I didn't talk to him. Suddenly, from about three meters away from me, he threw his wine glass at me. It missed my face by only about five centimeters. Startled, at that instant, I felt fearless. I went to the table, picked up the key, opened the locked door, and I walked out. His voice echoed from the house.

"You have nowhere to go! You will be back! You will be back!"

Reaching the street, I didn't know where to go. Fortunately my dear neighbor, Mrs. Brown, was at her window. I walked to her door and she invited me in and noticed my sobbing. She asked me to sit down, but I had to run into the bathroom to spit out more of the seeping blood from my mouth. She helped me to the chair and asked, "What has happened to you, dear?" I told her what happened. She wasn't surprised and feared for my life. She asked me to stay with them for a while. The next day, while Barni wasn't home, I got some of my personal belongings. During my stay with the Browns, I realized I could not survive with Barni. My health had failed, and I had to quit work and focus on saving my life. I filed for divorce.

Two months later at the trial, at the request of the attorney, I had to recount some of the most intensely painful episodes of my life. In February 1974, at the New Westminster Courthouse, my divorce was granted for physical and mental cruelty. Walking out of the courtroom I was exhausted, when a flash of words came to me, "I am free of the silent terror. I am free; I am now, truly free."

After twenty-one years of abuse I had to learn how to deal with my painful wounds. To ease my excruciating pain, I prayed constantly for relief. It felt like I was trapped in a world I didn't belong. Home alone, I fought the powerful temptation to use alcohol and tranquilizer drugs to ease the pain. One day, while taking sedatives and alcohol, I got overly emotional and began sobbing out of control, feeling sorry for myself, angry with God, blaming everyone and everything for my tragic life. Flashes of destruction haunted me: Try again! This time you can end it for sure. Try again! Suddenly, my crossroad cross flashed in front of me. On my knees I prayed to my childhood friend, Jesus Christ, pleading for help. Quickly I realized He saved me again by not letting the dark side take over my life. I poured the liquor down the sink and picked up the Bible. I found my most reassuring verse Heb.13:5, *I will never leave you nor forsake you.* Exhausted, I recited this verse until I fell asleep.

The next day I felt spiritual strength that I wasn't alone. I started to look for a job. Two days later I started to work in the merchandising office of Port Coquitlam's K-Mart department store. I was happy the merchandising manager, Mr. Jalberty, and the five office girls welcomed me with kindness. I buried myself in my work. I was afraid to break down and sob out my life story, which I wanted to keep to myself. Still afraid of Barni being nearby, after six months I accepted a transfer to Vernon's new K-Mart office about 350 km away.

By this time, the children were on their own. We kept contact, but I was worried about them being so far away. However, Attila encouraged me, "Mom, start a new life and don't look back. With your faith, you will make it."

After the hard move, I felt strange and sad again in the new city, but I got friendly with my bank teller, Anne Watson, who was also Hungarian. She was a delight and we became good friends. Later she introduced me to many other people. Finally settled in my house and surroundings, I adopted the Okanagan as my new home.

In August 1975, Attila came on his vacation and stayed with me for a week. I was happy that he came, this was just what I needed - his love. But somehow he seemed different, very quiet, and disturbingly distant. I asked him if he felt well. "Yes Mom, I am fine. I just have this feeling that I want to go somewhere, but I don't know where."

His statement puzzled me. During his visit, I felt extremely close to him. I also had a strange feeling myself, but I didn't tell him that. I wanted to keep him with me and hug him all the time. The next day when I got home from work he was playing Hungarian Gypsy records that he loved so much. Later we had a nice chicken paprikas dinner, his favorite. After that we played a Hungarian card game called *Zsiros*. However, at the end of the week our good times came to an end. And, he left.

I was deeply concerned about his mood and distant thoughts. While the summer passed we talked on the phone regularly, but as his mother I knew something greatly troubled him. He was so different. Deep in my heart I felt something was wrong. I said lots of prayers for him, and I thought he must be going through some changes. Maybe he had found a girlfriend. Was he in love?

October 2, 1975 was a windy, rainy night, typical of fall weather. At about 10:30 p.m. my doorbell rang. I said, "Now who could be out on a miserable night like this?" Leery to open the door I looked out of the peephole and saw two policemen standing outside. I opened the door, and one of them asked me if they could come in. I was hesitant and nervous, but he said they had to come in, as they wanted to talk to me, so I let them in. Worried, I asked, "What is wrong? What is going on?"

One of the officers led me by the arm to the couch, motioned me to sit down, and sat beside me. By this time I was getting upset with him. He looked at his partner, expelled a deep breath, and then he said, "Mrs. Bibok we have sad news for you. Your son, Attila, was in a car accident, and he was killed." The news hit me like a bolt of electric shock and I passed out. When I came to, I felt numb. I couldn't talk, I just cried. The officer said, "Attila was a passenger in a car with three other people. The driver was speeding, lost control, ran off the road, and hit a telephone pole. Attila was sitting in the front seat without his seatbelt and his body was cast out of the car through the windshield, while the rest went through the doors." They were very compassionate and hesitant to leave me alone. Shortly after the police car left my driveway, my neighbor, Mr. Cowan, came to inquire if I was in any kind of trouble. When I stuttered out my tragic story, he offered to drive me to Vancouver, where Attila's body was. Immediately I started to pack and early in the morning we left on the six-hour drive. By the time we reached Vancouver, I had no tears left. I couldn't even pray any more.

When I arrived at my daughter's house, Barni was in the living room sitting close to his new girlfriend. I was furious. How insensitive of Barni to bring a woman to this tragic occasion. I asked Beatrix to go with me to see Attila, but she quickly pushed me into the bathroom and said, "Mom, the casket is closed and you can't see him."

By this time I was out of control and ready to kill anyone who got in my way. I wanted to see my son. I didn't believe nor accept that he was dead. Beatrix saw my rage and in a quiet voice she said it again, "Mom, you shouldn't see him."

"Why not?" I asked.

She told me as Attila had been cast through the windshield of the car his face was badly mutilated. She had seen him and his face looked shocking. She didn't want me to see him like that. She continued, "Mom, I want you to remember him as he was. Remember how handsome he was."

I asked, "If his face looked so bad, how could you recognize him?"

"Mom, from the radiation mark on his face. The mark looked so clean, not even a drop of blood was on it."

At that moment I realized the reason for the mysterious mark. I remembered how upset I was in Budapest, for the radiation treatment when he was a baby. And all that anguish and heartache with the name-calling in school, because of that mark on his face. At that time I didn't know, but I realized it now. The mark was there for a reason: to be able to quickly identify him after this fatal accident.

My pain was so intense it felt like my flesh was being torn apart piece-by-piece. My mind was nowhere and everywhere at the same time. My heart was aching with a burning and squeezing sensation. I could not cry or plead with God any more. I just asked, "Help, as no power on earth can help me with this immense heartache. Only you my Lord, only you."

My children were my reason for escaping from the Communism, knowing my life would not be easy having to deal with Barni alone, not knowing the language, and having nothing but the clothes on our backs. But, I wanted a better life for the children in a free country. The Lord had different plans. He called him home early in life. Regardless of my heartache, I thanked him for the twenty-one years of love and joy Attila had brought into my life.

After the cremation I rushed home to Vernon, with agonizing grief and pain in my heart. I tried to understand and come to terms with my extreme bereavement. My friends tried to help me, but I was beyond human help. In my solitude, I reflected on my troubled life. "Why was life so cruel and unfair? Why Lord? Why? I don't demand. I just ask."

Silently sitting in the dark room for weeks, just rocking in my chair, it felt like my life was stuck in limbo. Not answering the door or the phone, I was too deeply hurt to comprehend reality.

I needed help - I needed God - I needed healing!

After weeks in this distraught state of existence, I had a vivid dream that I was sitting in *Szentkut's* church in Hungary in complete tranquility. The next morning I followed my dream: I went to church. The priest delivered this message, "Why tragedy happens to us we don't know. We are earth bound. We have limited knowledge about the larger picture of life. We can't comprehend what God can do. God is always working with a purpose. God uses his creations for his purpose. Rom: 9-17. For the Scripture says to Pharaoh..."

"For this very purpose I raised you up to demonstrate MY POWER in you, and that my name might be proclaimed THROUGHOUT the whole earth."

Just then I realized maybe God needed my son for whatever His purpose was. I completely surrendered to God and vowed to ask no more questions. Walking home from church, I was more at peace with myself.

Life will go on, regardless of how hard it will be, I have to bear it. It is in the testing that we move from speculation to reality, as we experience God's power. I had tried to go around grief, to make a short cut to healing, but I realized there is no way out but through. I also realized there is no exemption from pain, grief, and sorrow. It touches every one of us. Some less, some more, and why is that? We don't know. Life is a mystery, a hidden secrecy of the higher power. We have no choice, and we have to accept it. And let Mystery be a Mystery. Without my dire experiences, I would not have become self-realized. Hardships mold us, teach us, and advance us very quickly in life. To be healed I surrendered to God all my being and recited *The Lord's Prayer*, "And, *forgive* us our trespasses as we *forgive* those who trespass against us." Sometimes it is grim to handle the silent terrors of life, but with faith it is remarkably easier.